THE BEST OF NEWSPAPER DESIGN™

the 2004 competition of the Society for News Design

SOCIETY FOR NEWS DESIGN
1130 Ten Rod Road, F 104
North Kingstown, RI 02852-4177 USA

Judging takes place at the
S.I. NEWHOUSE SCHOOL OF PUBLIC COMMUNICATIONS
Syracuse University, Syracuse, N.Y.

First printed in the U.S.A. by Rockport Publishers Inc., Gloucester, Mass.

INTRODUCCIÓN

 SND.

Copyright © 2005
Society for News Design

Society for News Design
1130 Ten Rod Road, F 104
North Kingstown, RI 02852-4177 USA
(401) 294-5233
(401) 294-5238 fax
snd@snd.org
www.snd.org

Other distribution by Rockport Publishers, Gloucester, Mass., www.rockpub.com.

ISBN 1-59253-169-5   hardcover edition
ISBN 1-878107-17-8   softcover edition
ISSN 1520-4251

La 26ª edición de la competencia fue la más grande en la historia de la SND. Las cifras hablan por sí solas.

Lo que encontrará en las siguientes 272 páginas es el diseño que estimulará y hasta rejuvenecerá tanto a novicios como a profesionales.

La competencia, patrocinada por la Sociedad de Diseño de Noticias y la Escuela de Comunicaciones Públicas S.I. Newhouse de Syracuse University, distingue la excelencia en el diseño de diarios, los gráficos y la fotografía. Ninguna otra organización sirve al profesional del diseño como lo hace la SND. Este libro es uno de esos importantes servicios.

Se debe estar presente en la calificación de las piezas concursantes para darse cuenta cómo tantas pueden ser revisadas en tan poco tiempo.

Para llevar a cabo esta tarea, se requiere de una gran cantidad de gente, cientos de mesas, miles de fichas de votación multicolores, y cientos de vasos rojos, amarillos y azules para recolectar las fichas, además de jueces talentosos y calificados.

Los jueces pueden otorgar tantos premios como quieran en cada una de las 21 categorías representadas en la competencia. La definición de los premios se mantiene constante año a año, pero los estándares pueden aumentar cada año si los jueces tienen más piezas para evaluar. Así, el trabajo de selección de ganadores es, a la vez, importante y difícil.

Premio a la Excelencia. Este premio se otorga a un trabajo que es verdaderamente excelente. Este premio va más allá de la competencia técnica o estética. Sin embargo, para recibir este premio, estas piezas deben ser casi perfectas.

Medalla de Plata. Este premio se entrega a un trabajo que va más allá de la excelencia. El dominio técnico de la Medalla de Plata debería ampliar los límites del medio. Estas piezas deberían brillar.

Medalla de Oro. Este premio se da a un trabajo que define el estado de las artes. Una pieza de esta categoría debería expandir los límites de la imaginación. Debería ser imposible encontrar algo deficiente en una pieza ganadora de oro.

Reconocimiento Especial de los Jueces. Un grupo de jueces, o la totalidad de ellos, entrega este honor a un trabajo que es sobresaliente en un aspecto particular, pero que no necesariamente mencionado en las categorías del Premio a la Excelencia, o las medallas de oro o plata. Este reconocimiento puede ser entregado a cosas tales como el uso de la fotografía, el de los infográficos, y de la tipografía a lo largo del trabajo.

Cuando una categoría tiene muchas piezas para ser mostradas de una sola vez, se realiza una primera selección para que los jueces seleccionen las páginas que quieren ver de nuevo en un grupo más pequeño. Solo se necesita un voto para que una pieza permanezca en la competencia.

Una vez que se ha llevado a cabo la primera selección, y todas las piezas que quedan en una categoría pueden ser vistas a la vez, cada juez emite un voto con una ficha del color que se le ha asignado, y la pone en el vaso de "sí" o en el de "no". Se da vuelta los vasos para esconder los resultados mientras se realiza la votación.

Si ocurre un conflicto debido a que los jueces se encuentran con alguna pieza de su periódico, de un medio en el que han realizado una consultoría recientemente (18 meses o menos), o de una publicación con la cual compiten, se pone un vaso amarillo frente a la pieza para anunciar el conflicto existente. En ese momento, un juez "general" vota en vez del juez que tiene el conflicto.

Cuando una pieza recibe tres de los cinco votos posibles, se le da un Premio a la Excelencia. Si recibe cuatro, gana una Medalla de Plata y si obtiene los cinco votos – el voto unánime del panel de jueces – gana una medalla de oro.

Lo que viene a continuación, aunque sea subjetivo, representa lo mejor de lo mejor de 2004. Esperamos que sus savias creativas sean estimuladas mientras vea estas imágenes.

INTRODUCTION

The 26th Edition competition was the largest in SND's history. The numbers speak for themselves.

What you'll find in the next 272 pages are designs that will excite and even rejuvenate both novice and pro.

The competition, sponsored by the Society for News Design and Syracuse University's S.I. Newhouse School of Public Communications, recognizes excellence in newspaper design, graphics and photography. No other organization serves the design professional as does SND. This book is one of those important rewards.

One has to be at the judging to start to understand how so many entries can be reviewed in such a short time.

It takes busloads of people; hundreds of tables; thousands of multi-colored chips for voting; hundreds of red, blue and yellow cups to collect the chips; and talented, qualified judges to get the job done.

Judges may give as many awards as they wish in each of the 21 categories represented in the competition. Award definitions remain constant year after year, but the standards may increase from year to year as judges have more to choose from. Thus the job of selecting winners is both important and difficult.

Award of Excellence. This award was granted for work that is truly excellent. This award went beyond mere technical or aesthetic competency. But to receive an award, these entries need be near perfect.

Silver Medal. This award was granted for work that went beyond excellence. The technical proficiency of the Silver Medal should stretch the limits of the medium. These entries should shine.

Gold Medal. This award was granted for work that defines the state of the art. Such an entry should stretch all limits of creativity. It should be impossible to find anything deficient in a gold-winning entry.

Judges' Special Recognition. This honor was awarded by a team of judges or by all judges for work that is outstanding in a particular respect not necessarily singled out by the Award of Excellence, Silver or Gold award structure. This recognition may be granted for such things as use of photography, use of informational graphics and the use of typography throughout a body of work.

When a category has too many entries to be displayed all at once, a first cut is done as judges pick pages they'd like to see again in a smaller group. It takes only one vote for an entry to remain in the competition.

Once a first cut has been completed, and all remaining entries in a category can be viewed at once, each judge casts a vote with a chip, color coded for that judge, and placed in either a "yes" or a "no" cup. Cups are flipped to hide results while voting is underway.

If a conflict occurs because judges come across an entry from their publication, a publication at which they have performed recent (18 months or less) consulting work, or a publication with which they compete, the judges place a yellow cup on the entry, signifying a conflict exists. At this point, a "generalist" judge will vote instead of the judge with the conflict.

An entry receiving three of five possible votes is given an Award of Excellence. An entry receiving four votes wins a Silver Medal and one receiving five votes – a unanimous vote of the panel – wins a Gold Medal.

What follows, although subjective, represents the best of the best for 2004. We hope your creative juices are stimulated as you view these images.

Marshall Matlock
SND Competition Committee Director
Syracuse University (N.Y.)

Michael Whitley
26th Edition Coordinator
Los Angeles Times

Shamus Walker
26th Edition Audit & Entry Director
Syracuse University (N.Y.)

Ron Johnson
Editor
The Best of Newspaper Design™
Kansas State University

THE COMPETITION

Competition committee director
Marshall Matlock
Syracuse University
Syracuse, N.Y.

26th edition coordinator
Michael Whitley
Deputy design director for news
     and sports
Los Angeles Times

Special thanks to the
co-sponsor for the competition –
the S.I. Newhouse School of
Public Communications,
Syracuse University, Syracuse, N.Y.

Judging facilitators

Cassie Armstrong, senior designer,
Orlando Sentinel (Fla.)

Tim Ball, news design director,
The Indianapolis Star

Jonathon Berlin, assistant design
director, Rocky Mountain News,
Denver, and editor of SND's
Design journal.

Stanley Bondy, Syracuse
University, Syracuse, N.Y.

Audrey Burian, Syracuse
University, Syracuse, N.Y.

Elise Burroughs, SND executive
director, North Kingstown, R.I.

Steve Cavendish, assistant design
editor for news, Chicago Tribune

Matt Erickson, assistant sports
editor for design, Times of
Northwest Indiana, Munster, Ind.

Justin Ferrell, assistant news
editor, The Washington Post

Bill Gaspard, SND president and
news design director, Los Angeles
Times

Jeremy Gilbert, sports
presentation editor, St. Petersburg
Times (Fla.)

Scott Goldman, assistant
managing editor for visuals,
The Indianapolis Star

Darcy Greene, MSU/SND student
affiliate co-adviser, Michigan State
University, East Lansing, Mich.

Ron Johnson, editor and designer
of SND's The Best of Newspaper
Design™ book and faculty
member, Kansas State University,
Manhattan, Kan.

Andrea Jones, designer, The News
and Observer, Raleigh, N.C.

Kris Kinkade, interim design
director, Kalamazoo Gazette,
(Mich.)

Kenny Monteith, presentation
editor, Lexington Herald-Leader
(Ky.)

Tiffany Pease, news designer,
The Charlotte Observer (N.C.)

Cheryl Pell, MSU/SND student
affiliate co-adviser at Michigan
State University, East Lansing,
Mich.

Leslie Plesser, 1-A designer, Star
Tribune, Minneapolis, Minn.

Zoila Quezada, SND
administrative assistant, North
Kingstown, R.I.

Denise M. Reagan, news design
director, South Florida
Sun-Sentinel, Fort Lauderdale, Fla.,
and editor of SND's Update

Mike Rice, visual team leader for
design and graphics, Arizona
Daily Star, Tucson, Ariz.

Epha Riche, news design director,
The Indianapolis Star (Ind.)

Chris Rukan, sports design
director, The Palm Beach Post,
West Palm Beach, Fla.

Susan Santoro, SND membership
assistant, North Kingstown, R.I.

Jay Small, director of online
content and operations, E.W.
Scripps Newspapers, Knoxville,
Tenn.

Colin Smith, designer, Daily
Herald, Provo, Utah

Emmet Smith, designer, The Plain
Dealer, Cleveland, Ohio

Chiyono Sugiyama, writer and
designer, The Daily Yomiuri, Tokyo,
Japan

Gregory Swanson, assistant
managing editor for presentation,
Quad-City Times, Davenport, Iowa

Dennis Varney, sports designer
and copy editor, Lexington
Herald-Leader (Ky.)

Lila Victoria, newsroom artist,
Staten Island Advance (N.Y.)

Shamus Walker, SND audit and
entry director, Syracuse University,
Syracuse, N.Y.

Paul Wallen, managing editor for
visuals, Sun Journal, Lewiston,
Maine

Steve Wolgast, staff editor for
news design, The New York Times.

Syracuse University students –
Richetta Coelho, Melissa Dahne,
Jen Doop, Graham Fleming,
Mariel Hart, Katie Hollenbeck,
Isabella Kanjanapangka, Cortney
McMahon, Kara Race, Crystal
Rainey, Katie Schlientz and Sarah
Winn.

Michigan State University
students – Erica Frederick,
Kelsey Hildebrandt, Danny Lynn,
Nick Mrozowski, Karly Pence,
Blanca Prado, Lydia Weiss and
Krissi Xenakis.

THE BOOK

Editor
Ron Johnson
Kansas State University
Manhattan, Kan.

Todd Stewart, San Antonio
Express-News (Texas)

Phill Spiker, Tulsa World (Okla.)

Steve Wolgast, The New York
Times

Cristobal Edwards, Universidad
Catolica, Santiago, Chile

Katie Lane, Wichita Eagle (Kan.)

Kansas State University
students – Loni Woolery,
Ryan Flynn, Jennifer Newberry,
Kerry Fischer, Matt Gorney,
Nathan Ryerson and Anthony
Mendoza

THE SOCIETY

President
Bill Gaspard
Los Angeles Times

Vice president
Christine McNeal
Milwaukee Journal Sentinel
(Wis.)

Treasurer/secretary
Scott Goldman
The Indianapolis Star

Immediate past president
Susan Mango Curtis
Northwestern University
Evanston, Ill.

Executive director
Elise Burroughs
North Kingstown, R.I.

President / SND Foundation
Steve Dorsey
Detroit Free-Press

2004
is our competition year. Entries were published between Jan. 1 and Dec. 31, 2004. This book was published in 2005.

26th
edition of this book has 272 pages, plus cover, and more than 1,100 images. The first edition, published in 1980, contained 56 pages and 385 images.

15,020
entries judged for this 26th edition – a record.

3
circulation categories for individual awards –
175,000 and over,
50,000-174,999 and
49,999 and under.

4
circulation categories for The World's Best-Designed Newspapers™ awards –
175,000 and over,
75,000-174,999
25,000-74,999 and
24,999 and under.

21
categories of the competition. From World's Best-Designed Newspapers™, a mandatory category, through the category Miscellaneous, many of the categories include specialty subcategories, as well as the three circulation divisions.

JUDGES

 **Tonia Cowan**

 **Richard Curtis**

 **Heidi de Laubenfels**

 **Linda Eckstein**

 **Julie Elman**

 **Jeff Goertzen**

 **John M. Humenik**

 **Joseph Kieta**

 **David Kordalski**

 **Teresa Kriegsman**

Tonia Cowan, graphics director at the Toronto Star, has recently returned to her Canadian hometown after 10 years in Manhattan. In 1994 she moved to New York City to work for The Associated Press in a number of capacities, including deputy art director, before moving to Newsweek to do 3D graphics. She has served as a judge for the Malofiej awards in Pamplona, Spain. She has won many awards for her graphics and design work.

Tonia Cowan, directora de gráficos del diario Toronto Star, regresó recientemente a su ciudad de origen en Canadá después de pasar 10 años en Manhattan. En 1994 se mudó a Nueva York para trabajar en varios puestos de trabajo en la Associated Press, incluyendo la subdirección de arte. Luego se cambió a Newsweek para dedicarse a los gráficos en 3D. Ha sido jueza de los premios Malofiej en Pamplona, España. Ha ganado muchos premios por sus gráficos y su trabajo de diseño.

Richard Curtis, a USA Today founder, is managing editor for graphics and photography. He was also a founder of SND and its Design journal. His work has been noted in "Information Architects" and "1,000 Most Creative People in the USA." He has won many design awards from several organizations, including SND. He also is the winner of the Anton Majeri Award for Innovation and Leadership in Graphics Journalism and twice won the American Journalism Review's best-designed newspaper award.

Richard Curtis, uno de los fundadores del periódico USA Today, es el editor administrativo de gráficos y fotografía. También fue uno de los fundadores de la SND y la revista institucional Design. Su trabajo ha sido reconocido en "Information Architects" (Arquitectos de la Información) y "1,000 Most Creative People in the USA" (Las mil personas

más creativas en los Estados Unidos). Ha ganado muchos premios de diseño de varias organizaciones, incluyendo la SND. También es el ganador del premio Anton Majeri para la Innovación y el Liderazgo en el Periodismo de Gráficos, y dos veces ha recibido el premio de la American Journalism Review (Revista de Periodismo de los EE.UU.) al diario mejor diseñado.

Heidi de Laubenfels is assistant managing editor for visuals and technology at The Seattle Times, which she joined in early 1998 to manage a new publishing system and a two-year-long redesign that culminated in June 2004. de Laubenfels has worked in numerous capacities in newsrooms at The Denver Post, the Phoenix Gazette and The Bellingham Herald (Wash.).

Heidi de Laubenfels es editora administrativa asistente de elementos visuales y tecnología del diario norteamericano The Seattle Times, al cual se sumó al comienzo de 1998 para administrar un nuevo sistema de publicación e implementar un proceso de rediseño de dos años de duración que culminó en junio de 2004. De Laubenfels se ha desempeñado en varios puestos de trabajo en la sala de noticias de los diarios norteamericanos The Denver Post, Phoenix Gazette y The Bellingham Herald.

Linda Eckstein has been Fortune magazine's information graphics editor since 1995. She joined the business biweekly as a designer in 1984, after designing news graphics at United Press International.

Linda Eckstein ha sido la editora de gráficos informativos de la revista Fortune desde 1995. Se sumó a la publicación bimensual como diseñadora en 1984, luego de

diseñar gráficos noticiosos en la agencia de noticias United Press International.

Julie Elman is a designer at The Virginian-Pilot, Norfolk, Va. She has also worked as a picture editor and photojournalist at other newspapers. She has taught photojournalism at the University of Missouri and design at Virginia Wesleyan College. Elman has won numerous SND awards.

Julie Elman es una diseñadora del diario norteamericano The Virginian-Pilot, de Norfolk, Virginia. También se ha desempeñado como editora de fotografía y fotoperiodista en otros periódicos. Ha enseñado fotoperiodismo en la University of Missouri y diseño en Virginia Wesleyan College. Elman ha ganado numerosos premios de la SND.

Tim Frank, who started *Newspagedesigner.com,* worked to put the Sun Journal, Lewiston, Maine, onto the news-design map, collecting more than 60 awards in the process. In 2003, Frank joined The Arizona Republic, in Phoenix, to coach the news designers' staff and help drive a new direction for the paper.

Tim Frank, quien comenzó el sitio web *Newspagedesigner.com,* se dedicó a poner el periódico norteamericano Sun Journal, de Lewiston, Maine, en el mapa del diseño de noticias, proceso durante el cual ha recibido más de 60 premios. En 2003 Frank se sumó al periódico norteamericano The Arizona Republic para guiar el equipo de diseñadores de noticias y ayudar a dar una nueva dirección al diario.

Janet Froelich is creative director of The New York Times Magazine and of T: The New York Times Style Magazine. Under her direction, The New York Times Magazine has won more than 60 Gold and Silver

awards from SND, The Art Directors Club and the Society of Publication Designers.

Janet Froehlich es la directora creativa de la revista dominical del diario The New York Times y de la revista de estilo del mismo periódico, llamada T. Bajo su dirección, la revista del diario neoyorkino ha obtenido más de 60 premios de oro y plata de la SND, The Art Directors Club (Club de Directores de Arte) y la Society of Publication Designers (Sociedad de Diseñadores de Publicaciones).

Bill Gaspard is news design director at the Los Angeles Times and the Society for News Design's 2005 president. He previously worked as senior editor for readership and visuals at The San Diego Union-Tribune (Calif.), as art director at the Kansas City Star Sunday Magazine and as a features writer and designer at The State Journal-Register in Springfield, Ill. In 1997, Gaspard was site chair for the society's annual workshop and exhibition in San Diego.

Bill Gaspard es el director de diseño de noticias del diario Los Angeles Times y el presidente de la Sociedad de Diseño de Noticias (SND) en 2005. Anteriormente se desempeñó como editor jefe de lectoría y elementos visuales en el diario californiano The San Diego Union-Tribune, como director de arte de la revista dominical del diario norteamericano Kansas City Star, y como redactor de reportajes y diseñador del State Journal-Register de Springfield, Illinois, EE.UU. En 1997, Gaspard fue el director de la conferencia y el taller anual de la SND en San Diego.

Jeff Goertzen is a senior graphics reporter for the St. Petersburg Times (Fla.). He is a graphics consultant who has worked with more than 60 newspapers worldwide, training artists and building art

departments. He has worked at The Orange County Register (Calif.); The Detroit News; The Dallas Morning News; El Mundo, Madrid, Spain; and El Periódico, Barcelona, Spain.

Jeff Goertzen es el reportero de gráficos jefe del diario del estado norteamericano de Florida, St. Petersburg Times. Es un consultor de gráficos que ha trabajado con más de 60 diarios de todo el mundo, entrenando artistas y organizando departamentos de arte. Ha trabajado en los diarios norteamericanos The Orange County Register, de California; The Detroit News, de Michigan; The Dallas Morning News, de Texas; y los españoles El Mundo, de Madrid; y El Periódico, de Barcelona.

John M. Humenik is editor of the Quad-City Times, Davenport, Iowa. He also is publisher of On The River and editor of the Quad-City Business Journal. He is a former presentation/graphics editor at The Cincinnati Enquirer and assistant managing editor at the The Times of Northwest Indiana, Munster. He received the Suburban Newspapers of America's 2004 Editor of the Year award.

John M. Humenik es editor del diario norteamericano Quad-City Times, de Davenport, Iowa. También es el dueño y director de On The River y editor de la publicación sobre negocios norteamericana Quad-City Business Journal. Anteriormente fue editor de presentación y gráficos del diario The Cincinnati Enquirer, del estado norteamericano de Ohio, y editor administrativo asistente en el diario norteamericano The Times of Northwest Indiana, de Munster, Indiana. En 2004 la Asociación de Diarios Suburbanos de Estados Unidos le dio el premio al editor del año.

Joseph Kieta is editor of the Merced Sun-Star, a McClatchy-owned daily in California. Prior to the Sun-Star, Kieta worked

Tim Frank

Janet Froelich

Bill Gaspard

Marcy Mangels

Matt Mansfield

Alberto Nava

on redesign projects at The Tribune, San Luis Obispo, Calif., and the Times Leader, Wilkes-Barre, Pa. He has won numerous awards for his newspaper work.

Joseph Kieta es el editor del diario Merced Sun-Star, publicado en California por la empresa de diarios McClatchy. Antes de ese puesto, Kieta participó en proyectos de rediseño en los periódicos norteamericanos The Tribune, de San Luis Obispo, California; y Times Leader, de Wilkes-Barre, Pennsylvania. Ha recibido numerosos premios por su trabajo periodístico.

David Kordalski has been assistant managing editor for visuals at The Plain Dealer, Cleveland, Ohio, for five years, overseeing photography, graphics, news and feature design. He guided the paper's 2001 redesign. In his 20-plus years as a visual journalist, Kordalski has worked at large-, midsize- and small-circulation dailies, as well as at weeklies.

David Kordalski ha sido editor administrativo asistente de elementos visuales en el diario norteamericano The Plain Dealer, de Cleveland, Ohio, durante cinco años, y ha estado a cargo de la fotografía, los gráficos, y el diseño de noticias y reportajes. Lideró el rediseño de su diario en 2001. En sus más de 20 años de carrera como periodista visual, Kordalski se ha desempeñado tanto en diarios de gran, mediano y pequeño tiraje, como en semanarios.

Teresa Kriegsman is design editor of The News & Observer, Raleigh, N.C., named a World's Best-Designed Newspaper™ in 1998. During her 16 years there, she has designed news and sports sections and won several awards from SND and Associated Press Sports Editors.

Teresa Kriegsman es editora de diseño del diario norteamericano The News & Observer de Raleigh, Carolina

del Norte, reconocido como uno de los diarios mejor diseñados por la SND en 1998. Durante sus 16 años en el periódico, ha diseñado las secciones de noticias y deportes, y ganado varios premios de la SND y la Asociación de Editores de Deportes de Prensa de los Estados Unidos.

Marcy Mangels has been an assistant managing editor for three years at The Journal News, which serves the northern suburbs of New York City. Mangels designed the front page of the Connecticut Post for several years, winning several regional awards, and then she redesigned the Post in 1999 for a web conversion.

Marcy Mangels ha sido editora administrativa asistente durante tres años en el periódico The Journal News, que circula en suburbios al norte de la ciudad de Nueva York. Mangels diseñó la primera página del diario norteamericano Connecticut Post durante muchos años, por lo que obtuvo premios regionales, y luego rediseñó la publicación en 1999 para convertirla al nuevo tamaño estándar angosto.

Matt Mansfield is deputy managing editor of the San Jose Mercury News (Calif.). Mansfield directs the design, graphics and photography departments, as well as state, national and international reporting for the Silicon Valley newspaper. The Mercury News has been judged a World's ' Best-Designed Newspaper™.

Matt Mansfield es subeditor administrativo del diario californiano San Jose Mercury News. Mansfield dirige los departamentos de diseño, gráficos y fotografía, además de la investigación noticiosa sobre el estado de California, el país y los temas internacionales del diario de

Silicon Valley. El Mercury News ha sido reconocido por la SND como uno de los diarios mejor diseñados del mundo.

Alberto Nava is art director of Récord, the Mexican sports newspaper named World's Best-Designed Newspaper™ the past two years. He leads a 40-designer team there, and he has 12 years of journalism-design experience, having worked at Reforma, México City, and at the editorial company Notmusa.

Alberto Nava es el director de arte del diario deportivo mexicano Récord, que ha sido reconocido en los últimos dos años por la SND como uno de los diarios mejor diseñados del mundo. Ahí dirige un equipo de 40 personas, y en sus 12 años de experiencia en el diseño de noticias, ha trabajado en el diario Reforma, de Ciudad de México, y en la empresa editorial Notmusa.

32
judges worked on the competition at Syracuse, N.Y., in February 2005. Five judges devoted four days judging the World's Best-Designed Newspapers™ category. Twenty-seven judges spent three days on all other entries.

2,187
cumulative hours were required to complete the judging. That's not counting the thousands of hours devoted to preparing entries and producing the book.

423
entries in the World's Best-Designed™ competition category.

5
newspapers named World's Best-Designed™. This compares to five in the 25th edition and four in the 24th.

0
Best of Show in this edition. Best of Show is judged at the conclusion of individual judging. In 26 editions, judges have selected Best of Show in only 12 of the competitions.

JUDGES

Matt Petty

Evangelia Philippidis

Brian Plonka

David Puckett

Gladys Ríos

Buck Ryan

Rob Schneider

Bonnie Scranton

Phaedra Singelis

Stacy Sweat

Matt Petty is an art director at the San Francisco Chronicle (Calif.). He has worked in visual journalism for eight years, including news, features and information graphics. He has also worked at the San Jose Mercury News and The Examiner, San Francisco. His work has appeared in the SND and Print annuals.

Matt Petty es un director de arte del diario californiano San Francisco Chronicle. Ha trabajado en periodismo visual durante ocho años, incluyendo noticias, reportajes e infográficos. También ha trabajado en los periódicos San Jose Mercury News y The Examiner, este último de San Francisco. Sus trabajos han aparecido en los libros anuales de la SND y Print.

Evangelia Philippidis is an editorial features illustrator for The Columbus Dispatch (Ohio), where she has spent 18 years presenting visual stories of humanity and hubris, technology and spirituality, passion and pathos. Her award-winning images reflect both her Greek heritage and modern influences.

Evangelia Philippidis es una ilustradora de reportajes editoriales del diario norteamericano The Columbus Dispatch, del estado de Ohio, donde ha pasado 18 años presentando historias visuales de humanismo y orgullo, tecnología y espiritualidad, pasión y sufrimiento. Sus imágenes, que han sido premiadas, reflejan tanto su ancestro griego como influencias modernas.

Brian Plonka is a staff photographer for The Spokesman-Review, Spokane, Wash. During his 22-year career, Plonka has been named photographer of the year 10 times in local, regional and national contests. He was the 59th POY newspaper photographer of the year, and he has won several SND Gold awards.

Brian Plonka es un fotógrafo contratado por el diario norteamericano The Spokesman-Review, de Spokane, estado de Washington. A lo largo de sus 22 años de carrera, Plonka ha sido reconocido 10 veces como fotógrafo del año en competencias locales, regionales y nacionales. Fue el 59º fotógrafo de diario del año ganador de la competencia Pictures of the Year (Fotografías del Año) de la Univesity of Missouri, y ha ganado varios premios de oro de la SND.

David Puckett, senior artist at The Charlotte Observer (N.C.), has worked at newspapers for nearly 25 years. Publications include The Orange County Register (Calif.) and the Los Angeles Times. Puckett has received dozens of awards from several organizations. SND awards include seven Silvers, a handful of Awards of Excellence and a Judges' Special Recognition for his 1991 graphics on the Persian Gulf War.

David Puckett, artista jefe del diario norteamericano The Charlotte Observer, de Carolina del Norte, ha trabajado en diarios por casi 25 años, entre los cuales figuran The Orange County Register, de California, y el Los Angeles Times. Puckett ha recibido docenas de premios de parte de varias organizaciones. Entre los premios de la SND, figuran siete de plata, varios premios a la excelencia y un reconocimiento especial de los jueces por sus gráficos sobre la Guerra del Golfo de 1991.

Gladys Ríos is a design consultant and former design director at The Times of Northwest Indiana, Munster. She has overseen news, features and sports design during her career, and her experience includes redesign and creation of new sections and publications. She is a former features design director at the Austin American-

Statesman (Texas), and she's also worked at The Detroit News and the Chicago Tribune.

Gladys Ríos es una consultora de diseño y ex directora de diseño del diario norteamericano The Times, del noroeste del estado de Indiana. A lo largo de su carrera, ha estado a cargo del diseño de noticias, reportajes y deportes, y su experiencia incluye el rediseño y la creación de nuevas secciones y publicaciones. Fue la directora de diseño de reportajes del diario Austin American-Statesman, de Texas, y también trabajó en los periódicos norteamericanos The Detroit News y Chicago Tribune.

Sharon Roberts, assistant managing editor for presentation at the Austin American-Statesman (Texas), has had newsroom positions that include artist, Palm Beach Post; art director, The Dallas Morning News; and assistant managing editor for graphics, photography and design, The Press Democrat, Santa Rosa, Calif. She recently led the launch of ¡ahora sí!, the Statesman's Spanish-language weekly.

Sharon Roberts, editora administrativa asistente de presentación de noticias del diario norteamericano Austin American-Statesman, de Texas, ha ocupado varios puestos en la sala de noticias; como artista en el periódico norteamericano Palm Beach Post, de Florida; directora de arte en el diario Dallas Morning News, de Texas; y editora administrativa asistente de gráficos, fotografía y diseño en el The Press Democrat, de Santa Rosa, California. Recientemente lideró el lanzamiento de ¡ahora sí!, el semanario en español del Austin American-Statesman.

Alejandro Ros' clients include publications and entities such as Página/12, Radar, Las/12, the Goethe-Institut Buenos Aires, MTV, rock bands and recording

artists. He has won 22 SND awards as well as Garden Prizes for compact-disc covers. He was the 2002 Platinum Konex Prize winner for best Argentinean designer of the decade.

Alejandro Ros tiene entre sus clientes publicaciones y entidades tales como las argentinas Página/12, Radar y Las/12; el Goethe-Institut Buenos Aires, MTV, grupos de rock y otros artistas musicales. Ha obtenido 22 premios de la SND y también Garden Prizes por sus tapas de disco compacto. En 2002 ganó el Konex Prize por ser el mejor diseñador argentino de la década.

Eduardo Danilo Ruiz has worked in the media for more than 20 years as an art director, typographer, informational architect and technology strategist. He has received many awards for his design of newspapers, magazines and interactive media, and he is the author of the acclaimed design of the dailies Reforma and Mural in Mexico, both celebrated in SND's "25 Influential Moments in the History of News Design." He has led more than 100 redesign projects in Latin America, Europe and Asia.

Eduardo Danilo Ruiz ha trabajado en medios por más de 20 años como director de arte, tipógrafo, arquitecto de información y estratega de tecnología. Ha recibido muchos premios por su diseño de diarios, revistas y medios interactivos, y es el autor del celebrado diseño de los diarios mexicanos Reforma y Mural, que fueron destacados por la SND como uno de los 25 influyentes momentos históricos del diseño de noticias. Ha guiado más de 100 proyectos de rediseño en América Latina, Asia y Europa.

Buck Ryan, executive director of the University of Kentucky's First Amendment Center, is a newspaper consultant and

a co-author of "The Editor's Toolbox," which explains his Maestro Concept for story planning and newsroom organization adopted by newspapers here and abroad. He received the university's highest award for teaching in 2003.

Buck Ryan, director ejecutivo del First Amendment Center (Centro de la Primera Enmienda de la Constitución de EE.UU., sobre libertad de expresión) de University of Kentucky, es un consultor de periódicos y coautor de "The Editor's Toolbox" (La Caja de Herramientas del Editor), que explica su Concepto Maestro para la planificación de artículos y la organización de la sala de noticias adoptada por diarios de todo el mundo. En 2003 recibió el mayor premio que otorga su universidad a un educador.

Rob Schneider is the design editor for sports for The Dallas Morning News. After graduating from Truman State University (Mo.), Schneider has been a reporter, photographer, copy editor, section editor and designer for various-sized newspapers in Missouri, Nebraska and Texas. SND, Associated Press Sports Editors and Malofiej have honored his work.

Rob Schneider es el editor de diseño de deportes del diario norteamericano The Dallas Morning News, de Texas. Luego de graduarse por la Truman State University, de Missouri, EE.UU., fue reportero, fotógrafo, editor de textos, editor de sección temática y diseñador para periódicos de diverso tiraje en los estados norteamericanos de Missouri, Nebraska y Texas. La SND, la organización de apoyo a discapacitados APSE y Malofiej han reconocido su trabajo.

Bonnie Scranton has been at Newsweek magazine for 11 years as the graphics director and now as a senior art director. She has worked

Sharon Roberts

Alejandro Ros

Eduardo Danilo Ruiz

Juan Velasco

Chin Wang

Sherman Williams

for Richard Saul Wurman's "Understanding Business" and has taught graphic design at Yale University. She has worked for Edward Tufte on his books "Visual Explanations" and "Beautiful Evidence."

Bonnie Scranton ha trabajado en la revista noticiosa norteamericana Newsweek por 11 años como directora de gráficos, y actualmente como directora de arte principal. Ha trabajado para "Understanding Business" (Entendiendo los Negocios) de Richard Saul Wurman y ha enseñado diseño gráfico en Yale University. También ha trabajado para Edward Tufte en sus libros "Visual Explanations" (Explicaciones Visuales) y "Beautiful Evidence" (Hermosa Evidencia).

Phaedra Singelis, a multimedia producer, is deputy managing editor for multimedia at *washingtonpost.com,* where she is responsible for content development. She is liaison between the online product and the newspaper's award-winning photojournalism department. Prior to working on the site, Singelis worked as a picture editor at The Baltimore Sun and as staff photographer at The Plain Dealer, in Cleveland, Ohio, and The Cincinnati Enquirer.

Phaedra Singelis, una productora multimedial, es subeditora administrativa de multimedios en *washingtonpost.com,* donde es responsable del desarrollo del contenido. Hace de puente entre el producto online y trabajo fotoperiodístico del diario, que ha sido premiado muchas veces. Antes de trabajar en el sitio web, Singelis fue editora de fotografía en el diario norteamericano The Baltimore Sun, Maryland, y fotógrafa contratada en The Plain Dealer, de Cleveland, y The Cincinnati Enquirer, estos dos últimos del estado norteamericano de Ohio.

Stacy Sweat has been associate managing editor for design and graphics at the Chicago Tribune since 1992. In the 1980s, she was art director for the Sunday magazines of the Orlando Sentinel (Fla.) and The Atlanta Journal-Constitution. She led the redesign of both the Pioneer Press, St. Paul, Minn., in 1990 and the Chicago Tribune in 2001.

Stacy Sweat ha sido editora administrativa asociada de diseño y gráficos en el diario Chicago Tribune desde 1992. En los años 80, fue directora de arte de las revistas dominicales de los periódicos norteamericanos Orlando Sentinel, de Florida, y The Atlanta Journal-Constitution, de Georgia. Dirigió el rediseño tanto del diario norteamericano Pioneer Press, de Saint Paul, Minnesota, en 1990, como el del Chicago Tribune en 2001.

Juan Velasco is an infographics reporter, artist and consultant. He worked for El Mundo, Madrid, Spain, from 1991 to 1996 and later as a graphics art director at The New York Times. In 2002, Velasco established the infographics company 5W Infographic in New York and Madrid.

Juan Velasco es un reportero, artista y consultor de infográficos. Trabajó para el diario El Mundo, de Madrid, España, entre 1991 y 1996, y más tarde como director de arte de gráficos de The New York Times. En 2002 Velasco fundó su compañía de infográficos 5W Infographic en Nueva York y Madrid.

Chin Wang art directs and designs the Life at Home and Sunday Arts covers for The Boston Globe. She also works on news pages and special sections. Before coming to The Globe in 2001, Wang worked at The Charlotte Observer (N.C.) and the Orlando Sentinel (Fla.).

Chin Wang dirige el arte y diseña las tapas de las revistas Life at Home (Vida en Casa) y Sunday Arts (Artes del Domingo) del diario The Boston Globe, del estado norteamericano de Massachussets. También trabaja en páginas de noticias y secciones especiales. Antes de llegar a The Globe en 2001, Wang trabajó en los diarios norteamericanos The Charlotte Observer, de Carolina del Norte, y Orlando Sentinel, de Florida.

Sherman Williams, assistant managing editor for photography at the Milwaukee Journal Sentinel (Wis.), is a founding and current board member of the Associated Press Photo Managers, serving as president in 2004. Williams has been a guest faculty member at the American Press Institute and the Maynard Institute, teaching sessions on covering diverse communities, picture editing and ethics.

Sherman Williams, editor administrativo asistente de fotografía en el diario Milwaukee Journal Sentinel, del estado norteamericano de Wisconsin, es un miembro fundador y actual del directorio de Associated Press Photo Managers (Gerentes de Fotografía de la agencia noticiosa norteamericana), donde fue presidente en 2004. Williams ha sido un profesor invitado en el American Press Institute y el Maynard Institute, para dar charlas sobre la cobertura de comunidades diversas, así como sobre la edición y la ética fotográfica.

450
publications entered the competition.

6
Gold Medals awarded, defining the state of the art.

79
Silver Medals awarded, going beyond excellence and stretching the limits of the medium.

8
Judges' Special Recognitions, honoring a specific entry or body of work for superior excellence, as an adjunct to the other awards.

992
Awards of Excellence. Unless otherwise designated, winning entries are Awards of Excellence.

WHAT THE JUDGES SAW

Graphics judges

Tonya Cowan
Richard Curtis
Linda Eckstein
Jeff Goertzen
David Puckett

GOING FOR THE GOLD
What the judges looked for in the 1,340 graphics entries.

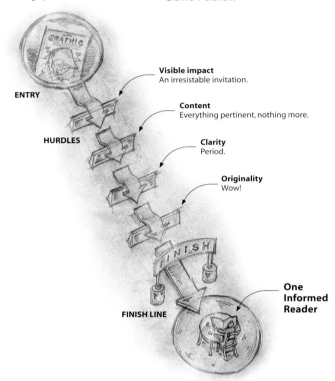

ENTRY

Visible impact
An irresistable invitation.

HURDLES

Content
Everything pertinent, nothing more.

Clarity
Period.

Originality
Wow!

FINISH LINE

One Informed Reader

Feature, magazine and illustration judges

Janet Froelich
Matt Petty
Evangelia Philippidis
Alejandro Ros
Chin Wang

We looked for work that presented a fresh view of culture in a graphic way. We looked for ideas — and for work that got to the essence of those ideas by stripping away the decoration.

As we walked down the rows of entries, we looked for work that had impact, clarity and one unified concept. As we looked further into the piece, all the details had to contribute to what we each viewed as the impact of the whole. Typography was really important to us, whether clean and elegant or raw and energetic.

Is it innovative, evocative, emotional, communicative, elegant, sophisticated, clear and fun?

Nos fijamos en trabajos que presentaran un punto de vista fresco sobre la cultura en forma gráfica. Buscamos ideas y también trabajos que representaran la esencia de esas ideas al eliminar la decoración.

Cuando caminamos a lo largo de las filas de las piezas participantes, buscamos trabajos que tuvieran impacto, claridad y un concepto único. Cuando observamos cada pieza más detenidamente, todos los detalles tenían que contribuir a lo que cada uno de nosotros vio como el impacto global. La tipografía fue muy importante para nosotros, tanto si era limpia y elegante, como bruta y energética.

¿Es innovador, evocativo, emocionante, comunicativo, elegante, sofisticado, claro y entretenido?

Photo and small-newspaper judges

Tim Frank
Joseph Kieta
Brian Plonka
Gladys Ríos
Phaedra Singelis

The competition revealed that design and photography are following the trend of the information age.

We need to remember the reasons why creative people are brought together to form a staff. Individuality, personal vision and craftsmanship truly make a special newspaper.

Many of the newspapers outside the United States are taking over where U.S. papers left off by giving subscribers a complete reading and visual experience. Although there were certainly some fine examples present, U.S. papers often forgot about putting individuals' vision into the content.

La competencia reveló que el diseño y la fotografía están siguiendo la tendencia de la era de la información.

Debemos recordar las razones por las cuales la gente creativa se reune para formar un equipo de trabajo. La individualidad, la visión personal y la habilidad artesanal realmente hacen que un periódico sea especial.

Muchos de los diarios no norteamericanos están sobrepasando a los de Estados Unidos en aspectos que los segundos habían desarrollado, al dar a los suscriptores una cabal experiencia de lectura y visual. Pese a que ciertamente hubo algunos buenos ejemplos presentes, muchas veces los diarios norteamericanos se olvidaron de incluir en el contenido el punto de vista de los individuos.

News and sports judges

Bill Gaspard
Teresa Kriegsman
Marcy Mangels
Matt Mansfield
Alberto Nava

Don't copy anything in this book. We mean it. Really.

Use this book for inspiration – not imitation.

Think for yourself. (Engage your mind before engaging your mouse.)

Edit yourself. (Find the best way to tell your story. Then plan it with clarity and execute it with precision.)

Be yourself. (Speak to your own community in your own voice.)

Enjoy yourself.

No copie nada de este libro. De verdad. En serio.

Use este libro para inspirarse, pero no para imitarlo.

Piense por su cuenta. (Aplique su mente antes de tomar el mouse del computador).

Edítese a sí mismo. (Encuentre la mejor forma de contar la historia. Luego, planifíquela con claridad y ejecútela con precisión).

Sea auténtico. (Hable con sus propias palabras a su propia comunidad).

Que le vaya bien.

Generalist judges
resolving conflicts of interest

Stacy Sweat
Juan Velasco

Long-form judges
judging longer entries

Heidi de Laubenfels
Julie Elman
David Kordalski
Rob Schneider
Sherman Williams

We responded to pages that made us think. These pages were absorbing; we were invited in and propelled to the message. When the page was clever, as readers, we felt clever as well.

All winners had an honest commitment to the content, absent cheap tricks. We rewarded strong thinking and innovation – not for innovation's sake, but rather because it offered a fresh perspective. This work was smart.

Clear communication transcends language. Great storytelling was key, and the story had to be told using appropriate tools – well-chosen pictures, tight graphics, powerful words. These pages had the cerebral might to back up the initial emotional resonance.

Consistent foundational elements were punctuated with personality, surprise, sophisticated typography, reserved color, clarity and strong organization.

Nos fijamos en páginas que nos hicieran pensar. Estas páginas eran absorbentes; nos invitaban al texto y nos llevaban al mensaje. Cuando la página era inteligente, también nos sentimos inteligentes como lectores.

Todos los ganadores tuvieron un honesto compromiso para con el contenido, sin trucos baratos. Premiamos las ideas fuertes y la innovación, no por el solo hecho de innovar, sino porque ofrecieron una perspectiva fresca. Este trabajo fue inteligente.

La comunicación clara trasciende el lenguaje. La narración de historias fue vital, y la historia debía ser relatada con las herramientas adecuadas; fotografías bien elegidas, gráficos concisos y palabras potentes. Estas páginas tenían el poder cerebral que sostenía la resonancia emocional inicial.

Los elementos fundamentales y consistentes fueron acentuados con personalidad, sorpresa, tipografía sofisticada, color restringido, claridad, y fuerte organización.

79

awards – the most of any publication – to the Los Angeles Times.

700

awards won in the United States. Of the 29 countries winning awards, these won 10 or more –
94 went to Spain,
58 to Canada,
44 to México,
35 to Portugal,
30 to Germany,
29 to Sweden,
16 to El Salvador, and
11 to Brazil.

68

facilitators and four auditors worked on the competition. They registered and organized entries, counted votes and assisted judges.

1,860

hours for six people to iron winning pages – preparing them to be photographed so they could sparkle in this book.

WHAT THE JUDGES SAW

World's Best-Designed Newspaper™ judges

John M. Humenik
Sharon Roberts
Eduardo Danilo Ruiz
Buck Ryan
Bonnie Scranton

If the design and architecture of a publication compose its score, then excellence is achieved through its performers. Of the 423 newspapers in this year's competition, five newspapers deliver an accomplished and inspiring performance.

After evaluating a record number of entries, the judges unanimously recognize the following publications as the World's Best-Designed Newspapers™. While these papers represent an array of format, scope and structure, they succeed because of their clarity of purpose and their commitment to engage their audience.

The winners excel in design — maintaining the highest standards of typography, page design, photography, illustration and color use. While each newspaper has a unique voice, all of them demonstrate passion, intelligence, imagination and rigor.

And to each publication — Bravo!

Si el diseño y la arquitectura de una publicación componen su partitura, entonces la excelencia se logra a través de sus intérpretes. De los 423 diarios de la competencia de este año, cinco presentan un rendimiento bien logrado e inspirador.

Luego de evaluar un número récor de piezas participantes, los jueces destacaron en forma unánime las siguientes publicaciones como los Periódicos Mejor Diseñados del Mundo™. Aunque estos diarios representan una variedad de formatos, coberturas y estructuras, logran el éxito debido a su claridad de propósito y su compromiso para enganchar a sus lectores.

Los ganadores se destacan por el diseño al mantener los más altos estándares en tipografía, diseño de página, fotografía, ilustración y uso de color. Pese a que cada periódico tiene una voz única, todos demuestran pasión, inteligencia, imaginación y rigurosidad.

Un ¡Bravo! a cada publicación.

FL

LOO
WONDE
TELLING
TO EA
ALWA

IRRESIST

WORLD'S BEST-DESIGNED NEWSPAPERS

chapter 1

LITERATUR

Ruhelos und unbeirrbar

Jürgen Habermas zum
75. Geburtstag

Die tote Tochter

Der niederländische Autor P. F. Thomése trauert um sein Kind
und erörtert all die großen Fragen des Lebens/Von Ines Barner

Eiskalter Aufstieg

Im Schweizer Ferienort Saas-Fee kraxeln Touristen gefrorene Wasserfälle hoch – 50 Meter in 25 Minuten
VON HANS GASSER

Information

Mörder für zwei Wochen

1982

Ein hoffnungsvoller Fall

Das politische Hoteljahr 2005: Weshalb Gerhard Schröder glaubt, im Wahljahr nichts mehr verlieren zu können. Und warum Angela Merkels Stern sinkt. VON GUNTER HOFMANN

Methode RWE
Der tägliche Anschlag:
Wie die Energiekonzerne ihre
politischen Freunde in Bund und
Gemeinden gewinnen. Seite 28

WIRTSCHAFT

Das Gesetz, das keiner merkt

Die Steuerreform wird vollendet –
bis fast nichts mehr übrig bleibt

Das deutsche Experiment beginnt

Von heute morgen an gibt es Hartz IV: Daten auf Arbeitslosen getroffen werden, soll selbst zu hartzen – mit allen Mitteln.
Die entscheidende Frage wird sein: Brauchen wir tatsächlich mehr Druck? VON KOLJA RUDZIO UND WOLFGANG UCHATIUS

Umtauscher

DOSSIER

Ohne jede Warnung kam die Flut übers Land

Wir haben versagt!

Die Zeit

Hamburg, Germany
Circulation: 450,000

A weekly newspaper with refined design and strong typography, Die Zeit invites readers to slow down and explore the many facets of life.

Bookish in its design, this paper reflects the country's history in fine typography and printing through the elegant, yet practical use of art and text.

Designers at Die Zeit succeed in the creative use of a strong grid structure, but also know how to break it to seduce the reader.

Die Zeit es un periódico semanal de refinado diseño y potente tipografía que invita a los lectores a relajarse y explorar la gran variedad de facetas de la vida.

De diseño tipo libro, este periódico refleja la historia de su país en una fina tipografía e impresión a través del uso de los elementos artísticos y el texto en forma elegante pero práctico.

Los diseñadores de Die Zeit logran el éxito en el uso de una potente estructura de retícula, pero también saben cómo romperla para seducir al lector.

SIBEL KEKILLI

»Ich spüre mein eigenes Gewicht nicht mehr und kann Dinge tun, die mir draußen, an Land, unmöglich sind. Unter Wasser kann man fliegen«

12 IN DER ZEIT

POLITIK

WISSEN

»Also waren wir eure Hereros«

Gruppenbild mit Nazis

Der Dschihad der Deutschen

WISSEN

Alles ist erlaubt

Die Mär vom Wasserstoff

2

DIE ZEIT

WOCHENZEITUNG FÜR POLITIK · WIRTSCHAFT · WISSEN UND KULTUR

Die Jahrhundertkatastrophe

Schuldlos in der Sintflut

Ohne jede Warnung

REISEN

Das Katerfrühstück

DIE ZEIT

WOCHENZEITUNG FÜR POLITIK · WIRTSCHAFT · WISSEN UND KULTUR

Nr.9 · 19. Februar 2004 · 59. Jahrgang

Propheten des Untergangs

»Deutschland in Not« singen die Schlagzeilen-Orakel. Unser Leitartikel kürzt ohne Angst nicht um. Die Katastrophenmacht. Schaßt und „die Politiker". Wieterie A. Fraßer und Göttz Hauwen untersuchen den Pessimismus der Strukturkrise.

Held unter Feuer

Karneval, Sex und Tod

Eine deutsche Blamage

Die Vereinsmeier

Geliebter Katzenjammer

Die Türkei passt rein

Der Klon, der ins Korea kam

„Aggressiv, effizient und zielorientiert"

Klon des Erfolgs

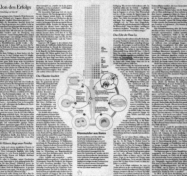

Zwischen Tönen wohnen

LEBEN

Umzingelt von Besserwissern

Überbezahlt, inkompetent, arrogant – über Berater schimpfen kann jeder. Bis man sie ganz dringend braucht VON BURKHARD STRASSMANN

E s war zwei Meter groß, trug helle, fast weiße Kleidung und hieß Burkhard. Wenn es kam, lege er eine Hand auf meine Schulter. Den Druck war leicht, ich kann mich heute noch jederzeit an das Gefühl erinnern...

Fortsetzung auf Seite 56

ECHTE BERATER von falschen zu unterscheiden ist nicht so leicht. Nur drei der auf dieser Seite abgebildeten Personen sind als professionelle Ratgeber tätig. Und zwar welche? Siehe nächste Seite, ganz unten

DEWA-Kundendienst: Beratung & Verkauf
K. Hannemann

LEBENSZEICHEN

G. i. B.

Gut im Bett? Diese Frage plagt auch Harald Martenstein

Mir wurde von einem Verlag ein Buch geschickt. Der Verlag heißt Rowohlt. Das Buch heißt *G. i. B. Gut im Bett*. Ich kenne die Autorin, sie war mal Auszubildende bei uns...

Lebensinhalt

CONSUMER, HEALTH & CULTURE

ONLINE MUSIC GOES LEGIT

BY JOHN M. MORAN • COURANT STAFF WRITER

If it weren't for Janet Jackson, Apple Computer's online music offer might have been the biggest shocker of the 2004 Super Bowl.

Apple, in a co-promotion with Pepsi-Cola, ran Super Bowl commercials offering to give away 100 million songs, free over the Internet, through Apple's iTunes online music service.

"This historic promotion to legally give away 100 million free songs will go down in history as igniting the legal download market," said Steve Jobs, Apple's chief executive.

He may turn out to be right. But the market for legally downloaded music was catching fire even before the kickoff.

After months of debate about the propriety of music file "sharing" and "swapping," consumers have begun flocking to sites that offer legal downloads for a price.

By early this year, more than three dozen services were selling music online, and more were planned. Prices for the music generally ranged from 25 cents to 99 cents a song, or about $10 for an album. Exact industry statistics are scarce, but it is clear that consumers are now legally downloading songs by the millions each month.

Even more services are coming. Wal-Mart recently begun testing a music download service selling songs at 88 cents

PLEASE SEE ONLINE, PAGE 125

A Nurse Across Town Will See You Now

BY HILARY WALDMAN • COURANT STAFF WRITER

Richard Moran was a newborn, swaddled in blankets, when his family moved into the Hartford house where he has lived for 87 years.

He settled his wife into this house, raised three children, retired to a recliner in the living room and has no plans to leave until he dies.

Moran suffers from asbestos-damaged lungs, prostate cancer, bladder cancer and congestive heart failure. Any one of his conditions could sentence him to a nursing home or hospital bed.

But a commercial-grade tanning bed that dominates his living room keeps Moran's skin as smooth and bronzed as a young lifeguard's. And a little white box on the end table keeps him well enough to remain at home.

The box is an electronic monitor that every morning relays Moran's medical vital signs to a nurse across town. If his weight, blood pressure or other indicators show signs of trouble, the nurse will call, visit or contact Moran's doctor.

In the twilight of his life, Richard Moran is riding the

PLEASE SEE MEASURING, PAGE 126

INSIDE Part 2 • BIG PLANS: The University of Connecticut Health Center has ambitious goals for cancer research and treatment. Page L18 • THE SHOW MUST GO ON: There are some bright lights in Connecticut's arts scene in 2004 — and more than a few challenges. Page L20 • RAMPING UP: Foxwoods and Mohegan Sun gear up for near-certain competition in gaming. Page L22 • ADMIT SOME: Getting accepted at the University of Connecticut is less of a sure thing. Page L24

THE HARTFORD COURANT • SUNDAY, FEBRUARY 22, 2004

FALL FASHION 2004 • NYC

Dapper Dans

DESIGNERS WANT MEN TO FORGET CARGO PANTS, GO FOR GLAMOUR

BY GREG MORAGO

BOOKS

In 'Oblivion,' Language Is Protagonist

A Gullible, Conniving Holy Man

THE EMBERS OF WAR

'A Ticket To Girl Island'

CONNECTICUT

Stability Not Just A Man's Province

SLAMMIN', JAMMIN'

At Wesleyan, A Big Plan On Campus

Partying With Family Across The Ocean

FIGHTING FOR AN EDUCATION

Danger Lurks On Walk Home

NATION / WORLD

Sparks Fly Over Latest Iraq Report

THE FIRST VOTE

Austrian Writer Wins Nobel

11am   6:10   6:30pm

The Sartorial Splendor Of Mourning In California

Voices Against The Grain

THE REAL BILL?

For lighthearted movie award, MTV's is heavy metal

America's Oldest Continuously-Published Newspaper

Hartford Courant.

WEATHER
Mostly Cloudy.
High Of 72. B12

VOLUME CLXVII, NUMBER 162   COPYRIGHT 2004, THE HARTFORD COURANT CO.   THURSDAY, JUNE 10, 2004   6★ | Metro $1.00 in Fairfield County and outside Connecticut   50¢

Focus Is On Timing Of Favors

Governor, Matthews Helped Each Other

By MARK PAZNIOKAS
COURANT STAFF WRITER

Gov. John G. Rowland touted Robert V. Matthews as a good risk for $9 million in private financing in 1997 as Matthews was secretly paying the governor $1,750 a month in rent for a condominium worth perhaps $500 a month, the House impeachment committee was told Wednesday.

Rowland stopped by a dinner at the Goodwin Hotel in Hartford on April 29, 1997, and assured bankers that Matthews would obtain state assistance to go with the private financing he sought, investigator Andrew Melnick testified.

"Don't worry about the state," Rowland reportedly told bankers from Norwest Business Credit. "The state will take care of its part. You take care of your part."

He was right. In June, a state agency approved a $1.15 million loan for Matthew's New Haven Manufacturing Co.

And the same month, lawyers closed a deal in which Matthews used a straw purchaser to secretly buy Rowland's Washington, D.C., condominium, then worth an estimated $25,000 to $30,000, for $68,500.

PLEASE SEE TIMING, PAGE A10

INSIDE

➤ Supreme Court to decide today on expediting Rowland appeal. **Page A10**

➤ Watching these hearings can be torture. Helen Ubiñas column, **Page B1**

➤ Updates are at **www.ctnow.com**

Rowland Steers Clear Of The Capitol

By CHRISTOPHER KEATING And JON LENDER
COURANT STAFF WRITERS

Gov. John G. Rowland's lawyers claimed this week that compelling him to appear before the House impeachment committee would distract the governor from "important issues affecting the interests of the state."

Whatever those interests are, they haven't required his presence at the state Capitol lately.

As the impeachment committee held its first public hearings Tuesday and Wednesday, Rowland completely avoided the Capitol building. He ducked out a rear entrance to avoid reporters at his one public appearance Tuesday — an annual Republican fund-raiser in Stamford — and had no appearances scheduled Wednesday or today.

His schedule included two meetings: a lengthy session in Avon Tuesday on homeland security, and a meeting of his commissioners Wednesday, which his office says he skipped.

Some light was shed on Rowland's whereabouts Wednesday when picketers

PLEASE SEE ROWLAND, PAGE A8

1911 ◆ RONALD REAGAN ◆ 2004

ASSOCIATED PRESS

DIGNITARIES GATHER in the Rotunda of the Capitol Wednesday as a military honor guard stands next to the casket of former President Ronald Reagan. Nancy Reagan, members of Reagan's former administration, U.S. lawmakers and other dignitaries attended the service. The former president's body will lie in state for two days in the Capitol Rotunda before his formal state funeral on Friday.

A SOLEMN DAY OF RITUAL

Combined Wire Services

WASHINGTON — The riderless horse with boots backward in the stirrups. The clop-clop of the horses' hooves along the avenue as the caisson carried Ronald Reagan's flag-draped casket to the Capitol.

The crowd of Americans five and six deep holding miniature American flags along both sides of a heat-hazed Constitution Avenue at twilight.

It was Wednesday's meticulously choreographed proceedings — replete with symbols dating back to the mid-19th century designed to display the nation's grief for a fallen leader — that will stick in the public mind.

Such somber traditions of a nation in mourning suffused the 40th president's last journey from California to the nation's capital as his flag-draped casket traveled to Washington for a formal cortege through the city.

Tens of thousands of citizens lined Constitution Avenue and the West Entrance to the Capitol, many

having waited for hours in wilting heat to pay their respects. Later, after an austere ceremony beneath the soaring dome, the first of an anticipated 150,000 mourners began walking past Reagan's coffin, which lay on the black velvet-covered catafalque first used under similar conditions at the death of Abraham Lincoln.

PLEASE SEE REAGAN, PAGE A3

WEST HARTFORD NATIVE TAKES ON A NEGLECTED 'DISEASE OF POVERTY'

Untwisting The Puzzle Of Hookworms

By WILLIAM HATHAWAY
COURANT STAFF WRITER

The farmers of northern Minas Gerais walk barefoot in the sandy, fecal-contaminated soil. Few in this Texas-size state in southeastern Brazil realize the soil is infested with hookworms, which bore into the soles of their feet, then suck blood from their intestines, sapping their energy and even their intelligence.

For two decades, the half-inch hookworm has been squarely in the scientific sights of West Hartford native Dr. Peter Hotez, who has used $18 million

from the Bill and Melinda Gates Foundation to create the world's first human hookworm vaccine.

Within two years, the former Yale professor who now heads the microbiology and tropical medicine department at George Washington University hopes to take the vaccine to Minas Gerais, to see whether it can begin to help eradicate the worm, which infects at least 740 million people worldwide.

If it works, the vaccine could be one of the first to offer protection against

what Hotez calls the world's orphan or neglected diseases — a loose collection of about a dozen ailments such as hookworm infection, river blindness, African sleeping sickness and dengue fever. These conditions sicken, cripple and maim the world's poor, though they do not kill in large numbers.

Experts on tropical diseases caution that even if the hookworm vaccine works, there is no guarantee that companies will make it in large quantities,

PLEASE SEE DOCTOR, PAGE A12

INSIDE

Lots Of Lemonade
Since setting up her first lemonade stand in West Hartford four years ago, an 8-year-old girl has raised $200,000 for cancer research. **Connecticut, Page B1**

The Real Bill?
Will Bill Clinton's new book contain any real news? **Life, Page D1**

CTnow.com Breaking news. All the time.

Business E1	Crossword D5	Lottery A4
Classified E7-E12	Editorial A14, A15	Movies .... Cal 18, 19
Connecticut B1	Life D1	Nation / World A2, A3
		Obituaries B10, B11
		Public Notices B6, E10
		Sports C1

40610
04209"00050

FLAVOR

By SHIRLEY O. CORRIHER · TRIBUNE MEDIA SERVICES

WHEN **FRUIT** LOOKS AND SMELLS **WONDERFUL**, NATURE'S TELLING YOU IT'S READY TO **EAT**. BUT IT'S NOT ALWAYS SO OBVIOUS.

How can fruit look and feel ripe but not be ripe at all? How can we tell if a piece of fruit is ripe? How can we get fruit to ripen? How can we slow down ripening when all of the bananas in that bunch on the counter are getting brown spots at once? As a food scientist, I should know the answers to all of these questions, but on occasion I slip up, too, and am drawn to a bright orange, soft apricot only to be devastated when I bite into it. There are guidelines that can help us all make better selections. And there are good and bad ways of storing fruit once it is chosen.

But first a little scientific explanation. Fruits are the seed-bearing ovaries of a plant. It's their mission to get their seeds as widely distributed as possible. If all of the seeds fall right under the plant, there will not be enough nutrients and sunlight for them to prosper. So several things must happen. Until the seeds are ready to plant, the fruit must stay hidden to keep the seeds safe. To that end, fruit remains hard, sour, inedible, often an almost invisible green among the leaves until the seeds are ready to be sown.

When this finally occurs, fruit needs to enlist the help of animals — humans included — to distribute those precious seeds. To attract animals, fruit becomes brilliantly beautiful, sweet and luscious with enticing aromas. Animals drawn by the gorgeous colors and smells pick the fruit and carry it away, eating the edible flesh but rejecting the hard, even poisonous seeds. Thus, animals distribute the seeds for the plant.

To become beautiful and irresistible, fruit ripens. It changes in color, texture, aroma, taste, size and nutrient content. All fruit does not change in the

PLEASE SEE RIPENING, PAGE G8

IRRESISTIBLY RIPE

PHOTO ILLUSTRATION BY CLOE POISSON / THE HARTFORD COURANT

SPORTS

A UNIT OF MEASURE

Sox Say No On Nomar

Deny That Trade With Cubs In Works

What's In It For The Unit

What's In It For The O'Banks

The Inside Pitch

Shaq Switches Coasts

Riley: Heat Acquire 'Best Player In World'

Janangelo Qualifies For State Open

3pm   2·22   4pm

IN

EX MARKS THE SPOT ON NET

What's Up With The Queen Of The Nuts?

The Search For A Lost Love: Putting Together The Pieces Of A Former Sweetheart's New Life From The Safety Of Your Computer

---

COURANT CLASSIFIED, PAGE E7

BUSINESS

Insurer Severing Last Tie To Charity

Foundation To Drop 'Anthem' From Name

Modest Pay Raises Likely

Rocco Budgeting Hikes Under 4%

High Demand, Storms Delaying Flights

MAD FOR MINIS

Want Apple's New Music Player? Good Luck Trying To Find One

THE GOSPEL
ACCORDING TO MEL

ALL EYES ARE ON JIM CAVIEZEL

STYLE

GO, DADDY-O

Hartford Courant.

Blasts In Egypt Kill 30

Boy Charged In Friend's Death

Blue Back Politicking: Both Sides Spend Big

Spinning The Unemployment Numbers

THE CAMPAIGN'S LAUGH TRACK

COMMENTARY

$3 Million For This?

By LAURENCE D. COHEN

On-and-off Litchfield County resident James Glassman, who writes on finance and technology and things political, had it right when he suggested that "one of the best ways to make money is to be standing around when large sums of cash are changing hands."

If the embarrassing spectacle of the Impeachment Investigation That Will Never End tells us anything, it tends to confirm the Glassman wisdom: There were a whole lot of people standing around when cash was changing hands.

For all the hype being churned out about the Let's Try to Beat Rowland Some Way Other Than Through Elections Because That Never Works impeachment inquiry, what is most remarkable is how mundane so much of the stirring revelations appear to be.

Sure enough, as with any large, bureaucratic nightmare of an organization, there's a lot of money sloshing around the of state of Connecticut government process, with squadrons of bosses and hangers-on and middlemen and pals and cousins and uncles and wives all coming away with a bit of change.

No one knows the drill better than legislators, who spend weeks of every session groveling for state money on behalf of their real employers: law-firm clients and universities and labor unions and nonprofit sob-sister agencies.

It has cost the taxpayers of Connecticut about $3 million so far to find out that Rowland has a part of it all — apparently committing such felonies as smoking expensive cigars not of his own choosing and bobbing up and down in a hot tub paid for

by a long-time friend and (gasp!) office-scheduling czar.

We've learned that Rowland has lots and lots of friends who are pretty good at winning state contracts; many, many friends who were winning state contracts when Rowland was still in the womb (known in the trade as partial-birth extortion); many, many friends who have acquired a bit more of the action since Gov. John took over.

Since the investigative committee isn't inclined to let us in on what may or may not be an impeachable offense, we are left

It has cost taxpayers $3 million to find out that Rowland has been committing such felonies as smoking expensive cigars not of his choosing.

to tsk, tsk, tsk at every Rowland chum-buddy transfer of affection with his pals.

What is remarkable about the spectacle thus far is that, in a

normal world, we could have sat John Rowland down with a 25-cent cup of coffee ($3 in West Hartford Center) and asked, "What the hell were you thinking, John?"

And if the feds weren't sniffing around with their own investigation, primed and ready

PLEASE SEE $3 MILLION, PAGE C6

Laurence D. Cohen is a public policy consultant who recently served as special assistant to Gov. John G. Rowland. His column appears every Wednesday and Sunday. He can be reached at cohencolumn@aol.com.

ILLUSTRATION BY PATRICIA COUSINS/SPECIAL TO THE COURANT
PHOTO BY STEPHEN DUNN/THE HARTFORD COURANT

Christianity's Widening Gulf

By RALPH LORD ROY

The overwhelming vote by a historic Wethersfield congregation to sever its ties with the United Church of Christ is symptomatic of the larger crisis confronting Christianity in this country.

American Catholicism had been facing its own challenges, with few new priests and declining attendance at Mass, further exacerbated by clergy sexual abuse and coverup by several bishops. All this has been accompanied by the mushrooming of "cafeteria Catholics" who identify with their church but ignore a variety of its teachings. Recently, a divisive debate has erupted over whether communion should be denied John Kerry and other pro-choice politicians.

The problems facing Protestant churches cannot be as easily summarized. These offspring of the Reforma-

SPIRITUAL LEADERS ON THE RIFT IN WETHERSFIELD, PAGE C3

tion always have been in a state of some disarray, with scores of denominations, large and small, crowding the religious landscape. This is the price they pay for the right of individual interpretation of Scripture and the lack of any overarching authority to enforce unity and hand down binding directives.

For decades, there has been tension between liberal/moderate Protestants and conservative/fundamentalist Protestants. The former group has dominated most mainline denominations (Congregationalists, Episcopalians, Methodists, Presbyterians, Lutherans) and has encouraged a faith that is flexible and open-minded. Assemble a dozen of them together for Bible study, and a wide assortment of interpretations emerges. Did Jesus really feed 5,000 or walk on water or raise Lazarus from the dead? Such topics can occasion spirited discussions, with many creative opinions aired in an amiable atmosphere of give-and-take.

Most of the growing congregations today, however, are in the conservative/fundamentalist camp, many of them charismatic, nondenominational and relatively new. The media glibly refer to the Christian right as evangelical — a misnomer, because Protestants are by definition evangelical. In Latin America, "Protestant" and "evangelical" are interchangeable terms.

The most important difference between the two species of Protestants is their view of Scripture. One attitude is well summed up in a bumper sticker that reads: "The Bible says it. I believe it. That settles it." Critics sometimes suggest that such obsessive veneration of the word of God is, in effect, a pious form of idolatry.

In reality, self-proclaimed Bible believers pick and choose among scriptural passages. They may focus on Old Testament texts that condemn homosexuality while ignoring other verses that forbid men from cutting their hair around their temples and warn women against wearing garments made of two different kinds of thread. Some pas-

PLEASE SEE CHRISTIANITY, PAGE C6

Ralph Lord Roy of Southington is a retired United Methodist minister.

The Last Laugh? Wait For The History Books

By MAX BOOT

Listening to the endless encomiums to Ronald Reagan, many from people who once derided him, I couldn't help wonder whether some day George W. Bush would receive similar tributes from his current enemies. It seems unlikely, even to me, but then it seemed pretty unlikely 20 years ago that the Gipper would ever win widespread acclaim as one of the greatest presidents in U.S. history.

It is bracing to the reader such as Dinesh D'Souza's Reagan biography and be reminded of what was actually said about him during his presidency. The man now eulogized as a giant was famously derided as an "amiable dunce" by Democratic elder Clark Clifford.

Robert Wright of the New Republic said he was "virtually brain-dead"; Nicholas von Hoffman called him an "unlettered, self-assured bumpkin" in Harper's magazine, and Kevin

Phillips complained he was trying to govern "based on maxims out of McGuffey's Reader and Calvin Coolidge."

Barbara Ehrenreich titled her book about the 1980s "The Worst Years of Our Lives." Reagan was accused of being a "reckless cowboy" and a "simple-minded ideologue" (Mark Hertsgaard) who was leading the nation toward nuclear annihilation.

These accusations were not particularly controversial among the chattering classes in the 1980s; they were (and in some quarters remain) received wisdom. The only wonder among the sophisticates was how Reagan fooled so many people into supporting him. Then-Rep. Patricia Schroeder provided the explanation when she said he was the "Teflon president" to whom no charge ever stuck. Garry Wills wrote that Reagan "cast a spell" that drew Americans into a "vast communal exercise in make-believe."

What was the source of all this animus? Part of it was personal: Reagan, a C student at Eureka College and a B-movie actor, couldn't win the respect of A-list intellectuals. They thought he wasn't up to running the country. But mostly it was ideological. Reagan's ideas flouted the intellectual fashions of his day.

When he came to office in 1981, the consensus was that the nation was suffering from "malaise." The best that could be hoped for, the smart set believed, was to strike an accommodation with the Soviet Union and to lower our economic expectations. Reagan scoffed at such pessimism. He set about reviving the economy with tax cuts and consigning the "Evil Empire" to the ash heap of history by raising defense spending and supporting anti-communist rebels abroad. He was not content to manage problems. He wanted to transcend them. And he did.

The similarities with George W. Bush are un-

canny. As Reagan was, he is thought to be an intellectual lightweight too stupid to understand how ruinous his policies are. He is getting as much grief as Reagan did for not bowing to the logic of deterrence and containment. Reagan's alternative was the Strategic Defense Initiative; Bush's, the doctrine of pre-emption. Reagan was derided for his stark depiction of the Cold War as a "struggle between right and wrong, good and evil." Bush used similar language in the war on terrorism — and earns similar derision.

On domestic policy, Bush is, as Reagan was, attacked for opposing abortion, appointing

PLEASE SEE LAST LAUGH, PAGE C6

Max Boot, a senior fellow at the Council on Foreign Relations, writes a weekly column for the Los Angeles Times, where this article first appeared.

INGER ATTERSTAM

Läkarstämma utan tingeltangel

Ursäkta, vad är klockan?

Atomuret fyller 50 år och börjar nå gränsen för hur bra det kan bli. Därför tävlar fysiker världen över för att skapa en "optisk klocka" så perfekt att när den väl dragit sig en hel sekund så har universum redan gått under. Men bra klockor räcker inte. Tiden måste skyddas så att den inte stjäls – av terrorister.

Håller tiden

Optiska klockan

2. Laserkammmen

Atomuren i världen

Europa tar upp kampen om tiden

SUSEN SCHULTZ
Reporter

Bigfoot skymtad på nytt i USA

13 000 nya arter upptäckta i havet

Hierarkin skapade torterare i Irak

Kylan slutet för mammutarna

Missa inte

BRA JUST NU

FILM · SCEN · BÖCKER · KONST · MUSIK

Vältalig triumf över rasismen

AV OLA SIGVARDSSON

Högtflygande drömmar med lite markkontakt

FREDRIK BRÄCKNER

Bantning ger stort manfall

I otakt med omvärlden

SVENSKA DAGBLADET

Fredag den 12 november 2004　　　　E4o | Sedan 1884 | Pris 15 kr

Zlatans konstverk var värt ett pris på galan JAN MAJLARD Sport sid 23

KVINNOR SÅLLAS BORT I MATTSSONS STYRKA Nyheter sid 11

Snabbmatskedjor gör stora förluster

SvD-undersökning visar att var femte franchisetagare är nära konkurs

Stora förluster, svag försäljning och allvarliga anmärkningar från revisorn. Det är vardagen för varannan företagare inom Stockholms största kiosk- och snabbmatskedjor. SvD har

granskat ekonomin hos 76 franchisetagare i Pressbyrån, 7-Eleven, Burger King, McDonalds, Taco Bar och Sandys. Vart femte företag står på konkursens rand. **Näringsliv sid 4–5**

FOTO: ABED OMAR QUSINI/REUTERS

Presidenten är död – symbolen lever

Yasser Arafat har inlett sin sista resa. I går flögs han till Kairo för dagens officiella begravningsceremoni. I eftermiddag kommer han till Ramallah för att jordfästas. "Alla de som i sina eftermälen

prisar Arafat borde betänka att det är det palestinska folket som borde hyllas", skriver SvD:s Cordelia Edvardson om sorgens dag i Ramallah. **Utrikes sid 18–19**

Autist rev upp rabatt – fick 5 år

Fem års rättspsykiatrisk vård efter att ha hjärjat och ryckt upp blommor i rabatter. Det blev straffet för 49-årige Kenneth som är utvecklingsstörd autist.

Svenska domstolar och rättsläkare klassar förståndshandikappade som sjuka för att de ska slippa fängelse. **Nyheter sid 6–7**

77 Redan på Losing my edge stod det klart att Murphy i grund och botten var en misslyckad musikjournalist.

Andres Lokko debuterar i SvD:s nya nöjespaket. **Kultur sid 15**

SvD guidar dig till bästa nöjet

Vilsen i kulturen? Vi har hjälpen. Kulturredaktionens medarbetare väljer sina favoriter i Stockholms utbud av film, konst, musik, scenkonst, och i böckernas värld.

Dessutom nio sidor fredagsläsning.
• Eminem vinglar till
• Underkänd persier
• Tecknade filmhjältar
• Lysande rysk filmdebut
• Gulliga figurer för vuxna

Kultur sid 6, 15–23

Näringsliv

NÄRINGSLIV

Måndag 6 december 2004 — Sveriges största affärstidning — Svenska Dagbladet

| +0,4 | +0,7 | +2,2 | 2,07 | 3,38 | $ 6,74 | € 8,96 |

Forseke räds inte avhopp

Carnegies vd Karin Forseke talar hellre om nyrekryteringarna

Även om konflikterna avlöser varandra på ledningsnivå och många chefer försvunnit är Carnegies vd Karin Forseke är säker på att det blir bra för bolaget.

Julklapparna finns på nätet

TVÅ SACO-FACK VILL BLI ETT

Dyrare ris hotar leda till matkris

FELREKRYTERING KAN BLI DYR

Rustar hellre upp än bygger nytt

---

8 KULTUR

SvD onsdag 1 december 2004

KOMMENTAR | Nyhetskänsla

Sorti för den goda tv-journalistiken

Till mullornas Iran för att läka exilens sår

Sakprosa

AZAR MAHLOUJIAN
Tillträde till Iran

TELEKOM | NYHETER 7

SvD onsdag 1 december 2004

Telia har bästa 3G-nätet i landet

| TELIA | .TELE2. | 3 | vodafone |

Millicom tvingas till nyemission

Ericsson får order från Cingular i USA

KULTUR

Fredag 12 november 2004 — SVENSKA DAGBLADET

Lennart Sjögren skriver Sveriges bästa poesi
KULTUR sid 9

LOKKO HITTAR REN POP HOS LCD SOUNDSYSTEM
FREDAG sid 15

Vrakplundrare kan dömas till fängelse sid 4

50 år i Vällingby sid 5

SvD:s recensenter guidar till kulturen sid 6–7

Befriad

Framtidens seriefigurer får eget värde sid 16–17

---

16 HELG | REPORTAGE

SvD söndag 28 november 2004   SvD söndag 28 november 2004   **REPORTAGE | HELG 17**

BILDEN AV AIDS I AFRIKA

BILDEN TALAR Hur berättar man om lidandet? Hur väcker man engagemang? Inför Världsaidsdagen försöker de internationella hjälporganisationernas fotografer få väst hur katastrofen ser ut, med hjälp av utsända fotografer.

FOTO: BRENT STIRTON TEXT: CHRIS BEESON

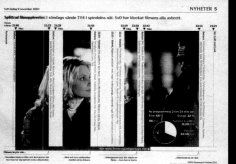

SvD tisdag 9 november 2004　　　　　　　　　　　　　　　　　　　　NYHETER 5

Splittrad filmupplevelse: I söndags sände TV4 i spindelns nät. SvD har klockat filmens alla avbrott.

Rättssal blev bio för en dag

Kända regissörer i strid med TV 4 om reklamavbrott i långfilmer

SVENSKA DAGBLADET

Söndag den 28 november 2004　　　　　　E4 | Sedan 1884 | Pris 15 kr

Etisk investering eller ideologi? **PJ ANDERS LINDER** Ledare sid 4

KAROLINA HÖJSGAARDS TRIPPEL KAN GE BRAGDGULD Sport sid 30–31

96 procent färre i försvaret på 17 år

År 1990 kunde försvaret mobilisera 730 000 man. Efter försvarsbeslutet, som väntas vara genomfört 2007, består insatsförsvaret som mest av 31 500 man. Även förbandsnedläggningarna är drastiska.

Trots minskningen betalar skattebetalarna fortfarande runt 40 miljarder kronor per år för försvaret vars framtid nu underkänns av flera experter. Nyheter sid 21–23

1985 73 förband　　**2007** 17 förband

FOTO: PETER HOELSTAD/SCANPIX

Fler fast i skuldfälla

Stockholm och Göteborg noterar i år en dramatisk ökning av antalet personer som söker skuldsanering. Uppgången ligger på 22 procent och bara i Stockholm handlar det hittills i år om närmare 700 fall. Näringsliv sid 18–19

Under ytan i Mexiko
Den mexikanska ön Cozumel är ett paradis för dykare, med klart och varmt vatten och möten med lekfulla delfiner.
• Tindrande julmarknad
• Till häst i Sydafrika
• Så äter du bra på Phuket
Resor, Kultur sid 23–29

Ukrainas parlament vill ha nyval

Ukrainas parlament ogiltigförklarar presidentvalet, skriver Peter Johansson, SvD:s medarbetare i Kiev. Högsta domstolen beslutar om valet imorgon.
Jan Blomgren analyserar det splittrade Ukraina. Väster om Dnepr dominerar nationalismen, öster om floden talar de ryska.
Utrikes sid 24–25

NYHETER Kritik mot förslag om barns skydd
Förslaget om vilka som ska kontrolleras mot brottsregistret för att skydda barn mot övergrepp får kritik för att inte inkludera alla vuxna som arbetar med barn. sid 6

NÄRINGSLIV Musik från Sony Ericssons inre
SvD har besökt Sony Ericssons stängda designavdelning i Lund. Där har de skapat flera framgångsrika modeller men nu är det dags för nästa: musikmobilen. sid 5–7

KULTUR Debutant vann Bronshäst
Som första kvinnliga regissör vann Lucile Hadzihalilovic Bronshästen vid Stockholms filmfestival med sin debutfilm. sid 4

Passa-på-pris nya Ford Mondeo. Vinterhjul medföljer.

KINDWALLS SVERIGES STÖRSTA FORDÅTERFÖRSÄLJARE

SvD fredag 12 november 2004　　　　　UTVECKLINGSSTÖRD OCH INLÅST | NYHETER 7

Sabotage av rabatt gav fem år

Autistiske Kenneth fick Sveriges längsta straff för brott mot naturvårdslagen

6 NYHETER　　　　　　UTVECKLINGSSTÖRD OCH INLÅST　SvD fredag 12 november 2004

Pr-grupp ska avslöja lungen

I dag döms Knutbypastorn

DNA löser 18 år gammalt mord

34 friska dömda till psykisk vård

Domstolar vill inte sätta utvecklingsstörda i fängelse

Många får felaktig behandling

KULTUR

SVENSKA DAGBLADET

Tisdag 9 november 2004

13-åriga Jojo redan en världsstjärna

PHILIP ROTH GÖR LINDBERGH TILL PRESIDENT

Politikens Bob Dylan sid 6–7

TV4 väljer reklamen framför filmerna sid 5
Kniven i hjärtat växer sid 12
Jackson Browne sid 13

THE BEST OF NEWSPAPER DESIGN 26 | WORLD'S BEST-DESI

2
MARCA, domingo
15 de febrero de 2004
PRIMERA REAL MADRID • VALENCIA

3
MARCA, domingo
15 de febrero de 2004
PRIMERA REAL MADRID • VALENCIA

PRIMERA

SEGUNDA

MARCA

Núñez vomita toda la bilis

Juan José Díaz SUBDIRECTOR DE MARCA

BECKHAM SABE QUE HOY SE DECIDE MEDIA LIGA

"Es el partido del año"

"Sí, es el partido más importante del año". Lo dice Beckham y lo dice todo lo que rodea al Madrid-Valencia: sus números en Liga, el duelo Pichichi-Zamora, los dos puntos de distancia...

MIGUEL ÁNGEL LARA | MADRID

ESPECIAL PARA BECKS

17-08-03
Su debut fue ante el Valencia

27-09-03
Primera derrota en Liga y críticas

21-01-04
Primera expulsión con el Madrid

Santiago Bernabéu · 21:00h · C+ DIGITAL+

Árbitro: Tristante Oliva

Así es un Real Madrid / Valencia

Se han enfrentado **68 VECES** en el Santiago Bernabéu

SÓLO PODRÁS VERLO EN CANAL+
902 170 902

Rally México

Víctor Muñoz: "Es algo que lo porque modifica la vida de las personas y de un país entero..."

Aurora Fajardo: "No tengo palabras. Mi condena total y absoluta. Toda mi solidaridad con todos los familiares, de toda mi familia."

R.C. Celta: "El Celta de Vigo, quiere trasladar su condena a los personas..."

YA GANÓ EN RALLIES DEBUTANTES COMO INDONESIA, CHIPRE Y TURQUÍA

México, desafío para Sainz

Loeb, el piloto a batir tras ganar en Montecarlo y **Suecia** El Mundial llega a la tierra con calor, gran altitud y un recorrido desconocido

1+1 GETAFE
Sólo pudo empatar contra nueve

MARCA

ATLÉTICO NUMANCIA
CON EL 'NIÑO', A EUROPA

EL MADRID **NECESITA GANAR AL BAYER LEVERKUSEN** PARA ASEGURAR LA CHAMPIONS Y RESARCIRSE DEL FORTÍSIMO VARAPALO RECIBIDO EN EL CAMP NOU

A LEVANTAR CABEZA

[Confidencial Marca] El vestuario madridista analizó la crisis y la forma de atajarla: "Necesitamos un mediocentro"

ACB 81-81 REAL MADRID-ETOSA HACÍA SEIS AÑOS QUE EL MADRID NO ERA LÍDER EN SOLITARIO

ADSL 512 24h + Llamadas locales y nacionales 24h **36€/mes** wanadoo

---

VOLEIBOL
Numancia aseguró el primer puesto

■ VOLEIBOL
Tenerife y Ávila, final copera

■ ATLETISMO
Higuero, Redolat y Fernández toman el Mundial en 1.500

■ ESQUÍ
Víctima mortal en las pistas de Candanchú

■ GOLF
John Daly se coloca en cabeza del Buick

LIGA NACIONAL
1ª JORNADA

EL ATLÉTICO SIGUE SIN FÚTBOL, PERO AYER AL MENOS TUVO GOL

Pablo y Torres evitan un 'thriller'

El central abrió el marcador en la segunda mitad y el Niño cerró el partido Pensó fue suficiente para conseguir a un correoso Numancia

CÉSAR AGUILERA

"Con la plantilla al completo podemos pelear por la Champions"

MÁXIMO HERNÁNDEZ

"Para mí el arbitraje ha sido una vergüenza; nos ha mediatizado"

M

MARCA

Viernes
12 marzo 2004
0,90 euros

HOY **SÓLO HAY LUGAR PARA LA REPULSA**
HOY **DEBEMOS RECORDAR A LAS VÍCTIMAS**
HOY **EL MENSAJE ES DE LIBERTAD Y VIDA**
HOY **EL DEPORTE QUEDA EN SEGUNDO PLANO**

ESPAÑA, DE LUTO
192 **MUERTOS**, 1.427 **HERIDOS**

LLORAMOS JUNTOS,
GANAREMOS JUNTOS

POLÉMICA
Juan Antonio Jiménez

Undiano Mallenco y el Clásico tranquilo

FALTA AL META   **PENALTI**

RESULTADOS [JORNADA 12]

CLASIFICACIÓN   **CALENDARIO**   **PRÓX. JOR.** [27-28/11/04]   **PICHICHI**   **ZAMORA**

JORNADA 12

MARCADOR

RESULTADOS [JORNADA 11]

QUINIELA

[JORNADA 12]   [PRÓXIMA JOR.]

Nuevo Fiat Doblò
con motor Multijet de 70 CV

Fiat Doblò desde 9.000 €

2B
GRUPO 1   **GRUPO 2**   **GRUPO 3**   **GRUPO 4**

SUPERLIGA FEMENINA

---

15 minutos de IMF

● **VOLEIBOL**
Tenerife y Ávila, final copera

Numancia aseguró el primer puesto

● **WATERPOLO**
Sabadell pierde en Berlín con estrépito

● **ATLETISMO**
Higuero, Redolat y Fernández toman el Mundo en 1.500

● **ESQUÍ**
Víctima mortal en las pistas de Candanchú

● **GOLF**
John Daly se coloca en cabeza del Buick

REAL SOCIEDAD 1-1 ATHLETIC

LA REAL NO SUPO CÓMO JUGAR DESDE QUE SE QUEDÓ CON UNO MÁS
La expulsión de Gurpegui hizo fuerte al Athletic

Dos postes de Kovacevic y Xabi Alonso pudieron sentenciar el derbi a los siete minutos Los de Valverde, con uno menos desde el 52'

CRÓNICA

DENOUEIX

EL APUNTE

VALVERDE

LA POLÉMICA
La expulsión del navarro fue justa

El mayor 'ESTADIO' deportivo del mundo

El campo de regatas de la Copa América 2007 de Valencia equivale a 83.000 campos de fútbol. Sus costas han cambiado en diez años la 'ruta del bakalao' por la competición más elitista.

El campo de regatas

Los protagonistas

USA 76   **SUI-64**   **ALINGHI**

BMW ORACLE RACING   Team Shosholoza

Sistema de competición

TV
[la entrevista del domingo]

JAVIER REYERO

"Me duele ser impopular entre un sector atlético"

PROGRAMACIÓN DEPORTIVA

DIGITAL+

LA PRIMERA   2   3   S   C   TM   C7

EXPANSIÓN TV

PRIMITIVA   EUROMILLONES   LA QUINIELA

RONALDO
AZOTE DEL
VALENCIA

LE HA HECHO SIETE GOLES EN SÓLO CINCO PARTIDOS DE LIGA

A Ronaldo le encanta jugar ante el Valencia

Ronaldo es un azote para el Valencia. Es el equipo que mejor se le da en la Liga española. Cinco partidos ante el cuadro de Mestalla le han bastado para hacer siete goles. Nadie ha sufrido tanto los goles goleadores del brasileño como Zubizarreta, Cañizares y Palop. A esos siete dumas suma otro en la Copa.

MANUEL ÁNGEL LARA | MADRID

"Sí, es verdad que se me da bien el Valencia, pero cada partido es diferente y ya veremos qué pasa en éste", Palabras de Ronaldo a la salida del último entrenamiento del Real Madrid antes de medirse al Valencia, un rival que el Partido de la Liga tiene marcado a fuego de goles desde que el 26 de octubre de 1997 hiciera por primera vez contra el cuadro de blanquillo. Desde entonces, cinco partidos de Liga y siete goles con su firma Real Madrid-Valencia.

'Es verdad que se me da bien el Valencia, pero cada partido es diferente y ya veremos qué pasa en éste'

Ronaldo

SIGUE LA PISTA...

Consigue el circuito **SUPERFÓRMULA**
con la garantía de Carrera
Incluye un **Ferrari** y un **Williams**

0-2 ZARAGOZA ATLÉTICO
El Atleti se crece tras el descanso y descubre a Jacobo

WOODGATE
"Me voy a dejar la piel por salir adelante"

ESPAÑA 21:45 • TVE1 BÉLGICA

SALEN JUNTOS

Luis apuesta por primera vez por Raúl y Torres titulares
• El capitán cumple hoy ocho años en la Selección

FÓRMULA 1 G. P. DE JAPÓN
El tifón Ma-On inunda Suzuka

MOTOCICLISMO G. P. DE MALASIA
Sete, por delante de Rossi

SANCHIS juega sin balón

El ex jugador del Madrid dirige un Curso Superior de Dirección y Gestión de entidades deportivas. Forma futuros presidentes. Pavón y 'Pato' Clavet, sus últimos alumnos.

¿QUÉ FUE DE LA QUINTA?

EL RECREATIVO SE ALEJA DEL SUEÑO DEL ASCENSO

La sequía tinerfeña dura ya 631 minutos

CONSIGUE EL CIRCUITO SUPER FÓRMULA DE MARCA

POR SÓLO 20 CUPONES + 55 €

Ferrari F2002
V10 Nº1

Marca te lleva la competición a casa

Consigue el mejor circuito Carrera de Fórmula 1: Más de cuatro metros de recorrido (5 rectas estándar, una recta de conexión y ocho curvas), dos mandos de velocidad mecánicos, vallas protectoras, son los coches, Ferrari y Williams, compatibles con cualquier tipo de pista. Todo lo necesario para revivir los mejores momentos de la F1 sin salir de casa. Completa la cartilla que encontrarás mañana en Marca, con los 20 cupones que publicaremos en el diario y, por sólo 55 euros, entra en competición.

10 RAZONES PARA ELEGIR EL MEJOR CIRCUITO

Si quieres más, MARCA ¡Qué fuerte!

WilliamsF1 BMW
FW24 2003

Carrefour
RECÓGELO EN TU CENTRO MÁS CERCANO

Im Labyrinth der steinernen Rosen

Wie man in vier Tagen am Roten Meer in Ägypten das Tauchen mit Pressluft lernt

Warmes Wasser das ganze Jahr

Zarengold

Diamant Afrikas

DER TAGESSPIEGEL
LESERREISE

DER TAGESSPIEGEL

Harald Schmidt weiß, wo es langgeht: Aber was machen seine Mitspieler? – *Medien, Seite 35*

Unsere Organe (1): Wie das Herz fit bleibt – *Seite 33*

16 Seiten Beilage: Alles zum neuen Tagesspiegel

Rau geißelt die Gier der Eliten

Zeitungen heute / Bilder brauchen Worte

Fischer drängt die USA: Zurück zur Moral

Amerika soll nach Folterskandal dem Weltstrafgerichtshof beitreten / Interview mit dem Außenminister

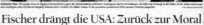

... die Deutschen Trojaner wurden

WM-Stadien kosten 50 Millionen mehr

Hohe Zinsen aber sicher

Premierenfieber

Warum man bei neuen Aktien achten sollte

Mit der Dampflok durch die Wüste

Vorträge, Führungen und zeitgenössische Musik

TAG DER DEUTSCHEN EINHEIT Wie Ost und West schon eins sind – und wo noch nicht

Die Bananenrepublik

Yoko Ono über Lennons Mörder und die wichtigsten Telefonate ihres Lebens – *Sonntag, Seite S 1*

Mit Reise und mit Stellenmarkt

Schwesternspiele: Was CDU und CSU trennt und verbindet – *Seite 8*

BERLIN, SONNTAG, 20. JUNI 2004 / 60. JAHRGANG / NR. 18 511   WWW.TAGESSPIEGEL.DE   BERLIN/BRANDENBURG 1,33 €, AUSWÄRTS 1,75 €

FUSSBALL-EM

Für Deutschland wird es jetzt eng

PORTO · Mit einem 0:0 gegen Lettland hat die deutsche Fußball-Nationalmannschaft ihre erste Ausgangsposition bei der Europameisterschaft in Portugal verspielt. Das Team benötigt nun im letzten Spiel der Vorrunden-Gruppe D am Mittwoch gegen Tschechien einen Sieg, um noch das Viertelfinale zu erreichen. Die Deutschen zeigten gegen die zuvor eingestellten Letten eine deutlich schwächere Leistung als beim 1:1 zum Auftakt gegen die Niederlande. Als erstes Team qualifizierte sich Tschechien für die nächste Runde. In einem hochklassigen Spiel besiegte das Team die Niederlande nach 0:2-Rückstand noch mit 3:2.   *Tsp*

— Seiten 17 und 18

GRUPPE D

Lettland – Deutschland	0:0
Niederlande – Tschechien	2:3

Verpasste Chance. Die deutsche Fußball-Nationalmannschaft kam beim 0:0 gegen Lettland nur zu wenigen Torchancen. Hier hat Arne Friedrich (links) von Hertha BSC im Zweikampf gegen Andrejs Rubins das Nachsehen. Im letzten Spiel gegen Tschechien brauchen die Deutschen nun einen Sieg, um das Viertelfinale zu erreichen.   Foto: ddp/Marcus Brandt

Europa mit Verfassung – aber ohne Chef

Erleichterung über den Gipfel-Kompromiss / Konservative wollen Kommissionspräsidenten bestimmen

BRÜSSEL/BERLIN – Als Meilenstein in der Geschichte Europas haben Politik, Wirtschaft und Kirchen in Deutschland die Verabschiedung der EU-Verfassung durch die Staats- und Regierungschefs bewertet. Allerdings gab es auch Kritik an den Beschlüssen, die einigen Europa-Politikern nicht weit genug gehen. Bundeskanzler Gerhard Schröder (SPD) wertete den bart umkämpften Kompromiss am Freitagabend als „historische Entscheidung". Dies sei „eine ungeheuerlich wichtige Zäsur", betonte Schröder und fügte hinzu: „Europa ist einiger geworden und politisch führbarer."

In der noch ungelösten Frage des neuen EU-Kommissionspräsidenten verlangten CSU-Chef Edmund Stoiber und der CDU-Europapolitiker Elmar Brok die Besetzung des Amtes mit einem Konservativen. Bis Ende Juni soll entschieden werden. Die bisherigen Kandidaten, der Belgier Guy Verhofstadt und der Brite Chris Patten, zogen ihre Kandidaturen in der Nacht zum Samstag zurück. Brok sagte dem Tagesspiegel, er sei „doppelt zufrieden" mit dem EU-Gipfel. „Erstens, weil wir eine Verfassung haben. Und zweitens, weil der Gipfel gezeigt hat, dass der Rat der Staats- und Regierungs-

chefs den Kommissionspräsidenten nicht mehr am Parlament vorbei bestimmen kann." Nun müsse der Rat auf die konservative EVP, die stärkste Fraktion im EU-Parlament Rücksicht nehmen.

Der EU-Gipfel hatte sich am späten Freitagabend in Brüssel auf die erste Verfassung für die Europäische Union geeinigt. Zwei wichtigste Bestandteile sind die Erweiterung von Mehrheitsentscheidungen und die größere Teilhabe des Straßburger Parlaments. In wichtigen Fragen der Außen- und Verteidigungspolitik bleibt aber weiterhin Einstimmigkeit aller EU-Mitglieder vorgeschrieben.

Stoiber kritisierte allerdings, dass die demokratische Legitimation europäischer Entscheidungen noch nicht ausreichend sei. Die FDP-Europaabgeordnete Silvana Koch-Mehrin bekräftigte die Forderung nach einer Volksabstimmung über die Verfassung. Für ein europaweites Referendum setzten sich auch die Grünen ein. Die Kirchen bedauerten das Fehlen eines Bezugs auf Gott in der Präambel. In dem Dokument wird jetzt verwiesen auf das „kulturelle, religiöse und humanistische Erbe" Europas.

Die EU-kritische Liga polnischer Familien bezeichnete die Verabschiedung der

Verfassung als „Tag der Schande und des Verrats" für die Regierung in Warschau. Der Chef der katholisch-nationalistischen Oppositionspartei, Roman Giertych, sagte, die Liga werde alles in ihrer Macht Stehende tun, um die Verfassung mit einer Volksabstimmung zu Fall zu bringen. Die Liga war bei der Europawahl mit 16 Prozent der Stimmen zweitstärkste polnische Kraft geworden. Konservative und katholische Kreise in Polen kritisieren das Fehlen eines Gottesbezugs in der Präambel.   *cvm/ddp/epd/dpa*

— Seite 5

Nach dem EU-Gipfel

Ruhe ist jetzt erste Pflicht

VON CHRISTOPH VON MARSCHALL

Berlin sei dazu verdammt, immerfort zu werden und niemals zu sein", Karl Scheffler Satz aus dem Jahr 1910 ist zum geflügelten Wort geworden – für die Dynamik auf dem Weg zur Weltstadt; Der Publizist hatte es freilich anders gemeint. Er traute Berlin die Kraft damals nicht zu. Er fürchtete, dass die Stadt sich an ihrem Ehrgeiz überhebt.

Immerfort werden und niemals sein: Das ist auch das Selbstverständnis der meisten Europa-Enthusiasten, der Berufseuropäer sowieso. Sie können sich die EU nur ständig unter Dampf vorstellen, vorwärts stürmend zur nächsten Erweiterung, zur nächsten Vertiefung. Nicht aber als Organismus, der mal innehält, wenn er eine neues Stadium erreicht, wenn genug ist, lange, bis sich die Verhältnisse gefestigt haben, bis Europa wieder in sich ruht.

Scheffers Zweifel an Berlins Selbstverständnis 1910 sollten Europa eine Warnung sein. Dafür muss man nicht gleich die fliegenden Katastrophen bemühen – die beiden Weltkriege, die Teilung des Kontinents und den Verlust seiner Führungsrolle in der Welt –, die ja auch Folge einer dramatisch falschen Selbsteinschätzung Deutschlands und seiner Hauptstadt waren. Es genügt, den jüngsten

Europa hat endlich eine Verfassung: Diese Schlagzeile wird vorerst die Gipfelbilanz bestimmen und den Ärger um die Kür eines Kommissionspräsidenten überstrahlen. Und da Erfolg man mal anziehend wirkt, wird sie vielleicht viele Bürger für Europa interessieren und das Wahldebakel vergessen machen. Nur ist diese Schlagzeile nicht ganz wahr, und der Erfolg wurde zudem mit Kompromissen erkauft, die viele Fortschritte, die diese Verfassung bringen sollte, wieder entwerten.

Europa hat noch lange keine Verfassung. Die Staats- und Regierungschefs haben den Entwurf des Konvents nach manchen Änderungen gebilligt; im Dezember harten sie ihn noch abgelehnt. Wird er die Volksabstimmungen in skeptisch gestimmten Ländern wie Großbritannien oder Polen sowie die Ratifizierung in allen 25 EU-Staaten überstehen? Und selbst wenn diese Verfassung weiter Erwarten so um 2009 in Kraft tritt: Was ist sie wert, nachdem der Gipfel sie nochmals kräftig gerupft hat, um die Einigung zu ermöglichen? Ja, sie ist ein Fortschritt, aber sie macht die EU nicht viel entscheidungsfähiger und auch nicht viel demokratischer. In Brüssel wurden jetzt einige Klauseln eingefügt, die gemeinsame Entscheidungen nicht erleichtern, sondern erschweren. Im Parlament muss Deutschland, das schon heute weniger Sitze hat, als ihm nach der Bevölkerungszahl zustehen, drei Sitze abgeben – zu Gunsten kleinerer Staaten, die bereits überrepräsentiert waren.

Im Stolz auf den gemeinsamen Außenminister zeigt sich der gravierendste Irrglauben: dass die EU substanzielle Meinungsverschiedenheiten überwinden könne, wenn sie eine neue Institution einrichtet. Die 25 EU-Staaten sind indessondere die großen sechs (Deutschland, Frankreich, Großbritannien, Italien, Spanien und Polen) haben aus gutem Grund in eigene außenpolitische Interessen. Die Gegensätze kann auch ein EU-Außenminister nicht aufheben. Und an eine gemeinsame Steuerpolitik ist schon gar nicht in denken angesichts der so gegensätzlichen Traditionen.

Die Verfassung illustriert das grundsätzliche Problem: Europa kann sich nicht selbst überholen. Um eine Macht in der Welt zu werden, müsste es schneller vorangehen, geeint auftreten. Das geht aber nicht, weil schon der jetzige Stand der Integration den Willen der Bürger, der Nationalstaaten und ihrer Regierungen überfordert. Gar nicht zu reden von der Erweiterung um 10 neue Staaten, die zwar vollzogen, aber noch lange nicht bewältigt ist. Wer da immer neue Projekte ausruft – die Türkei und jetzt Kroatien –, läuft vor dem Heute davon und riskiert, dass die EU irgendwann an den vielen ungelösten Problemen zerbricht. Ruhe ist jetzt Europas erste Pflicht. Sie, das ist am wenigsten, wird die Union stärken. Nur so, das erschließt ist, zu konsolidieren. Die EU muss auch mal sein dürfen, und nicht immerfort nur werden.

Heute teilen sich Sonne und Wolken den Himmel, ein Nachmittag gibt es vielleicht Schauer bei 20/23 maximal 20 Grad. Im Wochenverlauf wird es etwas wärmer.

Telefon-Faxe 75-C/DX / Seiten 5-34 / Schweiz 2,30 CHF / Spanien 1,90 € / Dänemark 18 DK / Tschechien 59 CZK / Polen 3,85 zł / Ungarn 380 HUF

Und was mache ich jetzt?

VON AXEL HACKE

Das Leben ist ein immerwährendes Aufsuchen und Verschwinden, daran sind wir gewöhnt. Eine Europameisterschaft kündigt sich an, dann ist sie plötzlich da, ein paar Wochen lang. Man schaut die Europameisterschaft an, dann ist sie wieder weg. Man kauft sich ein neues Hemd, trägt das Hemd, wäscht und bügelt es, aber eines Tages ist das Hemd nicht mehr da, und man weiß nicht: Hat man es im Hotel vergessen? Hat die Bermuda-Hose es während des Waschvorgangs gefressen? Man ist unter Men-schen kommen, verbringt Zeit mit ihm, dann meldet er sich nicht mehr, man selbst ruft auch nicht an, es hat schon interessantere Menschen gegeben, findet man – und dann ist er verschwunden, weg, weiß gar nicht mehr: Wo lebt er? Lebt er überhaupt?

So geht das Tag für Tag. Aber dass im Staate Missouri nun ein ganzer See verschwunden ist, wundert einen doch. Alles soll schnell gegangen sein, fast über Nacht war er weg, der See, Lake Chesterfield hatte er geheißen. Man hatte ihn vor längerer Zeit künstlich angelegt, Leute hatten sich Häuser mit Seeblick gekauft – nun blicken sie auf Schlamm und viel Fläche. Irgendwie ist durch heftige Regenfälle ein Schlauchloch entstanden, wird gemeldet, durch die habe sich der See davon gemacht. Das ist seltsam. Man bedenkt, dass Dörfer in Stau-Seen absaufen, aber dass nun die Seen selbst... Es be-

in der Sommer, man ginge gerne baden irgendwo – aber was geschieht mit einem Schwimmer, der sich just in dem Moment im See befindet, während der See beschließt zu geh'n? Wo findet man ihn dann wieder?

Das Dumme ist ja, dass immer nur Dinge verschwinden, die man gern hat oder die man braucht. Schlüssel, Telefonzellen. Briefkästen. Manche Tierarten, Jedenfalls fällt es einem in diesen Fällen auf, anderes ist sicher auch einfach weg, aber man merkt es nicht, jeder jedes-falls. Massenvernichtungswaffen zum Beispiel. So einen See hat jeder gern. In letzter Zeit hat man gehört, das oli werde verschwinden, hey, das ist interessant: Die Dinge, die verschwinden, werden immer größer, was? Die SPD war einmal eine Riesenpartei – nun ist sie beinahe weg. So wie die Leute um Lake Chesterfield gewohnt waren, morgens aus dem Fenster auf den See zu blicken, wohnte man an den Jahrzehnten in der Zeitung auf die SPD. Was wird dort sein, wenn es so weitergeht mit ihr? Was passiert mit den Leuten, die zufällig in der SPD sind, während die Partei im Erdreich versickert? Und wenn ein See, das öli, die SPD einfach so in hohem Tempo verschwinden können – was ist noch sicher? Werden sich die Alpen wieder zusammenrollen? Wird der Himmel einrollen? Wird der Asphalt uns schmatzend verschlucken, während wir auf ihm gehen?

22 Tote bei US-Angriff auf Falludscha

BAGDAD – Bei einem US-Luftschlag gegen mutmaßliches Versteck des als Top-Terroristen gesuchten Jordaniers Abu Mussab al-Sarkawi im Irak sind am Samstag mindestens 22 Menschen getötet worden. Wie US-General Mark Kimmitt sagte, wurde der Angriff auf das Gebäude in der westirakischen Stadt Falludscha mit einer Präzisionswaffe angegriffen. Ziel sei ein vermutetes Versteck und Waffenlager von Mitgliedern des Netzwerks von Sarkawi gewesen.   *dpa*

— Seite 5

Post verschiebt den Börsengang ihrer Bank

BERLIN – Die Deutsche Post hat es offenbar bisher nicht geschafft, genügend Anleger für die Aktien ihrer Tochter Postbank zu überzeugen. Der Konzern gab am Samstag bekannt, die Preisspanne für die Papiere zu senken. Privatanleger und Großinvestoren können bis kommenden Dienstag Aufträge zu den neuen Konditionen abgeben oder alte Orders ändern. Das Börsendebüt soll dann am kommenden Mittwoch erfolgen. Ursprünglich war es für Montag geplant.   *hop*

— Seite 24

SPD-Chef geht auf Distanz zu Rente ab 67

BERLIN/ULM – Nach der verheerenden Wahlniederlage streitet die SPD weiter über den Reformkurs der Bundesregierung. Vertreter des linken Flügels drängten auf einen Kurswechsel. SPD-Chef Franz Müntefering wies Forderungen nach Korrekturen zurück. „Wir gewinnen das Vertrauen nur zurück, wenn die Menschen das Gefühl haben: Die machen das ernsthaft, solide, auf Dauer angelegt", sagte er dem „Focus".

Allerdings kündigte Müntefering Änderungen in der Frage des Renteneintrittsalters und der Altersvorsorge an. Auf dem Katholikentag in Ulm sprach er sich am Samstag für einen flexiblen Rentenbe-

ginn zwischen 63 und 70 Jahren aus statt einer pauschalen Erhöhung des Renteneintritts etwa auf 67 Jahre. „Wir müssen weniger mit festen Daten arbeiten, sondern individuelle Lösungen suchen", sagte der SPD-Vorsitzende.

Der Vorsitzende der PDS, Lothar Bisky, äußerte sich besorgt über die Schwäche der SPD. „Wir können uns nicht freuen, wenn uns die SPD in den Keller geht", sagte Bisky dem Tagesspiegel am Sonntag. Bisky appellierte an die SPD, sie solle den Mut haben, ihre Reformen zurückzunehmen.   *AFP/dpa/ddp/hi.m.*

— Seiten 4 und 7

Fragen der Ehre

Zug um Zug

Kade Müller

Ulrich Timper

Rolf Moebius

Zur Buchmesse und ihrem Thema „Arabische Welten": Literaten im Café; arabisch Essen; der erste Kreuzzug – *Seiten S3, S6 und S7*

SONNTAG, 3. OKTOBER 2004 / NR. 18 610 · WWW.TAGESSPIEGEL.DE/SONNTAG · SEITE S1

„Keiner wäscht reiner"

Fragen an den Großlyriker F. W. Bernstein, etwa: Müssen sich Gedichte reimen?
Ein Werkstattgespräch über Poe, Hacks, Hölderlin, Grünbein, Reich-Ranicki, Lurchi…

Kostbare Rarität

Von den Vorfahren lernen

Wenn Beduinen Fassaden retten

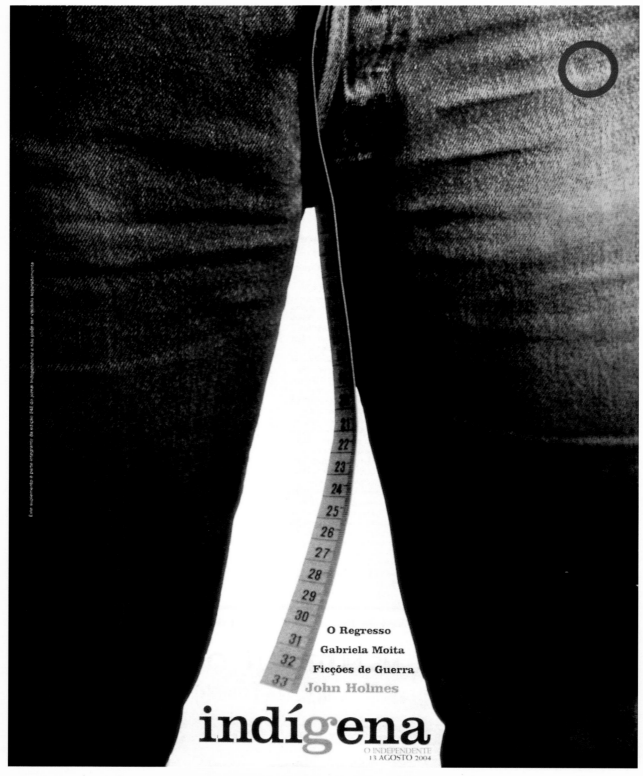

Este suplemento é parte integrante da edição 1642 do jornal Independente e não pode ser vendido separadamente.

O Regresso
Gabriela Moita
Ficções de Guerra
John Holmes

indígena
O INDEPENDENTE
13 AGOSTO 2004

**JUDGES' SPECIAL
RECOGNITION &
GOLD**

O Independente
Lisbon, Portugal

*Entertainment page design/
49,999 and under*

Sónia Matos, Art Director &
Designer; **Inés Serra Lopes,**
Editor-in-Chief; **Leonardo
Ralha,** Editor; **Patrick Grosner,**
Photographer

It's funny, sexy and unforgettable. The idea is perfect, the execution wonderfully subtle, and the printing flawless. It evokes a classic Andy Worhol Rolling Stone cover and shows you something that you can't really show. The jeans and body are a life-size slice of a real body. The cover then becomes interactive.

Es divertido, sexy e inolvidable. La idea es perfecta, la ejecución es maravillosamente sutil y la impresión no tiene falta alguna. Evoca la clásica tapa de Rolling Stone de Andy Warhol y enseña algo que uno no puede mostrar realmente. Los jeans y el cuerpo son una parte de tamaño real de un cuerpo de verdad. De esa forma, la tapa se hace interactiva.

DGES' SPECIAL RECOGNITION

chapter 2

SILVER

The New York Times
New York, N.Y.

Special coverage/Sections/With ads

Ken McFawlin, Art Director; **Staff**

Beginning with an incredibly powerful cover, this section delivers pages of smartly played, smartly edited images. The organization and design, with the subjects and copy blocks, allow the reader to spend time with each photo. It's also a nice touch to run photos over the gutter when the facing pages aren't a true double truck.

Comenzando con una tapa increíblemente poderosa, esta sección entrega páginas con imágenes bien puestas y editas inteligentemente. La organización y el diseño, con los temas y los bloques de texto, permiten que el lector dedique tiempo a cada foto. También es un buen toque llevar fotos sobre el doblez cuando las páginas opuestas no son una verdadera página doble.

JUDGES' SPECIAL RECOGNITION

The New York Times
New York, N.Y.

Photography/Project page or spread

Ashley Gilbertson, Photographer

This photograph by Ashley Gilbertson is one of the strongest photographs published this year. It has a terrible beauty that sums up two and a half years of war with eloquence and drama. The contrast and mix of art, news and vision are an example of what great photography is supposed to be.

Esta fotografía de Ashley Gilbertson es una de las más poderosas que fueron publicadas en el año. Tiene una terrible belleza que resume dos años y medio de guerra con elocuencia y dramatismo. El contraste y la mezcla de arte, noticias y visión son un ejemplo de lo que debe ser la excelencia en fotografía.

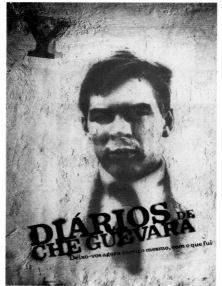

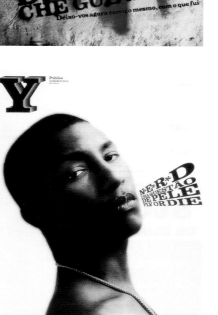

The typography is beautiful. The use of color is straightforward, immediate and restrained. The publication takes relatively ordinary subject matter and makes posters that develop ideas in a consistently strong way. The mix of photography and illustration is powerful. The editors take simple beginnings, such as handout art, and elevate them. It's a stunning use of the medium. The way the designers incorporate the logo adds a level of sophistication.

Es una linda tipografía. El uso del color es al grano, inmediato y restringido. La publicación toma un tema relativamente común y realiza afiches que desarrollan ideas de forma consistente y poderosa. Los editores parten con un inicio simple, como los elementos visuales entregados por las fuentes, y los ensalzan. Se trata de un sorprendente uso del medio. La forma en que los diseñadores incorporan el logo le da un nivel de sofisticación.

JUDGES' SPECIAL RECOGNITION & SILVERS

Público
Lisbon, Portugal
JSR for multiple covers
Silvers / Entertainment page design/50,000-174,999
Awards of Excellence / Entertainment page design/ 50,000-174,999

Vasco Câmara, Editor; **Hugo Pinto,** Designer; **Ivone Ralha,** Designer; **Jorge Guimarães,** Designer

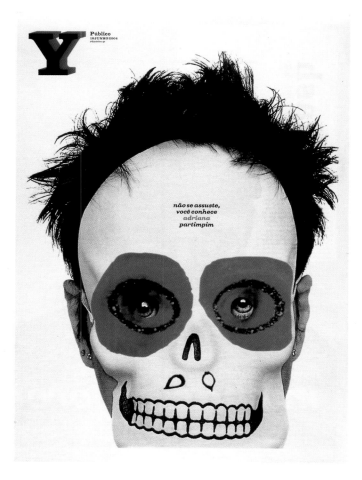

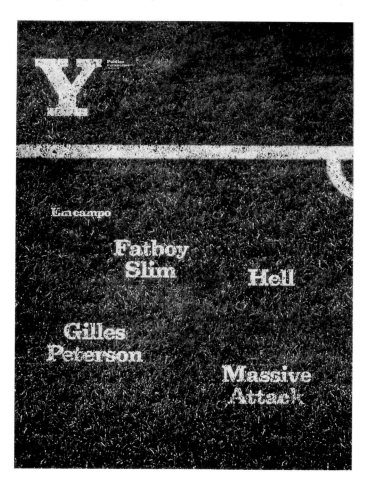

SILVER

The message is very complex. It pushes the limits to publish this kind of ironic metaphor about an artist who wants to shock you. It takes you to a confused and mysterious place. It's very dramatic.

El mensaje es muy complejo. Lleva al límite para publicar este tipo de metáfora irónica sobre un artista que quiere choquear. Te lleva a un lugar confuso y misterioso. Es muy dramático.

SILVER

This story is a designer's worst nightmare – an annual event with the same kind of handout art every year. But this design takes a fresh approach. The concept doesn't hit you over the head. The typography is lovely, with just enough of an effect to complete the illusion.

Este artículo es la mayor pesadilla de un diseñador – un evento anual con el mismo tipo de imágenesentregadas por las fuentes de todos los años. Pero este diseño tiene un enfoque fresco. El concepto no te asalta de pronto. La tipografía es muy linda, y apenas lleva un efecto para completar la ilusión.

(Homeless in Santa Fe)

the Dilemma
To give or not to give?

A man on the street approaches you.
You know he's homeless. He tells you
he needs gas money. Or food money.
Or beer money. But it's always money.
Do you give him any?

yes

Ethicist Randy Cohen, columnist for *The New York Times Magazine*, says absolutely.

"You can never go wrong by being too generous," he says. "The worst that will happen is that you will alleviate someone's suffering briefly."

But what if the man uses it for alcohol?

"So what?" Cohen asks, who also is the author of the book *The Good, The Bad & The Difference*. "These are people with tremendously difficult lives. Why should they be denied a drink or anything else that will ease their suffering? We don't deny ourselves that. Why should we hold them to a higher standard?"

But what about the argument that you're enabling the homeless?

"I think that's a lot of psychological hogwash," Cohen says. "It's not just claptrap, it's heartless claptrap."

People are homeless, he points out, because jobs are gone and housing is more expensive, not because you give them your spare change.

"So the poor don't use their money with utter prudence, do the rich?" he asks.

But while Cohen believes giving a panhandler money is the right thing to do, he also believes you must do more.

"You can give your quarters or your dollars to people you encounter on the street forever, and that won't change the circumstances that put them there," he says.

The only way to truly end homelessness is to give money to groups that offer rehab, counseling or housing.

"There are other people, among who I include myself, who prefer to do their giving in ways that don't just alleviate immediate suffering, but address the causes of homelessness," he says. "They like to give to groups that are making an organized and concentrated effort to do that."

Cohen believes that this giving — of time or money — is an absolute necessity ("an affirmative obligation, a moral duty") for every single person because it is our fault that people are homeless. We are, as Cohen likes to point out, a democracy, and we voted for the people who made the policies that created the homeless.

"We elected these guys. And you shouldn't get to turn your back on (homelessness)," he says. "These are the consequences of social policies in our society. Why should we be shielded from the view of the results of that?"

But even with all his advice, Cohen knows the crux of the giving problem.

"I can certainly understand why some people choose not to give," he says. "Everyone has tried to work out their own criteria for this. What I don't know is anyone who is happy with the standards they've established for themselves."

no

Capt. Jill Steiner from the Salvation Army in Santa Fe says absolutely not.

"I would never give them money," says Steiner. "The line is 'help me out with food,' but that money is destined for alcohol. I wouldn't ignore them, but I wouldn't enable them to get alcohol and drugs."

Carolyn Luna-Anderson from Life Link, which offers homeless services, isn't as stringent, however she suggests that instead of just handing out money, pay them for completing some task, such as cleaning up the parking lot they are sitting in. Or buy them food if they are hungry.

At the very least, when you are asked for money, ask a question back: "Do you see yourself doing this in six months or a year?" or "What do you want with your life?" Sometimes it is a simple interaction with another human that causes a homeless person to find a way out, she says. But, Anderson warns, make sure not to say anything in a judgmental way. Instead, say it with the kindest possible voice.

Another way to get that interaction, says Jim Black, who heads the soup kitchen at St. John the Baptist Catholic Church, is to come to the church for your lunch break.

Instead of going to McDonald's or Tomasita's, you can have a hot meal or fresh food at St. John's. You can leave a donation (or not) and engage whoever you sit next to in conversation. It might be just the spark they need to get off the street.

If none of these things appeal to you, but you still want to help, cut out this listing of homeless services and hand it to the next person who asks for money.

Cut this out and hand this out.

If you need food:	If you need a (free) doctor:	If you need a shower or to do laundry:
BREAKFAST Monday–Friday 6 a.m. to 8:30 a.m. The Salvation Army 525 W. Alameda St.	Healthcare for the Homeless Various times on Monday, Tuesday and Thursday 818 Camino Sierra Vista 988-1742	Monday–Friday 10 a.m. to noon; 1 p.m. to 3 p.m. The Salvation Army 525 W. Alameda St.
LUNCH Monday–Saturday 11:45 a.m. to 12:45 p.m. St. John the Baptist Church 1307 Osage Ave.	**If you need a place to stay:**	**If you're under 21:** SHELTER: If you're 10 to 17 years old La Otra Puerta 438-0502 5686 Agua Fria Street
Sunday noon Bienvenidos Ashbaugh Park On Cerrillos Road	St. Elizabeth's Shelter 804 Alarid St. 982-6611	**If you're 22 or older** FOOD, SHOWER, LAUNDRY: Street Outreach Resource Center 228 North Guadalupe 438-0502
DINNER Monday–Friday 5 p.m. to 5:30 p.m. The Salvation Army 525 W. Alameda St.	Winter Shelter for Men The Salvation Army 525 W. Alameda St. 986-8354 10 p.m. to 6 a.m.	Currently only open Tuesdays and Thursdays

JUDGES' SPECIAL RECOGNITION

The Santa Fe New Mexican
Santa Fe, N.M.

JSR for interactive and inventive storytelling

Award of Excellence / Special coverage / Sections/Without ads

Christine Barber, Page Designer

We honor this entry for its interactive, inventive storytelling. You have to handle this section, interact with it, turn it, touch it and get into it. The designer took a hands-on approach, with organic type and arrows. This fresh approach to a visually stale story added humanity and levity to link you to the subject.

Honramos esta pieza concursante por su narración interactiva e inventiva. Es preciso que uno maneje esta sección, interactúe con ella, la mueva, la toque y que se involucre con ella. El diseñador se decidió por un enfoque directo, con tipografía y flechas orgánicas. Este enfoque fresco de una historia visualmente añeja le dio humanidad y liviandad para crear un nexo entre el lector y el tema.

This project was a special effort in the use of photography and use of zoned publications. The ambition and planning necessary to take an idea that would have been thrown away in most newsrooms is to be applauded, as is the effort to reach out to a young readership. The photography and lighting are excellent, consistent and dramatic, and, yet, each portrait is special and different.

Este proyecto fue un esfuerzo especial en el uso de la fotografía y de la publicaciones zonales. Es destacable el objetivo y la planificación necesarios para esta idea, que podría haber sido descartada en la mayoría de las salas de noticias. Lo mismo se puede decir del esfuerzo para llegar a la lectoría joven. La fotografía y la iluminación son excelentes, consistentes y dramáticos, y, sin embargo, cada retrato es especial y diferente.

JUDGES' SPECIAL RECOGNITION & SILVERS

The Times of Northwest Indiana
Munster, Ind.

JSR for special effort

Silvers
Special news topics/Editor's choice, sports
Miscellaneous

Matt Erickson, Assistant Sports Editor/Design

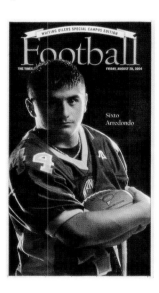

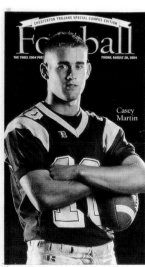

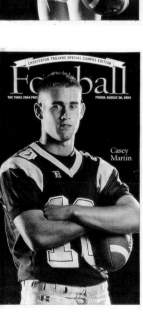

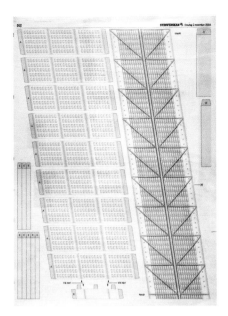

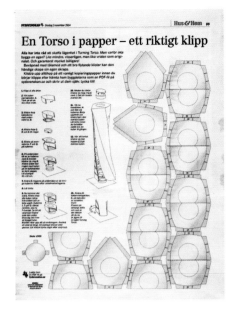

JUDGES' SPECIAL RECOGNITION

Sydsvenskan
Malmo, Sweden

Award of Excellence / Home/Real estate page design/50,000-174,999

Roger Brinck, Information Graphics Designer; **Christoffer Rehn,** Information Graphics Designer; **Krister Cronqvist,** Information Graphics Designer

This is an interesting way to look at a structure. In addition to the graphic, consecutive pages included templates for building that could be cut out and constructed by the reader. It's innovative and interactive, and it invites participation.

Ésta es una interesante forma de observar una estructura. Además del gráfico, las páginas consecutivas incluyeron formatos de edificios que podían ser recortados y armados por los lectores. Es innovador e interactivo, e invita a la participación.

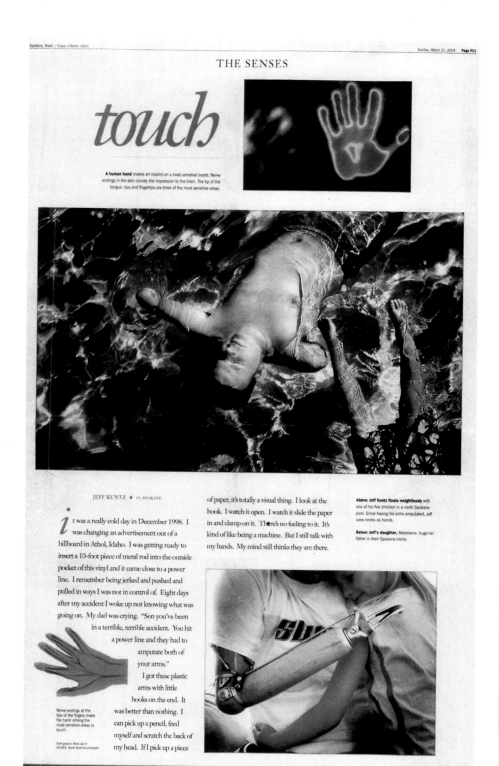

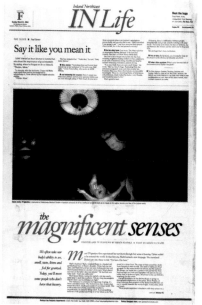

These photos are visual poetry done in a surprising way. The concept of illustrating the senses through subjects who have lost those senses is incredibly well executed. It makes us appreciate our own senses. The consistency of the design and secondary elements are well done.

Estas fotos son una poesía visual realizada de forma sorprendente. El concepto de ilustrar los sentidos a través de personas que los han perdido está increíblemente bien llevado a cabo. La consistencia del diseño y de los elementos secundarios están bien hechos.

JUDGES' SPECIAL RECOGNITION

The Spokesman-Review
Spokane, Wash.

JSR for photography & concept

Award of Excellence / Special news topics/Editor's choice, local/ regional

Ralph Walter, Page Designer; **Brian Plonka,** Photographer; **Molly Quinn,** Graphic Artist; **Geoff Pinnock,** Design Director; **Bart Rayniak,** Photo Editor

JUDGES' SPECIAL RECOGNITION

The Arizona Republic
Phoenix, Ariz.

JSR for use of illustration & storytelling

Awards of Excellence
Special news topics/Editor's choice, local/regional
A-section news design/175,000 and over

Tracy Collins, Deputy M.E.; **Christopher Kozlowski**, A.M.E.; **Tim Frank**, Senior Editor/News Design and Graphics; **Tony Bustos**, Graphic Artist; **Sam Milbee**, Page Designer

The exceptional illustrations take an impossible-to-illustrate story and put you inside the prison. The etchings are realistic like photos, but they do not distort reality. The typographical chaptering devices make the presentation less imposing and clearly break a long story.

Las excepcionales ilustraciones toman un tema imposible de ilustrar y te ponen dentro de la prisión. Los dibujos son tan realistas como las fotos, pero no distorsionan la realidad. La forma de separar los capítulos con recursos de la tipografía hace que la presentación sea menos imponente ya que claramente segmenta un largo artículo.

MULTIPLE WINNERS

chapter 3

GOLD & SILVER

The Globe and Mail
Toronto, Ontario, Canada

Gold / Photography/Use of photography

Silver / Photography/Project page or spread

AWARD OF EXCELLENCE
Opinion page design/ 175,000 and over

Cathrin Bradbury, Weekend Editor; **Erin Elder,** Director/Photography; **Jerry Johnson,** Focus Editor; **Brian Kerrigan,** Photo Editor; **Cinders McLeod,** Designer; **Louie Palu,** Photographer; **David Pratt,** Executive Art Editor; **Staff**

This paper is filled with dramatic and passionate photographs, way beyond the covers. Other papers do some fantastic splashes when they have something good, but this paper does it all the time. It's phenomenal work that takes really innovative and new risks. The editing, cropping, technical skill and toning are flawless, down to each mugshot.

Este diario está lleno de fotografías dramáticas y apasionadas, mucho más allá de las tapas. Otros periódicos hacen fantásticas muestras fotográficas cuando tienen algo bueno que dar, pero este diario lo hace todo el tiempo. Es un trabajo fenomenal, que realmente toma nuevos e innovadores riesgos.
La edición, el recorte, las habilidades técnicas y la armonización del color son impecables, incluso en los retratos pequeños.

Globe Focus

SWIFT BOAT TO VICTORY: HOW THE REPUBLICANS GET AWAY WITH SMEAR TACTICS, F3

IS THIS THE END OF B.C.'S FANTASY ISLAND? THE OUTSIDE WORLD INVADES SALTSPRING, F7

'PIPSQUEAK! SMALL FRY! SHRIMP!' A TALL ORDER FOR SHORT KIDS, F6

A HARD-ROCK LIFE

Canadian prosperity depends on the sweat of multitudes who do jobs their fellow citizens seldom see or even imagine. This Labour Day weekend, The Globe and Mail sheds light on some of those dark places with the work of staff photographer **LOUIE PALU,** who has spent years documenting the underground world of northern miners. For more, please see page F4

After being lowered by chain in a bucket (seen to his left), and through the never-ending rain caused by being below the water table, a miner signals the crew above him to begin moving the blasted rock from the bottom of Louvicourt Mine's shaft No. 1 in Val d'Or, Que. Shaft sinkers blast down by 10 to 20 feet a day — the miner shown is at 2,500 feet, but currently, shafts can go as deep as 7,000 or 8,000 feet, the equivalent of four CN Towers thrusting down into the earth. Most workers consider shaft sinking the most dangerous of all underground assignments.

MANAGING EDITOR, FEATURES, CATHRIN BRADBURY, FOCUS EDITOR, JERRY JOHNSON ■ FEEDBACK TO FOCUS@GLOBEANDMAIL.CA

GOLD

San Jose Mercury News
San Jose, Calif.

Special news topics/The Athens Olympics

AWARDS OF EXCELLENCE
Opinion page design/175,000 and over

Inside news page design/175,000 and over

Wayne Begasse, Picture Editor; **Chuck Burke,** News Designer; **Caroline Couig,** Picture Editor; **Kim Fararo,** Perspective Editor; **Jim Gensheimer,** Photographer; **HyunJu Chappell Hine,** News Designer; **Stephanie Grace Lim,** Artist; **Matt Mansfield,** Deputy M.E.; **Kevin Wendt,** News Design Director; **Staff**

Every photograph seems like a surprise. These pages display state-of-the-art portrait photography that mixes black-and-white and color successfully to pace the pages. The graphics and illustrations demonstrate smart conceptual work, and it seems as if they were done in conjunction with the other elements.

Cada foto parece una sorpresa. Estas páginas exhiben fotografía de retrato de primera línea que mezcla blanco y negro y color en forma exitosa para dar ritmo a las páginas. Los gráficos y las ilustraciones demuestran un trabajo conceptual inteligente, y parece como si hubieran sido hechos en conjunto con los demás elementos.

Synchronized swimming

SILVER

Sports page design/175,000 and over

The image, paired with its information, has incredible elegance and beauty. This page stands out as something extraordinary even in a section filled with great coverage.

La imagen, junto con su información, tiene una increíble elegancia y belleza. Esta página se destaca por ser algo extraordinario, incluso en una sección llena de gran cobertura noticiosa.

SILVERS

San Jose Mercury News
San Jose, Calif.

Breaking news topics/Obituaries
Special coverage/Sections/Without ads
Inside news page design/175,000 and over

AWARDS OF EXCELLENCE
Photography/Page design
Special coverage, section pages/Inside page or spread
Special news topics/Ronald Reagan's death and funeral
A-section news design/175,000 and over

Jonathon Berlin, Designer; **Caroline Couig**, Picture Editor; **Mark Damon**, Director/Photography; **Jeff Hindenach**, News Designer; **Matt Mansfield**, Deputy M.E.; **Kris Viesselman**, Creative Director; **Kevin Wendt**, News Design Director; **News Staff**; **Staff**

Many papers had the same information and photography to work with when Ronald Reagan died. With innovative photo editing, clear hierarchy, bold typography and a well-done closing page, the Mercury News made a truly special section.

Muchos diarios contaron con la misma información y fotografía para cuando Ronald Reagan murió. Con una edición fotográfica innovadora, una clara jerarquía, una tipografía con carácter y una página de cierre bien hecha, el Mercury News hizo una verdadera sección especial.

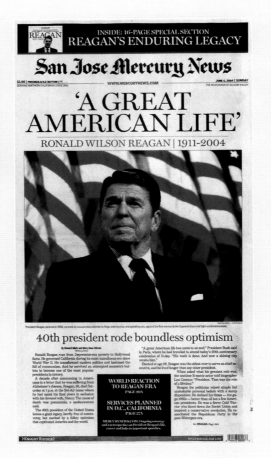

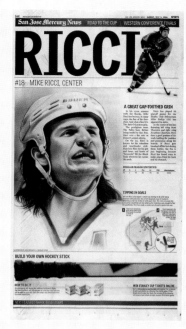

SUNDAY, JUNE 6, 2004   FC

San Jose Mercury News
A 16-PAGE COMMEMORATIVE SECTION

SECTION S

'My friends, we did it. We weren't just marking time, we made a difference. ... All in all, not bad. Not bad at all.'

REAGAN
1911–2004

1980: Ronald Reagan poses in Los Angeles during his presidential campaign.
GEORGE ROSE — SPECIAL TO THE MERCURY NEWS

The Californian
His adopted home shaped him, and in turn, he redefined it.
PAGE 5

The legacy
He showed an unwavering zeal for obliterating communism.
PAGE 10

The leader
Editorial: He had strong convictions and a talent for articulating his goals.
PAGE 14

SILVER

San Jose Mercury News
San Jose, Calif.

Special news topics/Editor's choice, sports

AWARDS OF EXCELLENCE
Special coverage/Single subject
Miscellaneous

Doug Griswold, Illustrator; **Matt Mansfield**, Deputy M.E.; **Kris Viesselman**, Creative Director; **Kevin Wendt**, News Design Director; **Javier Zarracina**, Deputy Graphics Director

The quality of the illustration, the consistency of the typography and the smart touches on the value of each player take a very pretty thing and enhance its value.

La calidad de la ilustración, la consistencia de la tipografía y los inteligentes toques en el valor de cada jugador hacen de este trabajo algo muy lindo y destacan su valor.

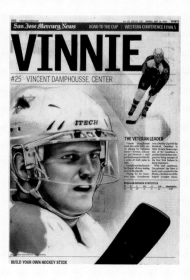

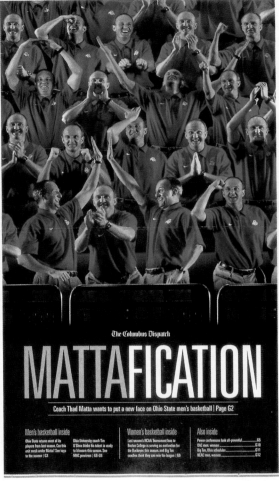

The Columbus Dispatch

MATTAFICATION

Coach Thad Matta wants to put a new face on Ohio State men's basketball | Page G2

Men's basketball inside

Ohio State returns most of its players from last season. Can this unit reach under Matta? See keys to the season | G3

Ohio University coach Tim O'Shea thinks his talent is ready to blossom this season. See MAC previews | G8-G9

Women's basketball inside

Last season's NCAA Tournament loss to Boston College is serving as motivation for the Buckeyes this season, and Big Ten coaches think they can win the league | G6

Also inside

Power conferences look all-powerful G5
OSU men's scene G10
Big Ten, Ohio schedule G11
NCAC men, women G12

RedEye
Chicago, Ill.

A-section news design/50,000-174,999
Combination portfolio/Individual/50,000-174,999 (Chris Courtney)

Chris Courtney, Designer; **Joe Knowles,** Co-Editor

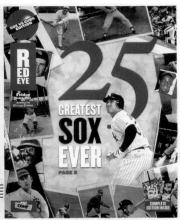

Herald on Sunday
Auckland, New Zealand

Sports page design/50,000-174,999
Photography/Sports

Rob Cox, Designer; **Chris Skelton,** Photographer; **Matthew Straker,** Art Director

SILVER

The Columbus Dispatch
Columbus, Ohio

Special coverage, section pages/Cover only

AWARD OF EXCELLENCE
Combination portfolio/Individual/175,000 and over (Todd Bayha)

Todd Bayha, Page Designer; **Barth Falkenberg,** Photo Director; **Scott Minister,** Art Director

The paper took a hard-to-illustrate subject and executed it seamlessly. The subject is the coach of a Big 10 basketball team, and the photographer was able to shoot him in nearly 50 positions. The resulting page is a delightful surprise.

El diario tomó un tema difícil de ilustrar y lo llevó a cabo sin faltas. El tema es el entrenador de un equipo de básquebol de la liga norteamericana Big 10, y el fotógrafo fue capaz de tomarle fotos en casi 50 posiciones. La página resultante es una agradable sorpresa.

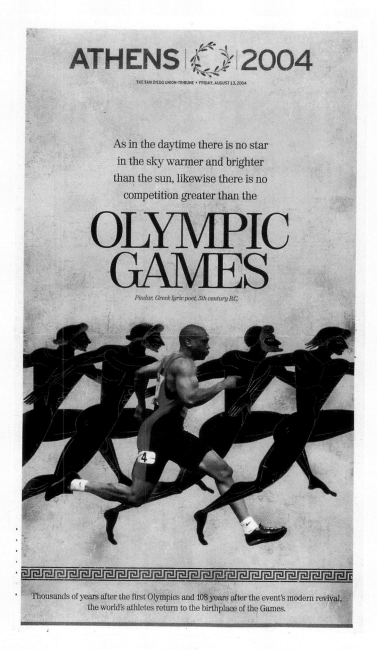

ATHENS 2004

THE SAN DIEGO UNION-TRIBUNE • FRIDAY, AUGUST 13, 2004

As in the daytime there is no star
in the sky warmer and brighter
than the sun, likewise there is no
competition greater than the

OLYMPIC GAMES

Pindar, Greek lyric poet, 5th century B.C.

Thousands of years after the first Olympics and 108 years after the event's modern revival, the world's athletes return to the birthplace of the Games.

ATHENS 2004

Thorpedoed

Phelps' golden dream over as he gets bronze

U.S. men take pride in effort for silver

American gymnasts applaud Japan's team

SILVERS

The San Diego Union-Tribune
San Diego, Calif.

Special coverage/Single subject
Special coverage, section pages/
Cover only

AWARDS OF EXCELLENCE
Sports page designer portfolio/
Individual/175,000 and over
Breaking news topics/Editor's
choice, sports

Sean M. Haffey, Photographer;
Bruce Huff, Sports Photo
Editor; **Greg Manifold,** Sports
Designer; **Christina Martinez,**
Illustrator; **Christopher
Meighan,** Page Designer;
Joshua Penrod, Sports
Designer; **Michael Price,**
Presentation Editor; **Chris Ross,**
News Design Editor; **Doug
Williams,** Deputy Sports Editor;
Dave Wilson, Page Designer;
Staff

The consistency and quality of these sections over the entire Olympics are impressive. The pages are elegant, and the volume is appropriate. The typography and energetic structure help navigation. The use of photography is great, with dramatic and exceptional cropping. The cover is one of the best in the competition.

La consistencia y la calidad de estas secciones respecto de la cobertura total sobre los juegos olímpicos es impresionante. Las páginas son elegantes y el volumen es apropiado. La tipografía y la energética estructura ayudan a la navegación. El uso de la fotografía es grandioso, y el recorte de la imagen es dramático y excepcional. La tapa es una de las mejores de toda la competencia.

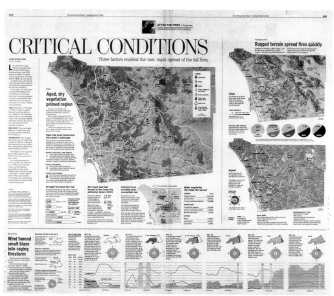

CRITICAL CONDITIONS

Three factors enabled the vast, rapid spread of the fall fires

The San Diego Union-Tribune
San Diego, Calif.

Information graphics, charting/175,000
and over
Information graphics, mapping/175,000
and over

Brian Cragin, Deputy Graphics Editor;
Michael Price, Presentation Editor

SILVERS

The Boston Globe
Boston, Mass.

*Illustration/Multiple
Special news topics/Editor's
  choice, sports*

AWARDS OF EXCELLENCE
Illustration/Single (2)

Ken Fratus, Assistant Sports
Editor; **Robert Goldstrom,**
Illustrator; **Josh Gosfield,**
Illustrator; **Brian Gross,** Designer;
Gary Kelly, Illustrator; **Chuck
Pyle,** Illustrator; **John Ritter,**
Illustrator; **Grant Staublin,**
Designer; **Mark Ulriksen,**
Illustrator; **Dan Zedek,** Design
Director

The illustrations
blow you away. The
cover, consistent
typography and
small elements
(like the pennant
page-toppers)
bring together the
disparate illustrative
styles. This section
really captures the
emotion of the event
— if you're a Red
Sox fan, you want
the pages as posters;
for non-sports fans,
they really grab you.

La ilustración es
admirable. La tapa,
la consistencia
de la tipografía
y los pequeños
elementos (como
las banderillas de la
parte de arriba de
la página) reunen
los diversos estilos
de ilustración. Esta
sección realmente
captura la emoción
del evento –incluso
si uno no es un
hincha de los Red
Sox, querría las
páginas como
afiches. Para quienes
no son hinchas
deportivos, defini-
tivamente les llama
la atención.

One strike away: The standard for booting victory is set

By Dan Shaughnessy

NEW YORK METS 4   **1986**   BOSTON RED SOX 3

Fall classics

Great
unknowns

SILVER

The Boston Globe
Boston, Mass.

*Sports page designer portfolio/Individual/175,000
  and over*

Brian Gross, Designer

This designer took what was a
great sports year in Boston and
captured that emotion. Whether
it was a news event or preview,
the pages are filled with variety,
range and surprises.

El diseñador tomó lo que fue
un gran año deportivo en
Boston y capturó esa emoción.
Haya sido una noticia de evento
o un avance, las páginas están
llenas de variedad, amplitud y
sorpresas.

Ideas
& Books

Are steroids as bad as we think they are?

BY DRAKE BENNETT

WHEN THE POOP HIT THE FANS
BY MARK SCHONE
How Hollywood sold kids' entertainment down the toilet

SILVER

The Boston Globe
Boston, Mass.

News page designer portfolio/Individual/175,000 and over (Gregory Klee)

AWARD OF EXCELLENCE
Opinion page design/175,000 and over

Gregory Klee, Designer; **Jennifer Schuessler**, Editor; **Dan Zedek**, Design Director

Each page has intelligent facts and figures that go beyond decoration. The headlines support the illustrations, and the typography is restrained and smart. In what could have been a safe section, the conceptual thinking is a risk, but clearly the risk has paid off.

Cada página cuenta con hechos y datos inteligentes que van más allá de lo decorativo. Los títulos sustentan las ilustraciones, y la tipografía es restringida y elegante. Esta sección podría haberse ido a la segura, pero el pensamiento conceptual toma riesgos que claramente han dado frutos.

Ideas
& Books

THE *God* GAP

How religion divides the Democrats

BY ALAN WOLFE

ZEN AND THE ART OF SLAM DANCING
Buddhist punks find enlightenment in the pit BY DAVID F. SNYDER JR.

CityWeekly
BOSTON SUNDAY GLOBE FEBRUARY 1, 2004

Please, thanks, and @!#!!#%!!!*

Despite Menino's pleas, Boston can't shake its uncivil reputation

House of hoops, Southern style
Fans of college b-ball find a home where blues reigned

Yo — freeloaders!
Neighbors have had enough, take aim at out-of-area plates

SILVER

The Boston Globe
Boston, Mass.

News page designer portfolio/Individual/ 175,000 and over

AWARDS OF EXCELLENCE
Local news section design/175,000 and over (2)

Lesley Becker, Designer

There is a lot of smart thinking in the pages of this portfolio. These are heavily formatted pages, but each feels fresh, and each is packed with skillful use of typography. The designer has prepared vibrant solutions to hard-to-illustrate stories.

Hay una buena dosis de decisiones correctas en las páginas de este portafolio. Son páginas tremendamente formateadas, pero cada una se siente fresca y evidencia un hábil uso de tipografía. El diseñador preparó soluciones vibrantes para historias difíciles de ilustrar.

CityWeekly
BOSTON SUNDAY GLOBE JULY 11, 2004

A banquet of memories, bittersweet

'**SECURITY** ON OUR TRAINS, BUSES AND BOATS HAS NEVER BEEN MORE IMPORTANT. IF YOU'D LIKE TO HELP PROTECT OUR MBTA, GET INVOLVED IN OUR TRANSIT WATCH PROGRAM. THIS IS DANIEL A. GRABAUSKAS, MASSACHUSETTS SECRETARY OF TRANSPORTATION. WE ASK YOU TO KEEP YOUR EYES OPEN FOR SUSPICIOUS ACTIVITY,' ABANDONED PACKAGES OR UNACCOMPANIED LUGGAGE. AND IF YOU SEE SOMETHING, **SAY SOMETHING.**'

Terror and the Ⓣ

With loudspeaker warnings, the MBTA puts citizens on alert and wary passengers report an outbreak of the heebie-jeebies

Stowaways
They went to Ireland with a taste for adventure and returned with a gift for blarney

The Boston Globe
Boston, Mass.

Home/Real estate page design/175,000 and over
Illustration/Single

Michael Prager, Editor; **Chin Wang,** Art Director; **Russ Willms,**
Illustrator; **Dan Zedek,** Design Director

The Boston Globe
Boston, Mass.

Entertainment page design/175,000 and over
Illustration/Single

David Johnson, Illustrator; **Hayley Kaufman,** Editor; **Gregory Klee,**
Deputy Design Director; **Chin Wang,** Art Director; **Dan Zedek,** Design
Director

The Boston Globe
Boston, Mass.

Features page designer portfolio/Individual 175,000 and over
Special coverage, section pages/Cover only

Wendy Fox, Editor; **Chin Wang,** Designer; **Dan Zedek,** Design Director

The Oregonian
Portland, Ore.

Inside news page design/175,000 and over
Information graphics, mapping/175,000 and over

Dan Aguayo, Assistant Art Director; **Steve Cowden,** Staff Artist

SATURDAY, APRIL 3, 2004
TORONTO STAR

Exclusive
fold-out guide to
Greater Toronto's
new Terminal 1
opening this week
at Pearson airport

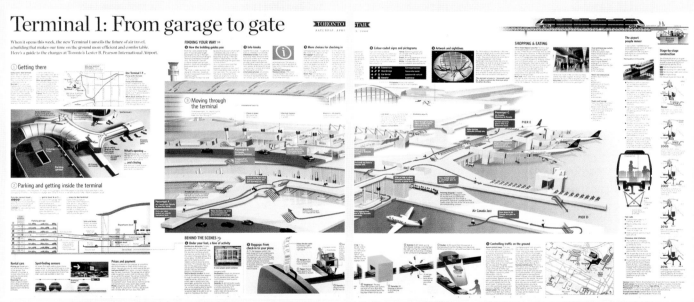

Terminal 1: From garage to gate

The graphic is huge – enormous – but more importantly it's easy to understand. It's clean, clear and polished, and it's a great surprise for readers. The type is perfect, and the color is restrained. Figuring out how to get a quad-truck is an accomplishment in itself.

El gráfico es enorme – más bien gigantesco – pero más importante que eso es que es fácil de entender. Es limpio, claro y ordenado, y es una gran sorpresa para los lectores. La tipografía es perfecta y el color es restringido. Conseguir realizar un reportaje de página cuádruple es todo un logro.

SILVER

Toronto Star
Toronto, Ontario, Canada

Special coverage/Sections/With ads

AWARD OF EXCELLENCE
Information graphics, Non-breaking/175,000 and over

Tonia Cowan, Graphic Director; **Mike Herman**, Artist; **Brian Hughes**, Artist; **Carl Neustaedter**, A.M.E. Design; **Lucas Oleniuk**, Photographer; **Kevin Scanlon**, Copy Editor; **Patty Winsa**, Researcher; **Spencer Wynn**, Designer;

GLAMOUR GIRL

CELEBRATE THE LUXE LIFE AND CHANNEL YOUR INNER
GODDESS WITH AN EMBARRASSMENT OF FURS

Five Items That Changed Modern Life

AVENUE

From the 1980s to the 1990s, the number of car models in North America went from about 140 to more than 260. There was an explosion of choices but precious little variety: All modern cars looked alike.

In 1999, car auctioneer Robert Shannon told the Australian Broadcasting Corporation, "Until you see the badge of a car on the road, you can't even tell what make it is. I can't, and I've been in the business 30 years ... I think they're all starting to look [like an] absolute cloning of each other."

The trouble was optimization. Computer modelling had allowed car manufacturers to find the ideal shape to minimize wind resistance, maximize trunk space and seat five people in optimal comfort. The unfortunate result was that every car started to look like the same tapered box on wheels.

Shannon clearly hadn't seen the Volkswagen New Beetle yet, though it had launched the previous year. The automotive malaise was over and vehicular style was back on the road.

To be fair, before the launch of the New Beetle, modern cars already said something about their drivers. A Volvo said, "I'm willing to pay for safety." A minivan: "I'm not as young as I used to be." An SUV: "I have contempt for humanity."

But in the '50s and '60s, cars were about coolness, sexiness and, in the original Beetle's case, cuteness. People gave their cars pet names, cuddled and customized them, and coaxed them to keep running. Cars and their owners forged an intimate connection of personalities. Somewhere along the way, though, that feeling took a wrong turn. It's hard to imagine the Beach Boys singing, "She'll have fun, fun, fun till her daddy takes the Civic away." Modern cars were efficient, but they weren't any fun.

That changed when the new Bug hit the road. The revamped Beetle has little in common with its massively successful precursor. The engine moved to the front, the interior was completely redone, and an ultra-modern, computerized diagnostic system meant that all those folks who used to lovingly tinker with their Bugs were out of luck.

But still, the new car had a flower on the dash and a friendly personality that was enough to revive VW's flagging North American sales. Even more important, it paved the way for other style-driven cars, including the PT Cruiser and the new Mini Cooper, both of which hit the pavement in 2000. If the times we live in are truly a golden age of design, it's because individuality and personality have begun to matter again. The New Beetle rides that wave and hurries it along. Anyone can pack humans into a car. Volkswagen packed humanity into theirs.

NOT LIKE THE OTHERS

The New Beetle brought a sense of fun to a car culture
bogged down in uniformity

By Patchen Barss

National Post
Toronto, Ontario, Canada

Other feature page design/175,000 and over
Lifestyle/Features page design/175,000 and over
Inside news page design/175,000 and over
Combination portfolio/Individual/175,000 and over (Gayle Grin)

Ben Errett, Arts and Life Editor; **Matthew Fraser,** Editor-in-Chief; **Gayle Grin,** A.M.E./Visuals

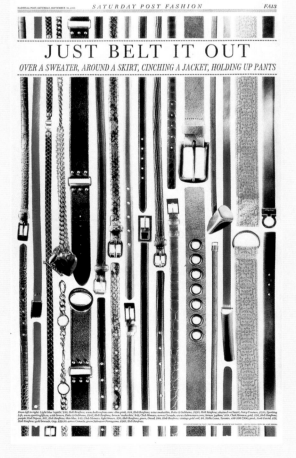

JUST BELT IT OUT

OVER A SWEATER, AROUND A SKIRT, CINCHING A JACKET, HOLDING UP PANTS

SILVER

National Post
Toronto, Ontario, Canada

Features page designer portfolio/
Individual 175,000 and over
(Christine Dewairy)

AWARDS OF EXCELLENCE
Lifestyle/Features page design/175,000
and over (2)

Christine Dewairy, Saturday Post
Fashion Art Director/Designer; **Matthew Fraser,** Editor-in-Chief; **Gayle Grin,** A.M.E./Visuals; **Shielagh McEvenue,** Saturday Post Editor; **Sarah Murdoch,** M.E./Features;

Perfect photos, typography and composition – it's a little bit retro but updated. The pages show products in a fun, innovative way that allows you to really look at the items. These are fresh, different kinds of newspaper pages.

Fotos, tipografía y composición a la perfección. Es un poquito retro pero actualizado. Las páginas muestan productos de forma divertida e innovadora, que permite que uno realmente se fije en los ítemes. Estas páginas de diario son frescas y diferentes.

These pages show some really innovative approaches. They take ideas we've seen before and treat them a different way. Each page is very smart, has a concept and offers a big effect. The more you read, the smarter it gets.

Estas páginas muestan algunos enfoques realmente innovadores. Toman ideas ya vistas y las tratan de otra forma. Cada página es muy elegante, tiene un concepto claro y entrega un buen efecto. Mientras más se lee, más inteligente se vuelve la lectura.

SILVER

National Post
Toronto, Ontario, Canada

Combination portfolio/Individual/175,000 and over
(Donna MacMullin)

AWARDS OF EXCELLENCE
Other feature page design/175,000 and over (2)

Ben Errett, Arts and Life Editor; **Matthew Fraser,** Editor-in-Chief; **Gayle Grin,** A.M.E./Visuals; **Donna MacMullin,** Features Presentation Editor & Designer

'Win Ohio, win the White House' is conventional wisdom,
and many think that's truer than ever for the 2004 presidential race.
But which Ohio? The state has distinct regions, each with its own social values
and economic woes. In a summerlong series The Plain Dealer examined ...

The Five Ohios

MIKE LEVY | THE PLAIN DEALER

A model Statue of Liberty greets customers at Peddler's restaurant, where Jonda Kennedy, left, and Cindy Barnes wait tables. Crippled by job losses, Ironton in Appalachia's Lawrence County remains proud and patriotic. "A lot of our young men join the military, and we just try to support them," Barnes said.

The Five Ohios' series and more information can be found on cleveland.com/fiveohios

THE PLAIN DEALER

THE FIVE OHIOS
The Farm Belt

STORIES BY BILL LUBINGER | PHOTOGRAPHS BY DALE OMORI | THE PLAIN DEALER

The foundation of Ohio's Farm Belt voters is as sturdy as the rumbling tractors that cultivate their fields, built on family, religion and education.

In a Plain Dealer poll taken in May, northwest Ohio was the one region among the five that identified moral and family issues as the most important in the presidential race — more important than even the economy and jobs.

And this despite the second-highest rate of job loss in the state last year behind Northeast Ohio.

The people of northwest Ohio — in Toledo and in Lima, Findlay, Fremont and Clyde — make autos and tires and glass and washing machines.

But the region is defined by its farms and farm families.

The population, much of it descendants of German immigration and with a work ethic to match, is heavily Catholic and Lutheran. Twelve of the 15 most religious counties in the state are found in northwest Ohio.

So voters here tend to be more conventional and conservative in their ethos — and show it.

Entering Fremont, the county seat of the region's bellwether Sandusky County, a white sign with black lettering welcomes visitors with, "See you in church!"

It's more than a greeting.

"People need a little more direction in their lives," said volunteer Tim Lee, setting up tents for the festival at Fremont St. Joseph Central Catholic Church, which his family attends and where his children go to school.

A direction, but not a directive. Especially about who should be president.

Endless fields of corn, soybeans and wheat meld from green to brown to gold in perfect rectangles like wrapping paper in northwest Ohio, which is a region of "also farms." The truck driver at the coffee shop "also farms." The factory worker running the register at the community social "also farms."

Olga Mendez manages the La Violeta gr who was born in Arkansas, moved to Po But she'd like to see more done for imm

A pocket of

FOSTORIA – The people of Ohio's Farm Belt are about as diverse as the flat landscape.

Even in Toledo's Lucas County, where about three-fourths of the 21-county region's black citizens live, the suburbs are overwhelmingly white.

But then there's Fostoria, a city oddly split among three counties.

Like northwest Ohio's other cities flanking Interstate 75 — Findlay, Fremont, Lima, Tiffin — Fostoria lured black families up from Dixie Highway from the South with its booming foundries and auto parts plants in the early 1900s.

Yet Fostoria retains a population especially diverse for its size: about 8 percent of the city's 13,900 residents are black and 8 percent are Latino, many

THE FIVE OHIOS

Southeast Ohio is the state's second least populated region with 2.2 million people.

THE FIVE OHIOS

The region is Ohio's Republican stronghold; Hamilton County is home to some of the Republican Party's top money givers.

Military issues drive stalwart county

The whole country was watching Ohio before the election. This project took the state apart piece by piece. The graphics helped explain the story. The pages are extremely well organized, clear from beginning to end. The design and photography give a sense of all the different regions. The whole newspaper must have been on board for this project — it couldn't do this if it weren't a real team effort.

Todo Estados Unidos estaba con los ojos en Ohio después de la elección presidencial. Este proyecto desarmó el estado pieza por pieza. Los gráficos ayudan a explicar la historia. Las páginas están extremadamente bien organizadas de principio a fin. El diseño y la fotografía dan una muestra de cada uno de las diferentes regiones. Todo el diario debe haberse dedicado a este proyecto –no podría llevarlo a cabo si no fuera un real trabajo en equipo.

OHIOS | The Farm Belt

...raped in Ohio's farmland

ONLINE: WWW.CLEVELAND.COM

PLAIN DEALER
SUNDAY

TRAVEL goes to Disney World
What if the FCC controlled the TV schedule? PDQ

SPORTS FINAL | $1.50

INDIANS FALL
REDS WIN, 4-2

FORUM Sheppard murder case still a mystery

HAPPY FOURTH OF JULY!

BOURDAIS WINS GRAND PRIX

Area alumni help fight 'brain drain'
Summer internships try to sell future grads on settling here

1 winning ticket sold in $290 million lottery

Differences create invisible borders

STORY BY ROBERT L. SMITH AND DAVE DAVIS | PLAIN DEALER REPORTERS

Militants say they beheaded Marine

Cheney bus makes stop in Parma

INSIDE

THE FIVE OHIOS

Appalachia

STORIES BY BILL SLOAT | PHOTOGRAPHS BY MIKE LEVY | THE PLAIN DEALER

Second in a series

THIS PLAIN DEALER SPECIAL REPORT CONTINUES ON #2, 7 AND 8

THE FIVE OHIOS

Five Ohios

REGION

THE FIVE OHIOS

State's isolated hill counties rich in minerals, poor in cash

SILVERS

The Plain Dealer
Cleveland, Ohio

Special coverage/Single subject
Special news topics/Editor's choice, local/regional
Reprints

AWARD OF EXCELLENCE
Photography/Photo series

Richard Conway, Picture Editor; Jeff Greene, Picture Editor; Lisa Griffis, Designer; Bill Gugliotta, Director of Photography; David Kordalski, A.M.E./Visuals; John Kuntz, Photographer; Mike Levy, Photographer; Ken Marshall, Graphics Editor; William Neff, Graphic Artist; Dale Omori, Photographer; Chris Stephens, Photographer; Lonnie Timmons III, Photographer

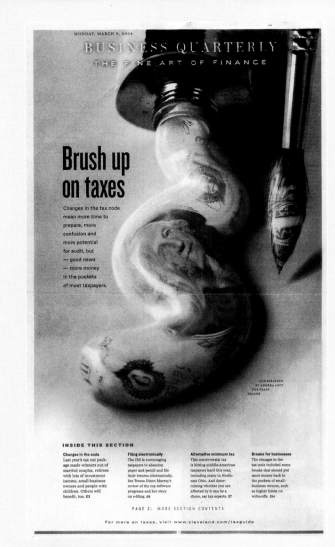

The Plain Dealer
Cleveland, Ohio

Photography/General news (planned)
Photography/Portfolio/Staff

Lonnie Timmons III, Photographer; **Staff**

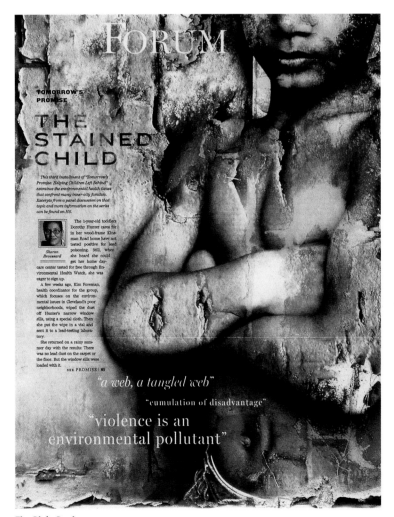

SILVER

The Plain Dealer
Cleveland, Ohio

Special coverage, section pages/Cover only

AWARD OF EXCELLENCE
Photography/Illustration

Terry Chapman, Designer; **Kristen DelGuzzi,** BusinessMonday Editor; **David Kordalski,** A.M.E./Visuals; **Andrea Levy,** Illustrator

The artwork defines the state of the art. Taxes are a messy concept for many people, and there's a subliminal messiness in this artwork. With the brush, the section then becomes the tool. The illustration is phenomenal.

El arte usado marca la excelencia del arte en general. Los impuestos son algo complicado para mucha gente, y hay una complicación subliminal en el arte del artículo. Con el pincel, esta sección se convierte en la herramienta. La ilustración es fenomenal.

The Plain Dealer
Cleveland, Ohio

Photography/Portfolio/Individual
Photography/Illustration

Andrea Levy, Photographer/Illustrator

SILVER

The Plain Dealer
Cleveland, Ohio

Photography/Portfolio/Individual (Andrea Levy)

AWARDS OF EXCELLENCE
Photography/Illustration
Photography/Illustration
Special coverage, section pages/Cover only

Andrea Levy, Illustrator; **David Kordalski,** A.M.E./Visuals

This is a portfolio. The clarity of vision, thinking and execution is remarkable. Each illustration is compelling, refined and well done.

Éste es un portafolio. La claridad de visión, pensamiento y ejecución es notable. Cada ilustración es llamativa, refinada y está bien hecha.

Los Angeles Times

Special reprint of a five-part series published December 5-10, 2004

The Troubles at King/Drew

ROBERT GAUTHIER Los Angeles Times

SYMBOL: *Patient Albert Johnson smokes at King/Drew Medical Center, which stands for justice to many black people in South L.A. It was founded to be the nation's "very best hospital," but by various measures is now one of the worst. Some call it "Killer King."*

Deadly errors and politics betray a hospital's promise

A Times investigation finds King/Drew far more dangerous than the public knows. Community pride, timid county leadership stand in the way of a remedy.

First of five parts

By Tracy Weber, Charles Ornstein and Mitchell Landsberg
Times Staff Writers

On a warm July afternoon, an impish second-grader named Dunia Tasejo was running home after buying ice cream on her South Los Angeles street when a car sideswiped her. Knocked to the pavement, she screamed for help, blood pouring from her mouth.

Her father bolted from the house to her side. An ambulance rushed her to the nearest hospital: Martin Luther King Jr./Drew Medical Center.

For Elias and Salma Tasejo, there was no greater terror than seeing their 9-year-old daughter strapped to a gurney that day in 2000. But once they arrived at King/Drew, fear gave way to relief.

Dunia's injuries were minor: some scrapes, some bruises and two broken baby teeth. The teeth would have to be pulled.

"They told me to relax," Salma recalled. "Everything was fine."

At least, it should have been.

What the Tasejos didn't know was that King/Drew, a 233-bed public hospital in Willowbrook, just south of Watts, had a long history of harming, or even killing, those it was meant to serve.

Over the last year, reports by journalists and regulators have offered stark glimpses of failings at King/Drew: Nurses neglecting patients as they lay dying. Staff failing to give patients crucial drugs or giving them toxic ones by mistake. Guards using Taser stun guns on psychiatric patients, despite an earlier warning to stop.

Over the same period, a team of Times reporters has been systematically examining the hospital. They conducted hundreds of interviews, studied years of malpractice cases and reviewed records of the hospital and its regulators. They looked closely at individual departments and physicians. And, to put their findings in perspective, they consulted outside experts in hospitals and medical care.

The investigation reveals that King/Drew is much more (See Hospital, Page 2)

VICTIM: *Dunia Tasejo was taken to King/Drew with some scrapes, bruises and two broken baby teeth. There should have been no reason to worry.*

About the series

PART ONE	PART TWO	PART THREE	PART FOUR	PART FIVE	ON THE WEB
Deep trouble: A hospital inspired by the civil rights movement fails — sometimes kills — those it was meant to serve.	**The myth of poverty:** King/Drew is not underfunded. It is mismanaged.	**Unheeded warnings:** How one pathologist got hired and remained on staff despite misdiagnoses and legal woes.	**Broad failure:** Beyond individual workers' shortcomings, whole departments are in disarray.	**Timidity at the top:** The county Board of Supervisors shies away from reform, paralyzed by community protest and racial politics.	**Learn more:** Additional photos and related articles are on the Times website at *www.latimes.com/kingdrew*.

SILVERS

Los Angeles Times
Los Angeles, Calif.

Special news topics/Editor's choice, local/regional Photography/Photo series

AWARDS OF EXCELLENCE
Special coverage/Single subject
Reprints

Gail Fisher, Senior Photo Editor; **Bill Gaspard,** News Design Director; **Robert Gauthier,** Photographer; **Joseph Hutchinson,** Deputy M.E.; **Michael Whitley,** Deputy Design Director

The traditional components — long narrative and photography — are brilliant, but the short items are also a great touch that pushed the project into something special. The photography keeps you involved and makes you want to read. The story is about an institution, but the photos make it personal.

Los tradicionales componentes –un largo relato y fotografías-, son brillantes, pero los elementos cortos también dan un buen toque que hace de este artículo algo especial. La fotografía lo mantiene a uno inmerso en la lectura. El tema es sobre una institución, pero las fotos le dan un carácter personal.

A38 WEDNESDAY, DECEMBER 8, 2004 LOS ANGELES TIMES

The Troubles at King/Drew

'I screamed and hollered. I tried to pull my baby out of the bed.'

BRENDA NELSON, *describing a visit to son Mario at King/Drew. She didn't know he'd been transferred to the ICU, and she was kept from entering for an hour. Nobody told her what she'd find when she was finally allowed in.*

Photographs by ROBERT GAUTHIER Los Angeles Times

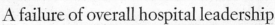

OVERCOME BY MEMORIES
Brenda Nelson, right, mourns her son Mario. His nurse allegedly silenced his vital-signs monitor and failed to notice his heartbeat fading. With Nelson are son Adrian Nelson and daughter Monique Pettigrew.

A failure of overall hospital leadership

POINT OF ENTRY

FORMER CHIEF

ENCOURAGING WORDS

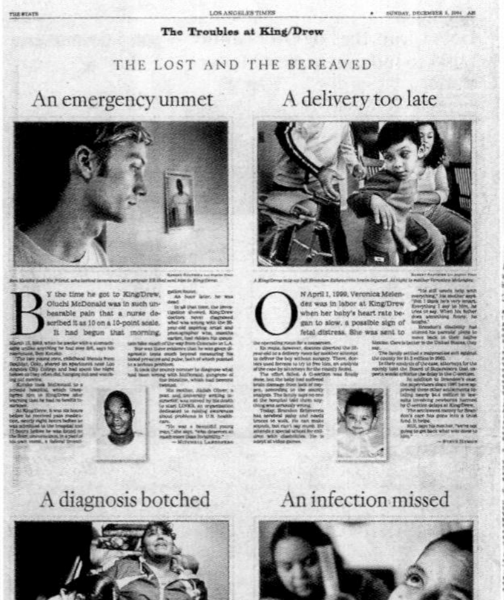

The Troubles at King/Drew

THE LOST AND THE BEREAVED

An emergency unmet

A delivery too late

A diagnosis botched

An infection missed

SUNDAY Los Angeles Times

SUNDAY, DECEMBER 5, 2004

FINAL

Proposal Would Hit Blue State Taxpayers

Global Nuclear Inquiry Stalls

The Troubles at King/Drew

Deadly errors and politics betray a hospital's promise

Militants

In the shadows, Palestinian fighters are poised to do battle with Israel.

Jerusalem

This holy city is at the heart of the Israeli-Palestinian struggle.

Security

Suicide attacks have altered life on both sides of the Israeli-Palestinian divide.

Refugees

SILVERS
Los Angeles Times
Los Angeles, Calif.

Photography/Use of photography
Special news topics/Editor's choice, international
Photography/Photo series
Special coverage/Single subject

AWARDS OF EXCELLENCE
Photography/Page design
Photography/Page design
Inside news page design/175,000 and over (3)
News page designer portfolio/Individual/175,000 and over
(Michael Whitley)
Photography/Project page or spread
Photography/Page design

Mary Cooney, Deputy Photo Editor; **Gail Fisher,** Senior Photo Editor; **Bill Gaspard,** News Design Director; **Joseph Hutchinson,** Deputy M.E.; **Rick Loomis,** Photographer; **Michael Whitley,** Deputy Design Director; **Staff**

This is all about strong photography and tight picture editing. The imagery is powerful, and the designer maximizes it with great play. Typographically, it works pretty well — the text blocks add valuable information. The disguised production bars at the top of each page leave a cradle of air at the bottom of the page.

Todo está centrado en fotografías de calidad y un buen nivel de edición de las imágenes. La visualidad es poderosa y el diseñador la maximiza dándole gran tamaño. Funciona bien en cuanto a la tipografía; los bloques de texto le añaden valiosa información. Las notables baras de producción en la parte alta de cada página dejan una cuna de aire al final de la página.

Los Angeles Times

THIRD OF SIX PARTS
Published Wednesday , July 14, 2004

[LIVING ON PENNIES]

For sale — cheap:
'Dead white men's clothing'

In Africa, the West's castoff clothes are de rigueur, not demeaning.
Nearly everyone has to buy used.

DRESSED TO SELL: *Athletic wear is popular at this Lagos merchant's used-shirt stand. Customers will part with $8 — more than a week's pay — for a Shaquille O'Neal jersey.*

BY DAVAN MAHARAJ ; PHOTOGRAPHS BY FRANCINE ORR ; TIMES STAFF

Lagos, Nigeria

Tossed off a flatbed truck, a 100-pound bale of used panties and bras, worn socks, DKNY suits and Michael Jordan jerseys lands with a thud amid a jostling swarm of shoppers.

Okech Anorue slits the plastic wrap on the refrigerator-size bundle he bought for $95 and dives in. There's bound to be a gem in there — like the faded leather bomber jacket once worn by Tiffany of Costa Mesa High School. That piece now hangs on the premium rack in his 5-foot-by-5-foot stall with a $25 price tag.

"These clothes make people's dreams come true," says Anorue, chairman of the vendors association at Yaba Market. "Everyone wears them, from insurance women, vendors, poor people to parliamentarians. When they put them on, you can't tell rich from poor."

Much of Africa was once draped in fabrics of flamboyant color and pattern, products of local industry and a reflection of cultural pride. But with half of its people surviving on less than a dollar a day, the continent has become the world's recycling bin. People scramble for 10-cent underpants, 20-cent T-shirts and dollar blue jeans discarded by Westerners.

A young man in the Congolese jungle wears a T-shirt that pleads: "Beam me up, Scotty." In a Lagos nightclub, a Nigerian ingenue models a used red negligee over a hot-pink halter top. A young Liberian fighter with an AK-47 assault rifle wears a tan bathrobe like a trench coat. In Togo, the castoffs are called "dead white men's clothing." Few people in that West African country believe that a living person would throw away anything this good.

Consumers in Uganda, Kenya and Tanzania call the used clothing *mitumba*, the Swahili word for bale.

"Without *mitumba*, most Ugandans would be walking naked in the countryside," lamented an editorial in that country's leading newspaper, the Monitor.

Insatiable demand from village shops and sprawling urban markets has turned the West's castoffs into an industry that generates hundreds of millions of dollars annually. Clothing is only the most visible example. Polluting refrigerators and air conditioners, expired medicines and old mattresses also are routinely shipped and resold here. Used vehicles imported from Japan dot African roads. Antiquated secondhand computers power many African governments.

[See Africa, Page 15]

Photographs by Francine Orr Los Angeles Times

AIDS has marked even the landscape in Africa. On a roadside in Masaka, Uganda, coffins are for sale, in a scene that is repeated across the continent. Elsewhere, land lies fallow because the disease has struck so many farmers, and deaths among teachers have closed schools.

[LIVING ON PENNIES]

When the push for survival is a full-time job

What is it like to live on less than a dollar a day? Hundreds of millions in sub-Saharan Africa know. Their work is an endless cycle of bartering, hawking and scrounging to get by until tomorrow.

PRIMITIVE SYSTEM: In Congo, the chukudu, a homemade wooden scooter, is the workhorse of men who ferry goods through the marketplace, earning a few cents a trip and perhaps a small handout of food from merchants.

FRANCINE ORR Los Angeles Times

FIRST OF SIX PARTS

By Davan Maharaj
Times Staff Writer

GOMA, Congo

Every day is a fight for pennies. ¶ At sunrise, Adolphe Mulinowa is out hauling 10-gallon cans of sand at a construction site. It takes him an hour to earn 5 cents. Then he hustles to a roadside with a few plastic bottles of pink gasoline, which he hawks alongside dozens of other street vendors. ¶ "Patron! Boss man! Gas! Gas! Gas!" Mulinowa barks as a battered Peugeot shudders past, kicking a spray of loose rocks at his face. ¶ The car does not stop. Mulinowa, a short man in his mid-30s with sad, reddened eyes, squats down again beside his bottles. It is a scene repeated many times in the four hours it takes to sell them. Mulinowa pockets an additional 40 cents. Then, as the sun goes down, he heads to his evening job hawking used shoes and live chickens. A few more pennies. ¶ After a 12-hour day, he returns home to his wife and six children with his earnings: about 70 cents and a bag of cornmeal swinging from his hand. "We beat the belly pains today," he says in a tired mumble. "Tomorrow, more hard work." ¶ Up and down the teeming streets of Goma, there is no real work as it is known in the West. There is only what everyone here calls se debrouiller — French for getting by, or eking a living out of nothing. ¶ Decades of war and disease, followed by a volcanic eruption that entombed nearly half the city beneath a rough crust of lava, have reduced work to a mishmash of odd jobs and scheming. Civil servants survive on bribes. A lawyer moonlights by making pastries. A single mother of four turns to prostitution in her living room, decorated with pictures of Jesus and Mary. ¶ They are among the poorest people on Earth, surviving on less than a dollar a day. ¶ In the United States, an individual who makes less than $9,310 a year is considered poor. The World Bank sets its poverty [See Africa, Page A10]

DOUG STEVENS Los Angeles Times

About this series

Six articles over the next two weeks:

PART 1: Today - Eking out an income.
PART 2: Monday - Staving off hunger.

Coming later:

PART 3: Settling for castoff clothes.
PART 4: Living in 100 square feet.
PART 5: Locked out of school.
PART 6: Surviving AIDS.

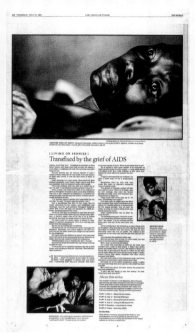

[LIVING ON PENNIES]
Transfixed by the grief of AIDS

SILVERS

Los Angeles Times
Los Angeles, Calif.

News page designer portfolio/Individual/175,000 and over (Joseph Hutchinson)
Photography/Feature
Photography/Photo series
Special coverage/Single subject (2)
Reprints

AWARDS OF EXCELLENCE
A-section news design/175,000 and over
Photography/Project page or spread (2)
Special news topics/Editor's choice, international (2)

Mary Cooney, Deputy Director of Photography; **Gail Fisher,** Senior Photo Editor; **Bill Gaspard,** News Design Director; **Joseph Hutchinson,** Deputy M.E.; **Francine Orr,** Staff Photographer; **Michael Whitley,** Deputy Design Director

These are striking and haunting photographs and incredible designs. The pacing is excellent, and the black-and-white palette, even on the front page, holds the project together. It's worth noting that the paper's commitment to the story, in time and space, is remarkable.

Estas fotos son impresionantes y cautivantes, y el diseño es increíble. El ritmo es excelente, y la paleta de blanco y negro, incluso en la tapa, unifica el proyecto. Vale la pena mencionar que el compromiso del diario para con la historia, en tiempo y espacio, es destacado.

CALENDAR

Ringing endorsement

SILVERS

Los Angeles Times
Los Angeles, Calif.

Breaking news topics/Editor's choice, local/regional
Features page designer portfolio/ Individual 175,000 and over (Paul Gonzales)
News design/Page(s)/Other 175,000 and over
News page designer portfolio/Individual/ 175,000 and over (Joseph Hutchinson)
Photography/Use of photography
Special news topics/Editor's choice, local/regional

AWARDS OF EXCELLENCE

Entertainment page design/175,000 and over
Entertainment section design/175,000 and over
Photography/Project page or spread
Special coverage, multiple sections/With ads
Special coverage, section pages/Cover only
Special coverage/Sections/With ads (2)
Special coverage, multiple sections/ With ads

Wes Bausmith, Design Editor; **Steve Banks,** Design Editor; **Laura DeAnda,** Design Editor; **Richard Dirk,** Photo Editor; **Bill Gaspard,** News Design Director; **Paul Gonzales,** Design Editor; **Steven Hawkins,** Deputy Design Director; **Cindy Hively,** Photo Editor; **Calvin Hom,** Deputy Director of Photography; **Tim Hubbard,** Design Editor; **Joseph Hutchinson,** Deputy M.E.; **Pete Metzger,** Design Editor; **Kirk McKoy,** Senior Photo Editor; **An Moonen,** Design Editor; **Christian Potter Drury,** Features Design Director; **Judy Pryor,** Design Editor; **Iris Schneider,** Photo Editor; **Kelli Sullivan,** Deputy Design Director; **Sue Timmons,** Design Editor; **Hal Wells,** Photo Editor

Los Angeles Times

CALENDAR

SUNDAY : PART I

September 12, 2004

calendarlive.com

jude's law

The glam Englishman rules Hollywood with six new parts, from a cameo as Errol Flynn to a libidinous star turn in "Alfie." PAGE 4

fall movie sneaks

A trippy take on world affairs: The "South Park" guys are stirring up trouble again — putting the finishing touches on their global puppetry romp. PAGE 14 How they make real Texas men: After many fumbles, Peter Berg gets "Friday Night Lights" with Billy Bob Thornton over Hollywood's goal line. PAGE 25 And more: Lunch with Queen Latifah; Colin Farrell becomes "Alexander"; the godfather of Japanese anime; and a complete guide to more than 100 new films.

The format is very handsome. Each page reinforces the identity of the section, and yet all are different. They nailed a lot of different approaches — handout photos, illustrations, art direction and staff photography. They have perfected every way you can illustrate a page. The fonts are strong and create a nice contrast.

El formato es muy atractivo. Cada página refuerza la identidad de la sección, y sin embargo, todas son diferentes. Se determinaron muchos y variados enfoques; fotos de fuente externa, ilustraciones, dirección de arte y fotografía producida por los fotógrafos de la planta del medio. Han perfeccionado todas las formas en que se puede ilustrar una página. La tipografía es poderosa y crea un buen contraste.

NEW DAY IN HAITI

Residents celebrate alongside triumphant rebels, but chaos persists

Los Angeles Times
NBA FINALS
LAKERS VS. PISTONS

Sunday, June 6, 2004

ALL FOUR ONE NOW

At times divided, Lakers' lineup of Hall of Famers is on the verge of an NBA title.
■ STORIES, S9-13

Los Angeles Times
Los Angeles, Calif.

Breaking news topics/Terrorist attacks
Inside news page design/175,000 and over (2)
Photography/Page design
Photography/Portfolio/Staff
Photography/Project page or spread
Sports page design/175,000 and over
Special coverage, section pages/Cover only

Alex Brown, Designer; **Carolyn Cole,** Photographer; **Mary Cooney,** Deputy Director Photography; **Colin Crawford,** A.M.E./ Photo; **Gail Fisher,** Senior Photo Editor; **Bill Gaspard,** News Design Director; **Alan Hagman,** Senior Photo Editor; **Calvin Hom,** Deputy Director Photography; **Joseph Hutchinson,** Deputy M.E.; **Rick Loomis,** Photographer; **Bill Nelson,** Illustrator; **Francine Orr,** Photographer; **Dan Santos,** Designer; **Lee Sinco,** Photographer; **Steve Stroud,** Photo Editor; **Michael Whitley,** Deputy Design Director

TERROR IN MADRID

Nearly 200 Die in Bombings; Spain in Shock

Basque Separatists Are Prime Suspects

El Gráfico
Antiguo Cuscatlán, El Salvador

Sports page design/49,999 and under (2)

José Jaén, Designer; **Ulises Martínez,** Illustrator; **Agustín Palacios,** Design Coordinator; **Cristian Villalta,** Editor-in-Chief

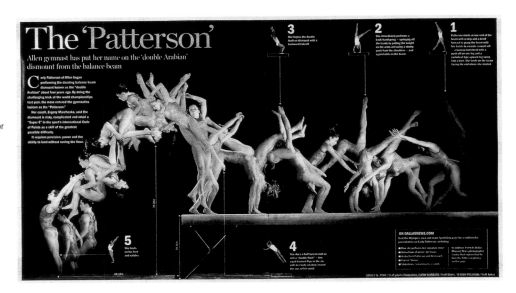

The Dallas Morning News
Dallas, Texas

Sports page design/175,000 and over
Special coverage, section pages/ Inside page or spread

Sergio Pecanha, Graphic Artist; **Smiley N. Pool,** Photographer; **Rob Schneider,** Design Editor/ Sports; **Chris Wilkins,** Photo Editor

Detroit Free Press
Detroit, Mich.

Inside news page design/175,000 and over
A-section news design/175,000 and over

Steve Anderson, News Designer; **Steve Dorsey,** Director/Design & Graphics; **John Fleming,** Deputy Graphics Director; **Fred S. Fluker,** News Graphic Artist; **Jeff Taylor,** A.M.E. Investigations

El Correo
Bilbao, Spain

Information graphics, breaking news/50,000-174,999
Information graphics/Portfolios/Extended coverage/ 50,000-174,999

Fernando G. Baptista, Editor; **José Miguel Benitez,** Co-Editor; **Gonzalo de las Heras,** Infographic Artist

Star-Telegram

BASEBALL04

SECTION N | SUNDAY, APRIL 4, 2004

The core of the game

.406 Ted Williams, right? 56? Joe DiMaggio. Numbers have always been a huge part of baseball, and their importance is growing. Average and ERA aren't enough? Let's add runs created, holds and OPS. Baseball people are immersing themselves in numbers to improve their game.

The love for numbers just keeps growing
As Paul Molitor says, "Everybody in baseball is fascinated by statistics." And the fascination is growing. **3**

Symbols of superiority shine in six numbers
You know the magic numbers (56, 715, .400, etc.) that define the game, but do you know the stories behind them? **10-11**

Bill James became baseball's king of stats
His ideas, and his analysis of which stats matter, have helped change the way baseball and fans use statistics. **6**

In computer game, fantasy is like reality
Forget Rotisserie leagues. The Diamond Mind game gives "fantasy" players a chance to really manage. **Gil LeBreton, 7**

AMERICAN LEAGUE PREVIEWS 13-16   **NATIONAL LEAGUE PREVIEWS 17-20**

STAR-TELEGRAM PHOTO ILLUSTRATION/RALPH LAUER AND JOHN T. VALLES

SILVER

Fort Worth Star-Telegram
Fort Worth, Texas

Special coverage, section pages/Cover only

AWARD OF EXCELLENCE
Sports page designer portfolio/Individual 175,000 and over (Michael Currie)

Cody Bailey, Senior Deputy Sports Editor; **Michael Currie,** Assistant Sports Editor; **John T. Valles,** Illustrator

This is a cool idea executed very well. It creates the illusion that the section will be revealing in the way the ball comes open. If you're a baseball junkie, it's a real treat.

Ésta es una gran idea bien ejecutada. Crea la ilusión de que la sección se irá revelando de tal forma como se abre la pelota. Si uno es un fanático del béisbol, es todo un obsequio.

The Hartford Courant
Hartford, Conn.

Entertainment page design/175,000 and over
Features page designer portfolio/Individual/175,000 and over

Chris Moore, Assistant Director/Design

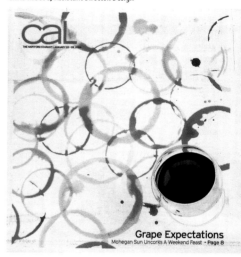

Grape Expectations
Mohegan Sun Uncorks A Weekend Feast • Page 8

THE SUNDAY MAGAZINE OF THE HARTFORD COURANT | DECEMBER 5, 2004

NORTHEAST

THE LAST WORD

LOWELL WEICKER, JACK DAVIS, KATHLEEN CAHILL, JEFF SCHULT, JERRY DUNKLEE AND KEVIN RENNIE SAY THEIR PIECE ABOUT THE ELECTION AND WHAT COMES NOW. PLUS: MIKE SWIFT EXAMINES EXACTLY WHY NEW ENGLAND IS SO BLUE.

The Hartford Courant
Hartford, Conn.

Magazine designer portfolio, combination/Individual 175,000 and over (Melanie Shaffer)
Magazines/Cover design

Michael McAndrews, Photographer; **Thom McGuire,** A.M.E. Graphics/Photo; **Suzette Moyer,** Design Director; **Melanie Shaffer,** Assistant Director/Design

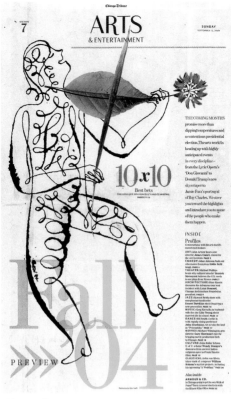

Chicago Tribune
Chicago, Ill.

Entertainment page design/175,000 and over
Illustration/Single

Joan Cairney, Art Director; **Scott Powers**, Editor; **Heidi Stevens**, Associate Editor; **Elvis Swift**, Illustrator

---

Chicago Tribune
Chicago, Ill.

Illustration/Single
Features page designer portfolio/Individual 175,000 and over

Stephen Ravenscraft, Art Director/Illustrator

ESSAY
Hearts of darkness

50 years later, 'Lord of the Flies' still resonates as it examines the loss of innocence

By Alan Cheuse

The first time around—that was in 1954—everyone seemed to know that William Golding's "Lord of the Flies" was an important book. E.M. Forster praised it. Malcolm Bradbury praised it, and The New York Times praised it, all of the voices speaking about the novel's universality and the success of its paradigm: A planeload of British schoolboys crashes on a remote tropical island, and the boys quickly revert to barbarism despite some desperate moves by a few of them to stand in the way of the downward slide.

Fifty years—and a rereading—later, the novel still holds high its emblem of our social despair, that "obscene thing," as Golding calls it, the Lord of the Flies, a fly-covered boar's head that one of the more brutish boys impales on a sharpened stick, with its "white teeth and dim eyes" and "the blood," which expresses "the ancient, inescapable recognition" that without the safeguards we desperately need to protect ourselves, humankind can go nowhere but down.

The political pessimism that spawned such a dark novel as this has its roots in the 20th Century's two awful world wars and the passive-aggressiveness of the Cold War period that followed World War II. The literary motif of the marooned man on a tropical island goes back, of course, to Robinson Crusoe. But Golding himself may have been thinking about darkly revising the old 19th Century children's classic by R.M. Ballantyne called "The Coral Island," an adventure novel about some schoolboys who survive a shipwreck on a Pacific island.

Whatever his sources, Golding certainly makes this classic fable his own, beginning with the island's light and climate, a subject, in other hands, easily turned to romantic fluff. But not here:

"The first rhythm that they [the marooned boys] became used to was the slow swing from dawn to quick dusk. They accepted the pleasures of morning, the bright sun, the whelming sea and sweet air, as a time when play was good and life so full that hope was not necessary and therefore forgotten. Toward noon, as the floods of light fell more nearly to the perpendicular, the stark colors of the morning were smoothed in pearl and opalescence; and the heat—as though the impending sun's height gave it momentum—became a blow that they

Alan Cheuse is a book commentator for NPR's 'All Things Considered,' a writing teacher at George Mason University and the author, most recently, of the short-story collection "Lost and Old Rivers."

PLEASE SEE **GOLDING**, PAGE 4

Tribune Illustration

Chicago Tribune
Chicago, Ill.

Opinion page design/175,000 and over
Illustration/Single
News page designer portfolio/Individual/175,000 and over (Mike Miner)

Charles M. Madigan, Editor; **Mike Miner**, Art Director

Chicago Tribune
Chicago, Ill.

Photography/Portfolio/Staff
Special coverage, section pages/Cover only

Bill Adee, Sports Editor; **Nuccio DiNuzzo**, Photographer; **Michael Kellams**, Associate Sports Editor; **John Konstantaras**, Photo Editor; **Dan McGrath**, A.M.E./Sports; **Jason McKean**, Art Director; **Steve Ravenscraft**, Art Director; **Scott Strazzante**, Photographer; **Keith Swinden**, Photo Editor; **Chris Walker**, Photographer

---

Chicago Tribune
Chicago, Ill.

Food page design/175,000 and over
Features page designer portfolio/Individual/175,000 and over (Catherine Nichols)

Bob Fila, Photographer; **Carol Haddix**, Editor; **Catherine Nichols**, Art Director

The New York Times
New York, N.Y.

*Information graphics, breaking news/175,000
and over*
Information graphics, mapping/175,000 and over

James Bronzan, Graphics Editor; **Joe Burgess,**
Graphics Editor; **William McNulty,** Graphics Editor

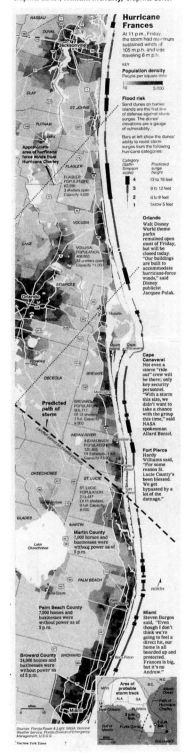

Hurricane Frances

At 11 p.m. Friday, the storm had maximum sustained winds of 105 m.p.h. and was traveling 6 m.p.h.

KEY

Population density
People per square mile

10 — 5,000

Flood risk
Sand dunes on barrier islands are the first line of defense against storm surges. The dunes' elevations are a gauge of vulnerability.

Bars at left show the dunes' ability to resist storm surges from the following hurricane categories:

Category (Saffir-Simpson scale)	Predicted surge height
4	13 to 18 feet
3	9 to 12 feet
2	6 to 8 feet
1	below 5 feet

Orlando
Walt Disney World theme parks remained open most of Friday, but will be closed today. "Our buildings are built to accommodate hurricane-force winds," said Disney publicist Jacquee Polak.

Cape Canaveral
Not even a storm "ride out" crew will be there; only key security personnel. "With a storm this size, we didn't want to take a chance with the group this time," said NASA spokesman Allard Bentel.

Fort Pierce
Hardy Williams said, "For some reason St. Lucie County's been bypassed. We get bypassed by a lot of the damage."

Miami
Steven Burgos said, "Even though I don't think we're going to feel a direct hit, our home is all boarded up and protected. Frances is big, but it's no Andrew."

Martin County
7,000 homes and businesses were without power as of 5 p.m.

Palm Beach County
7,000 homes and businesses were without power as of 5 p.m.

Broward County
24,000 homes and businesses were without power as of 5 p.m.

Sources: Florida Power & Light; NASA; National Weather Service; Florida Division of Emergency Management; U.S.G.S.

The New York Times

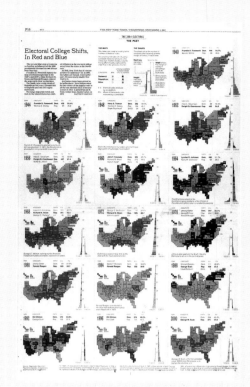

Electoral College Shifts, In Red and Blue

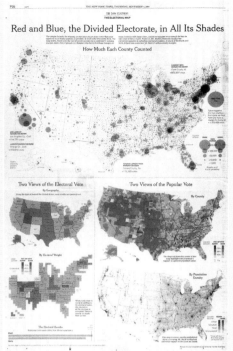

Red and Blue, the Divided Electorate, in All Its Shades

SILVER

The New York Times
New York, N.Y.

*Information graphics/Portfolios/
Extended coverage/175,000 and
over (Matthew Ericson)*

AWARDS OF EXCELLENCE
*Information graphics,
charting/175,000 and over*
*Information graphics, breaking
news/175,000 and over*
*Information graphics,
mapping/175,000 and over*

Matthew Ericson, Graphics Editor;
William McNulty, Graphics Editor;
Archie Tse, Graphics Editor

These graphics let the beauty of the information shine and don't get in the way of the statistics with unnecessary illustration. It took considerable effort to find numbers that would be illustrative. The planning for this kind of presentation on deadline is immense. They covered it as perfectly as an election story can be covered.

Estos gráficos permiten que se destaque la belleza de la información y que no se entrometan en los datos estadísticos con un exceso de ilustración. Tomó un gran esfuerzo encontrar los datos ilustrativos. La planificación de este tipo de trabajo bajo presión es enorme. Se cubrieron las elecciones con toda la perfección posible para este tema.

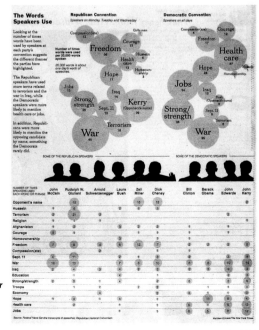

The Words Speakers Use

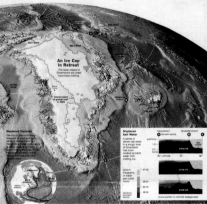

An Icy Riddle as Big as Greenland

The New York Times
New York, N.Y.

*Information graphics/Portfolios/Non-breaking
news (individual)/175,000 and over*
Information graphics, charting/175,000 and over
*Information graphics, breaking news/175,000
and over*

Matthew Ericson, Graphics Editor

The New York Times
New York, N.Y.

Information graphics, mapping/175,000 and over
Information graphics, Non-breaking/175,000 and over

Hannah Fairfield, Graphics Editor; **William McNulty,**
Graphics Editor

THE INDEPENDENT

WHITEWASH?
THE HUTTON REPORT
A SPECIAL ISSUE

Eight months ago, BBC reporter Andrew Gilligan broadcast his now infamous report casting doubt on the Government's dossier on Iraq's weapons capability; a vital plank in its case for war...

The Independent
London, England

A-section news design/175,000 and over (tabloid version)
A-section news design/175,000 and over (broadsheet version)
News page designer portfolio/Individual/175,000 and over

Kevin Bayliss, Art Director

MISSOURI BASKETBALL GETS PROBATION | SPORTS

ST. LOUIS POST-DISPATCH

COUNT HIM IN
BUSH LOOKS TO A SECOND TERM

President George W. Bush addresses supporters Wednesday at the Ronald Reagan Building in Washington.

MARK WILSON / GETTY IMAGES

TALK OF UNITY
Bush asks for trust as Kerry concedes
BY BILL LAMBRECHT
Post-Dispatch Washington Bureau

ANALYSIS
President can claim stronger mandate
BY JON SAWYER
Post-Dispatch Washington Bureau

IN MISSOURI
State has joined ranks of the "red"
BY JO MANNIES
Post-Dispatch Political Correspondent

MORE ELECTION COVERAGE ON PAGES A7-16 AND IN METRO, SECTION C

Kidnappers seize second U.S. citizen in Iraq this week

Arafat is rushed to intensive care in France, aides say

Argosy Gaming sells its business to another firm

New formulation of flu shot works with less vaccine

St. Louis Post-Dispatch
St. Louis, Mo.

Breaking news topics/Elections
Combination portfolio/Individual/175,000 and over (Chris Snider)

Chris Snider, Design Director; **Larry Coyne,** Director of Photography; **Wade Wilson,** Director/Design & Graphics

---

YOUR LIFE
COMING SUNDAY
FRIENDS & FAMILY In Your Life

RELIGION
& ETHICS

FRIDAY, OCTOBER 1, 2004

INSIDE **COMICS** Page 11

JOURNAL-COURIER • PAGE 12

Religious activists on opposite sides of the political aisle are sneaking around to bring down churches that endorse candidates

Church spies

BY TERRY MATTINGLY
Scripps Howard News Service

Call it church-state espionage. Unitarians and other activists in the religions left have been slipping into evangelical pews to endure altar calls, praise songs and sermons against gay marriage.

The Kansas-based Mainstream Coalition has a simple reason for doing this. If preachers openly endorse President Bush, its agents can report these crimes to the IRS...

SPIES, see page 6 ▶

Literary SPIRIT
BOOKS, MUSIC, ETC.

THE DEVIL'S INBOX
By Barbara Layman
(Augsburg Books, 123 pages, $10.99)

This novel, modeled after "The Screwtape Letters" by C.S. Lewis, has a contemporary twist. E-mail, not snail mail, is used...

— *Jeff Zell*

PITCHING MY TENT
By Anita Diamant
(Scribner, 223 pages, $24)

Before she became a novelist, Diamant spent two decades as a newspaper and magazine columnist...

— *Robin Galiano Russell*

The Dallas Morning News (KRT)

CROSS TALK

Monthly service
▶ PRAIRIE LAND LIBERTY CHURCH will hold its monthly service Sunday at 5 p.m. The Hendricker family will provide the program.

Speakers and concerts
▶ THE REV. LLOYD DUNAWAY will speak Sunday at the 10 a.m. and 6 p.m. services at Harvest Temple United...

Call to prayer
▶ INTERCESSORS FOR AMERICA, a national prayer organization, has issued a call to prayer to Christians of all faiths...

Jacksonville Journal-Courier
Jacksonville, Ill.

Other feature page design/49,999 and under
Features page designer portfolio/Individual/49,999 and under (Larry Rowe)

Steve Copper, Design Director; **Larry Rowe,** Designer

ESPECIAL

CLAROSCURO DE MARADONA
Diego Armando, 'El Pelusa', es hoy por hoy uno de los máximos símbolos argentinos de todos los tiempos

La Opinión
Los Angeles, Calif.

Sports page design/50,000-174,999
Combination portfolio/Individual/50,000-174,999 (Tadeo Guerrero)

Genoveva Guerrero, Section Editor; **Tadeo Guerrero,** Designer/Design Editor; **Rubén Keoseyan,** Editor

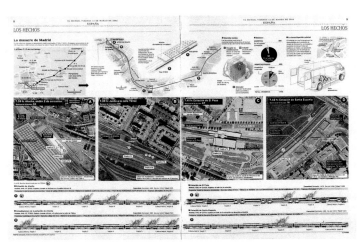

El Mundo Del Siglo XXI
Madrid, Spain

Information graphics/
Portfolios/Non-breaking
news (staff)/
175,000 and over
Information graphics/
Portfolios/Non-breaking
news (individual)/
175,000 and over
(Rafa Estrada)

Arturo Asensio, Illustrator;
Juantxo Cruz, Graphics Chief
Editor; **Rafa Estrada,** Graphic
Artist; **Isabel González,** Graphic
Artist

El Mundo Del Siglo XXI
Madrid, Spain

Information graphics, breaking news/175,000 and over
Information graphics/Portfolios/Extended coverage/175,000 and over

Juantxo Cruz, Graphics Chief Editor; **Graphics Staff; Research Staff**

El Mundo
Madrid, Spain

Special coverage/Sections/With ads
Special coverage, section pages/Inside page or spread

Carmelo Caderot, Design Director; **Ulises Culebro,** Illustrator; **Manuel De Miguel,** Art Director & Designer; **Luis Perez Ortiz,** Illustrator

SILVER

El Mundo
Madrid, Spain

Special news topics/The Athens Olympics

AWARD OF EXCELLENCE
Special coverage, section pages/Cover only

Raul Arias, Illustrator; **Carmelo Caderot,** Design Director; **Manuel De Miguel,** Art Director & Designer

Clear, consistent and restrained. This section is understated, but exceptional in typography and elegance. The photography is clean and direct, mixing cutouts and square photographs. The graphics are smart and interesting. The section is an exercise in using resources as smartly as possible.

Clara, consistente y acotada. Esta sección está presentada con un estilo restringido, pero excepcional en tipografía y elegancia. La fotografía es limpia y directa, y mezcla recortes y cuadrados fotográficos. Los gráficsos son inteligentes e interesantes. La sección es un ejercicio de uso de recursos lo más inteligentemente posible.

South Florida Sun-Sentinel
Fort Lauderdale, Fla.

A-section news design/175,000 and over (3)
Breaking news topics/Natural disasters
Breaking news topics/Natural disasters
News design/Sections/Local 175,000 and over
Photography/Portfolio/Staff
Photography/Portfolio/Individual (Michael Laughlin)
Special coverage/Single subject

Nicole Bogdas, Designer; **Robert Duyos,** Photographer; **Andres Gonzalez,** Photographer; **Dave Horn,** Designer; **Michael Laughlin,** Photographer; **Melissa Lyttle,** Photographer; **Rolando Otero,** Photo Editor; **Mike Perkins,** Designer; **Tim Rasmussen,** Photo Editor; **Carl Seibert,** Photographer; **Mike Stocker,** Photographer; **Mary Vignoles,** Photo Editor; **Anastasia Walsh Infanzon,** Photographer; **Staff**

Business
After the Storm
SOUTH FLORIDA SUN-SENTINEL | SATURDAY | SEPTEMBER 4, 2004 | SECTION B

If Frances strikes,
here's how to pick up the pieces.

WAITING: A crowd gathers Friday in front of 84 Lumber in Davie, one of the last places to find plywood for storm shields against the hurricane's winds. Staff photo/Andres Gonzalez

FOOD
KNOW WHAT TO KEEP, THROW OUT. **2B**

WATER
HOW TO DISINFECT YOUR SUPPLY. **3B**

SHELTER
PUT SAFETY FIRST WHEN REPAIRING YOUR HOME. **4B**

BELONGINGS
PROTECT YOUR CAR FROM FLOODING. **3B** BOAT REPAIRS REQUIRE PATIENCE. **2B**

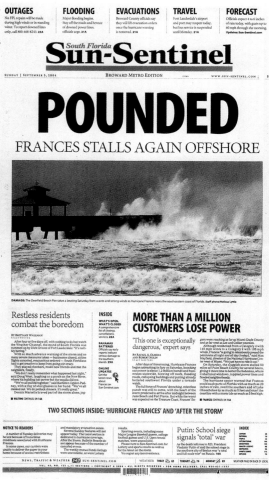

South Florida Sun-Sentinel
SUNDAY | SEPTEMBER 5, 2004   BROWARD METRO EDITION   WWW.SUN-SENTINEL.COM

OUTAGES	FLOODING	EVACUATIONS	TRAVEL	FORECAST

POUNDED
FRANCES STALLS AGAIN OFFSHORE

DAMAGE: The Deerfield Beach Pier takes a beating Saturday from waves and strong winds as Hurricane Frances nears the southeastern coast of Florida. Staff photo/Melissa Lyttle

Restless residents combat the boredom

MORE THAN A MILLION CUSTOMERS LOSE POWER

'This one is exceptionally dangerous,' expert says

TWO SECTIONS INSIDE: 'HURRICANE FRANCES' AND 'AFTER THE STORM'

Putin: School siege signals 'total' war

South Florida Sun-Sentinel
SUNDAY | AUGUST 15, 2004   BROWARD METRO EDITION   WWW.SUN-SENTINEL.COM | $1

CHARLEY'S WAKE
HELP RUSHES IN AS DEATHS MOUNT, COSTS CLIMB

NO DWELLING SPARED: A mobile-home community in Port Charlotte lies in ruins after Hurricane Charley roared through Southwest Florida. Staff photo/Carl Seibert

A TRAIL OF RUIN

THE DAMAGE

Carving a path of destruction through the heart of Southwest Florida, Hurricane Charley killed at least 13 people, left thousands homeless, 2 million without power and damage estimates as high as $20 billion. As thousands of rescuers began picking through the debris and helping survivors in the aftermath, state and local officials conceded they still don't have a complete picture of the devastation.

THE PEOPLE

Destroyed docks

Shipwrecked: The Fort Pierce City Marina is littered with smashed docks and boats after Hurricane Frances blew through, battering the waterfront with 100 mph winds.

Hurricane Jeanne

Images
OF THE
Storm

PALM BEACH POST
SPECIAL SECTION
SUNDAY, OCTOBER 3, 2004

Sky light: George Henderson sits and stares up at the sky through his missing roof. He lives with his son in Pleasure Cove mobile home park in Fort Pierce.

GREG LOVETT/Staff Photographer

UNBELIEVABLE: A SECOND HURRICANE IN THREE WEEKS

Powerful Jeanne follows Frances' path,
...ready-reeling Treasure Coast
...s of winds up to 120 mph

HURRICANE FRANCES

Indian River citrus is one of Hurricane Frances' biggest casualties.

SILVER

The Palm Beach Post
West Palm Beach, Fla.

Photography/Portfolio/Staff

AWARDS OF EXCELLENCE
Photography/Spot news
Photography/Spot news
Photography/Photo series
Photography/Portfolio/Individual (Greg Lovett)

Bruce R. Bennett, Photographer; **Rich Graulich,** Photographer; **Damon Higgins,** Photographer; **Taylor Jones,** Photographer; **John J. Lopinot,** Photographer; **Greg Lovett,** Photographer; **Paul J. Milette,** Photographer; **Cydney Scott,** Photographer; **Staff**

Fine art, straight news, news with creativity, great use of color palette — the range of photography at The Palm Beach Post is a near-perfect complement. The quality and diversity of the staff have blended into a shining portfolio.

Buen arte, noticias al grano, noticias con creatividad, gran uso de la paleta de color; el rango de la fotografía en The Palm Beach Post es un complemento casi perfecto. La calidad y la diversidad de la planta de trabajadores se han fundido en un brillante portafolio.

Sun Journal
Lewiston, Maine

A-section news design/49,999 and under (2)

Pete Gorski, News Artist; **Heather McCarthy**, Senior Designer; **Jason Rathbun**, Design Editor; **Daryn Slover**, Photographer; **Paul Wallen**, M.E./Visuals

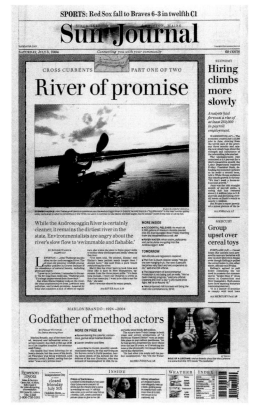

Sun Journal
Lewiston, Maine

Combination portfolio/Individual/49,999 and under (Paul Wallen)
A-section news design/49,999 and under
Breaking news topics/Editor's choice, sports

Keith Hagel, M.E./Nights; **Paul Wallen**, M.E./Visuals

Puls Biznesu
Warsaw, Poland

Business page design/49,999 and under
News page designer portfolio/Individual/49,999 and under (Jacek Utko)

Grzegorz Kawecki, Photographer; **Tadeusz Markiewicz**, Editor; **Jacek Utko**, Art Director

Diario de Sevilla
Sevilla, Spain

Information graphics, Non-breaking/49,999 and under
Information graphics/Portfolios/Non-breaking news (staff)/49,999 and under

Manuel Romero Tortosa, Graphics Editor; **Cristina García Rivera**, Graphic Artist; **Raquel Feria Legrand**, Graphic Artist; **Francisco Barquilla García**, Graphic Artist; **David Uribarri Paguillo**, Graphic Artist

Star Tribune
Minneapolis, Minn.

Photography/Photo series
Special news topics/Editor's choice, local/
regional
A-section news design/175,000 and over

Jerry Holt, Photographer; **Vickie Kettlewell,**
Photo Editor; **Peter Koeleman,** Director/
Photography; **Brian Peterson,** Photo Editor;
Leslie Plesser, Designer; **Cory Powell,**
Presentation Director

The Star-Ledger
Newark, N.J.

Photography/Photo series
Special coverage/Single subject
Reprints

Fran Dauth, Editor; **Robin Gaby Fisher,** Reporter; **Linda**
Grinbergs, Designer; **Kelly King,** Copy Editor; **Matt Rainey,**
Photographer; **Sharon Russell,** A.M.E. Design; **Pim Van**
Hemmen, Photo Editor

The Wall Street Journal
South Brunswick, N.J.

Illustration/Single
Illustration/Individual portfolio (Craig Frazier)
News page designer portfolio/Individual/175,000 and over (Craig Frazier)
Special coverage, section pages/Cover only

Craig Frazier, Illustrator; **Orlie Kraus,** Art Director; **Greg Leeds,** Executive Art Director

The Wisconsin State Journal
Madison, Wis.

Information graphics, charting/50,000-174,999
Information graphics, breaking news/50,000-174,999

Tim Ball, Design Editor; **Laura Sparks,** Graphics Editor; **Jason Klein,** News Artist; **Jason Stein,** Reporter

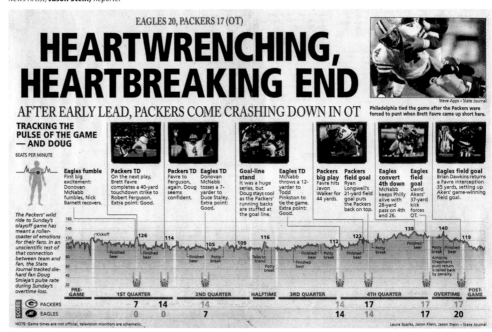

San Francisco Chronicle
San Francisco, Calif.

Entertainment page design/175,000 and over
Features page designer portfolio/Individual/175,000 and over (Matt Petty)

Nanette Bisher, Creative Director; **Joe Brown,** Pink Editor; **Matt Petty,** Art Director

San Francisco Chronicle
San Francisco, Calif.

Photography/Photo series
Special news topics/Editor's choice, local/regional

Nanette Bisher, Creative Director; **Deanne Fitzmaurice,** Photographer; **Susan Gilbert,** Deputy M.E.; **Randy Greenwell,** Acting Director of Photography; **Kathleen Hennessy,** Photo Editor; **Heather Jones,** Copy Editor; **David Lewis,** Project Editor; **Frank Mina,** Senior Art Director News; **Matt Petty;** Senior Art Director/Design; **Steve Proctor,** Deputy M.E. Metro; **Joe Shoulak,** Graphic Artist

NEWS

chapter 4

The Virginian-Pilot
Norfolk, Va.

A-section news design/175,000 and over
Staff

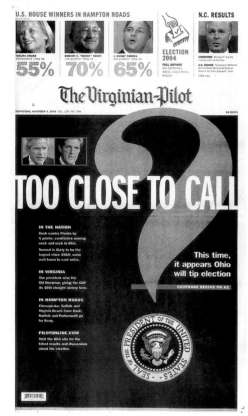

Bergens Tidende
Bergen, Norway

A-section news design/50,000-174,999

Arne Edvardsen, Editor; **Walter Jensen,** Chief of Presentation; **Tore Sehl,** Page Coordinator; **Anne Hovden,** Page Editor; **Anne Britt Kilvik,** Page Editor; **Oddmund Holmelid,** Page Designer

The Seattle Times
Seattle, Wash.

A-section news design/175,000 and over

Denise Clifton, Designer; **Ted Basladynski,** Designer; **Heather McKinnon,** Designer; **Teresa Scribner,** Designer; **Fred Nelson,** Photo Editor

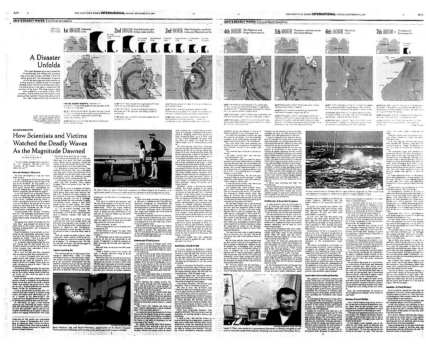

The New York Times
New York, N.Y.

A-section news design/175,000 and over
Staff

Bergens Tidende
Bergen, Norway

A-section news design/50,000-174,999
Staff

Sunday Herald
Glasgow, Scotland

News design/Sections/Sports 50,000-174,999

David Dick, Deputy Editor; **Stephen Penman,** Deputy Sports Editor; **Kandy Course,** Production

San Antonio Express-News
San Antonio, Texas

News design/Sections/Sports 175,000 and over

Dennis Ochoa, Assistant Art Director/Features

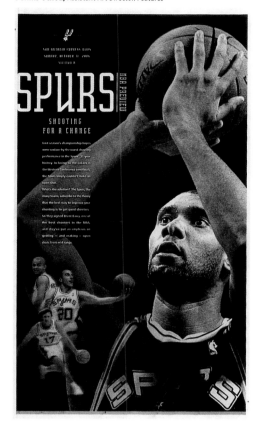

The Independent on Sunday
London, England

News design/Sections/Sports 175,000 and over

Carolyn Roberts, Art Director; **Elissa Millhouse,** Deputy Art Director; **Tristan Davies,** Editor; **Neil Morton,** Section Editor

The New York Times
New York, N.Y.

News design/Sections/Sports 175,000 and over

Wayne Kamidoi, Art Director; **Lee Yarosh,** Art Director; **Staff**

The New York Times
New York, N.Y.

Business page design/175,000 and over

Staff

The State
Columbia, S.C.

A-section news design/50,000-174,999

David Montesino, Design Director

Knoxville News Sentinel
Knoxville, Tenn.

A-section news design/50,000-174,999

Jennifer Dedman, Designer; **Michael Apuan,** A.M.E. Presentation

The State
Columbia, S.C.

A-section news design/50,000-174,999

David Montesino, Design Director

Estado de Minas
Belo Horizonte, Brazil

A-section news design/50,000-174,999

Rogério Carnevali, Design Editor; **Álvaro Duarte,** Art Director; **Paulo De Araújo,** Photographer; **Vera Schmitz,** Assistant Editor

Correio Braziliense
Brasilia, Brazil

A-section news design/50,000-174,999

Josemar Gimenez, News Room Director; **Carols Marcelo,** Executive Editor; **João Bosco Adelino de Almeida,** Art Director; **Kleber Sales,** Illustrator; **Divino Alves,** Page Designer; **Ana Dubeux,** Editor-in-Chief

El Universal
México City, México

A-section news design/50,000-174,999

Francisco Vega, Designer; **Carlos Morales,** Editor; **Óscar Santiago,** Art and Design Director; **Raymundo Rivapalacio,** International Coordinator; **Rubén Álvarez,** Information Director; **Francisco Santiago,** Edition Director; **Roberto Rock,** General Editorial Director

The Palm Beach Post
West Palm Beach, Fla.

A-section news design/50,000-174,999

Greg Lovett, Photographer; **Mark Edelson**, Presentation Editor; **Sabrina J. Starrett**, Page Designer; **Rick Robb**, News Editor

The Times-Picayune
New Orleans, La.

A-section news design/175,000 and over

Adrianna Garcia, Designer; **Daniel Swenson**, Graphic Artist; **Ted Jackson**, Photographer; **Michael DeMocker**, Photographer; **Doug Parker**, Photo Editor; **Terry Baquet**, News Editor; **Dan Shea**, M.E.

South Florida Sun-Sentinel
Fort Lauderdale, Fla.

A-section news design/175,000 and over

Jonathan Boho, Designer; **Michael Francis McElroy**, Photographer; **Mary Vignoles**, Photo Editor

The Palm Beach Post

Panhandle pounded

At least 20 die as Ivan rips through

Region told to keep close watch on Jeanne

The long haul: Debris cleanup to last months

The Times-Picayune

DEVASTATION

13 DIE AS IVAN'S TIDAL SURGE SMASHES GULF COAST

South Florida Sun-Sentinel

STORM WEARY

| Congress urged to OK $2 billion for 'urgent needs' | Millions remain without power across Florida | Almost all Broward schools closed today | Gasoline begins flowing, although shortages persist |

Good riddance, Hurricane Frances

Outages signal trouble for millions in S. Florida

AVENUE
Arts, Culture & Society

TIE ONE ON WITH THE LEADERS

National Post
Toronto, Ontario, Canada

A-section news design/175,000 and over

Gayle Grin, A.M.E./Visuals; **Laura Koot**, Designer; **Ben Errett**, Avenue Editor

MORGAN STANLEY SETTLES SEXUAL DISCRIMINATION LAWSUIT FOR $54 MILLION

The Times-Picayune

'Roadless' rule headed for dead end

Christopher Reeve believes no one has to live like this. Unfettered research is his answer.

Stepson, woman arrested in killing

THE FIGHT of HIS LIFE

Iraqi president warns militants of 'sharp sword'

Study lowers cholesterol threshold

The Times-Picayune
New Orleans, La.

A-section news design/175,000 and over

Anne Webbeking, Designer; **George Berke**, Design Director; **Terry Baquet**, News Editor

South Florida Sun-Sentinel

Measure targets senior services

Special taxing district would collect funds

THE WAR IN IRAQ

ONE YEAR LATER

WHAT BEGAN AS 'SHOCK AND AWE' HAS EVOLVED INTO A COSTLY OCCUPATION WITH ALMOST-DAILY CASUALTIES AND A BITTER SPLIT AMONG AMERICANS

Visa cap panics seasonal employers

Daily Digest

South Florida Sun-Sentinel
Fort Lauderdale, Fla.

A-section news design/175,000 and over

Jonathan Boho, Designer

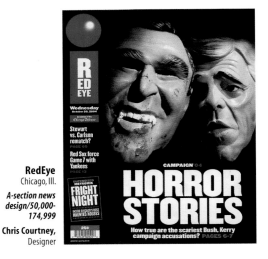

RedEye
Chicago, Ill.

*A-section news
design/50,000-
174,999*

Chris Courtney,
Designer

Heraldo de Aragón
Zaragoza, Spain

*A-section news
design/50,000-174,999*

Javier Errea, Art
Director; **Ana Perez,**
Designer; **Kristina
Urresti,** Designer; **Asier
Barrio,** Designer; **Pilar
Ostale,** Design Editor;
Carmelo Roy, Designer;
Cristina Salvador,
Designer

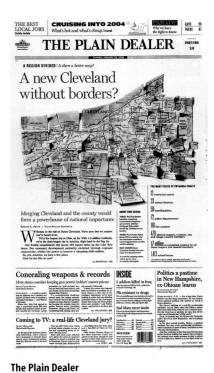

Toronto Star
Toronto, Ontario, Canada

A-section news design/175,000 and over

Staff

The Plain Dealer
Cleveland, Ohio

A-section news design/175,000 and over

David Kordalski, A.M.E./Visuals; **Lisa Grifffis,** Designer;
Chuck Caton, News Editor; **Christine Jindra,** Sunday Editor

Lexington Herald-Leader
Lexington, Ky.

A-section news design/50,000-174,999

Dennis Varney, Designer

Detroit Free Press
Detroit, Mich.

*A-section news
design/175,000 and
over*

Robert Huschka,
News Designer; **Rick
Nease,** Illustrator;
Steve Dorsey, Design
& Graphics Director;
Nancy Laughlin,
News Editor

Detroit Free Press
Detroit, Mich.

*A-section news
design/175,000 and over*

Amy Etmans, Designer;
Craig Porter, Photo
Editor; **Steve Dorsey,**
Designer/Design &
Graphics Director; **Diane
Weiss,** Photo Editor; **Chris
Clonts,** Deputy Design
Director/News

Hartford Courant
Hartford, Conn.

A-section news design/175,000 and over

Tim Reck, Designer; **Suzette Moyer,** Director/Design & Graphics; **John Scanlan,** Director/Photography; **Thom McGuire,** A.M.E. Graphics/Photography

Hartford Courant
Hartford, Conn.

A-section news design/175,000 and over

Vada Crosby, Designer; **Suzette Moyer,** Director/Design & Graphics; **Greg Harmel,** Designer; **Bruce Moyer,** Photo Editor; **Thom McGuire,** A.M.E. Graphics/Photo

Hartford Courant
Hartford, Conn.

A-section news design/175,000 and over

Greg Harmel, Designer; **Suzette Moyer,** Director/Design & Graphics; **John Scanlan,** Director/Photography; **Thom McGuire,** A.M.E. Graphics/Photography; **Patrick Raycraft,** Photographer; **MinJung Kim,** Artist; **Stephanie Heisler,** Photo Editor

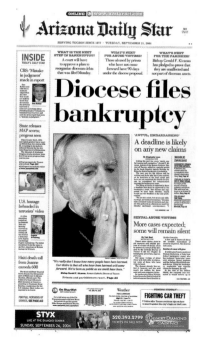

Arizona Daily Star
Tucson, Ariz.

A-section news design/50,000-174,999

Michael Rice, Assistant Design Director; **José Merino,** Design Director; **Victor Vaughan,** A.M.E./Visuals; **Staff**

El Diario de Hoy
San Salvador, El Salvador

A-section news design/50,000-174,999

Juan Durán, Art Director; **Teodoro Lira,** Graphics Editor; **Jorge Castillo,** Infographic Editor; **Mario Gonzáles,** Editor; **Remberto Rodriguez,** Graphics Co-Editor; **Hugo Rodriguez,** Designer; **José Santos,** Infographics

Arizona Daily Star
Tucson, Ariz.

A-section news design/50,000-174,999

Michael Rice, Assistant Design Director; **Victor Vaughan,** A.M.E./Visuals; **Staff**

The Oregonian
Portland, Ore.

A-section news design/175,000 and over

Mark Friesen, Designer; **Linda Shankweiler,** Design Director

The Oregonian
Portland, Ore.

A-section news design/175,000 and over

Mark Friesen, Designer; **Linda Shankweiler,** Design Director

The Boston Globe
Boston, Mass.

A-section news design/175,000 and over

Dan Zedek, Design Editor; **Charles Mansbach,** Layout and Production; **Paula Nelson,** Picture Editor

El Diario de Hoy
San Salvador, El Salvador

A-section news design/50,000-174,999

Juan Durán, Art Director; **Teodoro Lira,** Graphics Editor; **Jorge Castillo,** Infographic Editor; **Luis Lainez,** Editor; **Remberto Rodriguez,** Graphics Co-Editor/Designer; **Hugo Rodriguez,** Designer; **Tirsa Mendoza,** Designer;

The Times of Northwest Indiana
Munster, Ind.

A-section news design/50,000-174,999

Mike Rich, News Designer; **Gladys Rios,** Design Director

The Gazette
Montreal, Quebec, Canada

A-section news design/50,000-174,999

Jeanine Lee, Design Editor; **Roland-Yves Carignan,** Design Director; **Jack Romanelli,** M.E.; **Dave Sidaway,** Photographer; **Lynn Farrell,** Photo Editor

San Jose Mercury News
San Jose, Calif.

A-section news design/175,000 and over

Kevin Wendt, News Design Director; **Matt Mansfield,** Deputy M.E.; **Chuck Burke,** News Designer; **Wayne Begasse,** Picture Editor; **Mark Damon,** Director/Photography

San Jose Mercury News
San Jose, Calif.

A-section news design/175,000 and over

Kevin Wendt, News Design Director; **Matt Mansfield,** Deputy M.E.; **Jeff Hindenach,** News Designer; **Caroline Couig,** Picture Editor; **Wayne Begasse,** Picture Editor

The Ledger
Lakeland, Fla.

A-section news design/50,000-174,999

Steve Antley, Design Editor; **DeWayne Wilson,** Assistant Design Editor

Estado de Minas
Belo Horizonte, Brazil

A-section news design/50,000-174,999

Julio Moreira, Page Designer; **Valfredo Macedo,** Graphic Artist

Dagens Nyheter
Stockholm, Sweden

A-section news design/175,000 and over

Staff

Correio Braziliense
Brasilia, Brazil

A-section news design/50,000-174,999

Josemar Gimenez, News Room Director; **Ana Dubeux,** Editor-in-Chief; **Carlos Marcelo,** Executive Editor; **João Bosco Adelino de Almeida,** Art Director; **Luís Tajes,** Photo Editor; **Marcelo Ramos,** Page Designer

The Boston Globe
Boston, Mass.

Local news section design/175,000 and over

Lesley Becker, Designer; **Dan Zedek,** Design Director

The Boston Globe
Boston, Mass.

Local news section design/175,000 and over

Lesley Becker, Designer

The Boston Globe
Boston, Mass.

Local news section design/175,000 and over

Grant Staublin, Designer; **Carolyn Ryan,** Metro Editor; **Thea Breite,** Photo Editor; **Steve Wilmsen,** Assistant City Editor; **Dan Zedek,** Design Director

Reforma
México City, México

Local news section design/50,000-174,999

Alejandro Sosa, Designer; **Gustavo Cabrera,** Infographic Artist; **Óscar Mireles,** Photographer; **Arturo Páramo,** Photographer; **Alejandro Ramos,** Editor; **Ignacio Guerrero,** Graphics Editor; **Ricardo Del Castillo,** Art Director; **Ricardo Elizondo,** Section Director; **René Delgado,** Managing Director; **Lázaro Ríos,** General Managing Director

Savannah Morning News
Savannah, Ga.

A-section news design/50,000-174,999

Stephen Komives, Planning Editor; **Anita Sue Hagin,** Planning Editor; **Steven Austin,** Senior Editor; **Steve Bisson,** Photographer; **Bob Morris,** Photographer

Die Zeit
Hamburg, Germany

A-section news design/175,000 and over

Staff

The Palm Beach Post

West Palm Beach, Fla.

Local news section design/50,000-174,999

Mark Edelson, Presentation Editor; **Bruce R. Bennett,** Photographer; **Damon Higgins,** Photographer; **Tonya Favata,** Page Designer; **Jennifer Podis,** Photo Editor; **Caroline DiPaolo,** Metro Editor

---

What I Want To Be…

… when I grow up

In 1986, Grade 1 students at Howard public school shared their childhood dreams with Star readers. Eighteen years later, they open a window to their adult world

Sarah Sumi: Ballerina

"I dance at home on one leg"

Alessandra Nosko: Doctor

"I want to make people get well"

Sara Chang: Ballerina

"When you're a ballet teacher, you get a lot of money. About $20,000"

Anita Basu: Art teacher

"Coz you do nice paintings"

Niki MacRae: armoured truck driver

"They get money and bring it to the bank."

Matthew Munk: Baseball player

"Hoped to play for the Blue Jays

'Dreams stick around'

The Palm Beach Post — LOCAL / BUSINESS

ELECTION 2004

Palm Beach's council unaltered

Mecca holds off on Scripps pact

DUI retrial witnesses ID suspect as driver

West Palm, Ibis enclave settle dispute over services

'OUT OF BUSINESS'

Toronto Star
Toronto, Ontario, Canada

Local news section design/175,000 and over

Jo-Ann Dodds, Designer; **Bernard Weil,** Photographer; **Jordan Heath-Rawlings,** Reporter; **Greg Smith,** Editor

---

Metro/Portland

Burgerville founder George Propstra dies

STEVE DUIN

Worked over by the workers' comp system

A jail deputy hopes to use his disturbing collection of mug shots documenting the ruinous effects of methamphetamine to send an irrefutable message to Oregon schoolchildren

The faces of meth

The Oregonian
Portland, Ore.

Local news section design/175,000 and over

Ev Hu, Designer; **Kelly Yan,** Designer

THE NEW YORK TIMES METRO

Neither Time Nor a Harlem Storefront Stands Still

Beer for the Babe, and a Frenzy for Another Red Sox-Yankees Championship Series

Building an animosity that reached a fever pitch a year ago.

The New York Times
New York, N.Y.

Local news section design/175,000 and over

Michael Kolomatsky, Art Director; **Camilo Jose Vergara,** Photographer

---

PROSTITUCIÓN CALLEJERA

CÓMO SON...

Buscan legislador y organizaciones de sexoservidores regular actividad para combatir la extorsión en cerca de 50 sitios de trabajo sexual en la vía pública

Toma avenidas el sexoservicio

POR ERIKA HERNÁNDEZ

De la calle...

TÉRMINOS Y PROPUESTAS

Reforma
México City, México

Local news section design/50,000-174,999

Adriana Kaim, Designer; **Juan Jesús Cortés,** Infographic Artist; **Fernando Ortega,** Photographer; **Lázaro Ríos,** General Managing Director; **Alex Castillo,** Editor; **Ignacio Guerrero,** Graphics Editor; **Ricardo Del Castillo,** Art Director; **Ricardo Elizondo,** Section Director; **René Delgado,** Managing Director

SILVER

Sunday Herald
Glasgow, Scotland

Sports page design/50,000-174,999

David Dick, Deputy Editor; **Elaine Livingston,** Picture Editor

The aggressive black-and-white photo use and the multiple layers of gray in the typography made the page come alive, framing the boxers in a sophisticated way. The spread shows how effective design can place a moment in time.

El agresivo uso de la foto en blanco y negro, y las múltiples capas de gris en la tipografía dieron vida a esta página, al enmarcar a los boxeadores de forma sofisticada. Esta página doble muestra lo efectivo que puede ser el diseño para ubicar un momento en el tiempo.

The New York Times
New York, N.Y.

Sports page design/175,000 and over

Wayne Kamidoi, Art Director; **Joe Zeff,** Illustrator

Récord
México City, México

Sports page design/50,000-174,999

Alejo Nájera, Design Editor; **José Luis Barros,** Graphics Editor; **Alejandro Belman,** Design Editor; **Alberto Nava,** Art Director; **Alejandro Gómez,** Editorial Director; **Aarón Zúñiga Castañeda,** Section Designer/Designer; **Luis Enrique Gutiérrez,** Editor

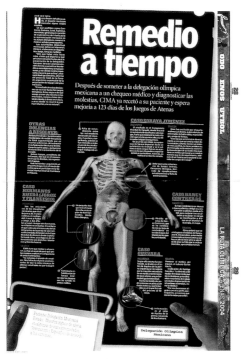

Récord
México City, México

Sports page design/50,000-174,999

Alejo Nájera, Design Editor; **José Luis Barros,** Graphics Editor; **Alejandro Belman,** Design Editor; **Alberto Nava,** Art Director; **Alejandro Gómez,** Editorial Director; **Aarón Zúñiga Castañeda,** Section Designer/Designer; **José Luis Tapia,** Editor

Correio Braziliense
Brasília, Brazil

Sports page design/50,000-174,999

Josemar Gimenez, News Room Director; **Ana Dubeux,** Editor-in-Chief; **Carlos Marcelo,** Executive Editor; **João Bosco Adelino de Almeida,** Art Director; **Luís Tajes,** Photo Editor; **Cláudio de Deus,** Page Designer; **Amaro Júnior,** Photo Illustrator

Récord
México City, México

Sports page design/50,000-174,999

Aarón Zúniga Castañeda, Designer/Section Designer; **Carlos Jalife,** Editor; **Alejandro Belman,** Design Editor; **José Luis Barros,** Graphics Editor; **Alejo Nájera,** Design Editor; **Alberto Nava,** Art Director; **Alejandro Gómez,** Editorial Director

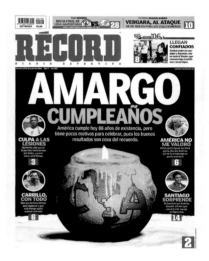

El Universal
México City, México

Sports page design/50,000-174,999

Guillermo Chávez Garrido, Section Designer; **Alejandro Asmitia,** Section Editor; **Pedro Iván Quintana,** Section General Editor; **Óscar Santiago Méndez,** Art and Design Director; **Sergio Fraire,** Designing Coordinator; **Rubén Álvarez,** Information Director; **Francisco Santiage,** Edition Director; **Roberto Rock L.,** General Editorial Director

Récord
México City, México

Sports page design/50,000-174,999

Ricardo Flores, Photographer; **Alejo Nájera,** Design Editor; **José Luis Barros,** Graphics Editor; **Alejandro Belman,** Design Editor/Designer; **Alberto Nava,** Art Director; **Alejandro Gómez,** Editorial Director

Récord
México City, México

Sports page design/50,000-174,999

Alejo Nájera, Design Editor/Designer; **José Luis Barros,** Graphics Editor/Artist; **Alejandro Belman,** Design Editor; **Alberto Nava,** Art Director; **Alejandro Gómez,** Editorial Director

Récord
México City, México

Sports page design/50,000-174,999

Alejandro Belman, Design Editor; **José Luis Barros,** Graphics Editor; **Alejo Nájera,** Design Editor; **Alberto Nava,** Art Director; **Alejandro Gómez,** Editorial Director

Los Angeles Times
Los Angeles, Calif.

Sports page design/175,000 and over

Michael Whitley, Deputy Design Director; **Bryan Volk,** Designer; **Dan Loumena,** Campus Times Editor

Rocky Mountain News
Denver, Colo.

Sports page design/175,000 and over

Brian Clark, Designer

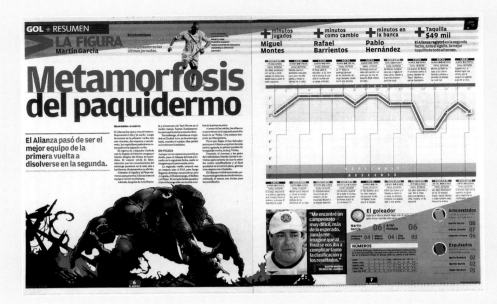

El Gráfico
Antiguo Cuscatlán, El Salvador

Sports page design/49,999 and under

Agustin Palacios, Coordinator of Design; **José Jaén,** Designer; **Ulises Martinez,** Illustrator; **Rodrigo Baires,** Journalist; **Carlos Vides,** Journalist; **Óscar Guerra,** Journalist

In this section, a superhero or supervillian represents each soccer team's star. Supporting these characters are super-graphics that tell how each team has done. The execution and aesthetic are also super. The section pushes the envelope.

En esta sección, un superhéroe o supervillano representa a la estrella de cada equipo de fútbol. Súper gráficos apoyan estos caracteres, y muestran cómo les ha ido a cada equipo. La ejecución y la estética también son súper. Esta sección va más allá del límite.

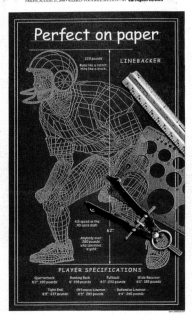

The Augusta Chronicle
Augusta, Ga.

Sports page design/50,000-174,999

Nate Owens, Graphic Artist; **Andrew Festa,** Sports Designer; **Dan Spears,** Weekend Sports Editor; **John Gogick,** News Editor; **Adam Smith,** Night News Editor; **Ling Low,** Presentation Editor

Diário de Notícias
Lisbon, Portugal

Sports page design/50,000-174,999

José Maria Ribeirinho, Art Director; **Cristina Santos,** Infographics Editor; **Paulo Oliveira,** Infographic Artist

San Jose Mercury News
San Jose, Calif.

Sports page design/175,000 and over

Shan Carter, Artist; **Eric Pinkela,** Sports Designer; **Craig Lancaster,** Sports Editor; **Kevin Wendt,** News Design Director; **Matt Mansfield,** Deputy M.E.

BOMBA NADAL

Mundo Deportivo
Barcelona, Spain

Sports page design/50,000-174,999

Joan Lanuza, Subdirector;
Ferran Morales,
Infographic Designer

SportsThursday

The New York Times

I.O.C. Ignores Snub, But Israel Stands Tall

Israelis Revel in First Taste of Gold

New Generation Dims the Glow of Sydney

A Tearful Retiring Image Is Bronzed for Gardner

The New York Times
New York, N.Y.

Sports page design/175,000 and over

Wayne Kamidoi, Art Director

SPORTS

Ouch!

THE BROWNS' BLACK SUNDAY

DE | COURTNEY BROWN | Torn foot ligament

TE | KELLEN WINSLOW | Broken right leg

CB | DAYLON McCUTCHEON | Broken finger

RT | RYAN TUCKER | Strained right quadriceps

DT | GERARD WARREN | Strained pectoral muscle

RG | PAUL ZUKAUSKAS | Strained left knee

Winslow, Brown top roll call of injured; Davis 'disgusted'

A shattering weekend places team's hopes in Garcia, Davis

Wedge hammers home importance of last games

The Plain Dealer
Cleveland, Ohio

Sports page design/175,000 and over

Staci Andrews, Assistant Sports Editor/Design; **Roy Hewitt,** Sports Editor

UNITED STATES VS. EUROPE

RYDER CUP 2004

EUROPE 6½, UNITED STATES 1½

Euro thrash

Woods, Mickelson 0-2 as U.S. proves no match

Cup opener turns into day of infamy

Detroit Free Press
Detroit, Mich.

Sports page design/175,000 and over

Christoph Fuhrmans, Sports Designer; **Tom Panzenhagen,** Assistant Sports Editor; **Steve Dorsey,** Design & Graphics Director; **Gene Myers,** Sports Editor; **Diane Weiss,** Sports Picture Editor

Pittsburgh Post-Gazette
Pittsburgh, Pa.

Sports page design/175,000 and over

Bill Pliske, Associate Editor/Design & Graphics

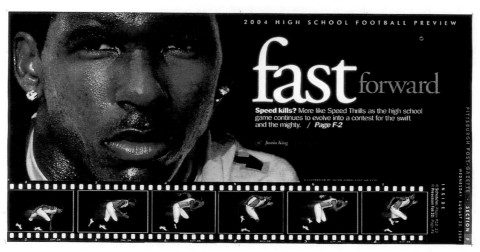

2004 HIGH SCHOOL FOOTBALL PREVIEW

fast forward

Speed kills? More like Speed Thrills as the high school game continues to evolve into a contest for the swift and the mighty. / **Page F-2**

The Boston Globe
Boston, Mass.

Sports page design/175,000 and over

Brian Gross, Designer; **Ken Fratus,** Assistant Sports Editor; **Joe Sullivan,** Sports Editor

The Boston Globe
Boston, Mass.

Sports page design/175,000 and over

Grant Staublin, Designer; **Ken Fratus,** Assistant Sports Editor; **Scott Thurston,** Assistant Sports Editor; **John Bohn,** Photographer; **Dan Zedek,** Design Director

Hartford Courant
Hartford, Conn.

Sports page design/175,000 and over

Tim Reck, Designer; **Thom McGuire,** A.M.E. Graphics/Photo; **John Woike,** Photographer; **Suzette Moyer,** Director/Design & Graphics

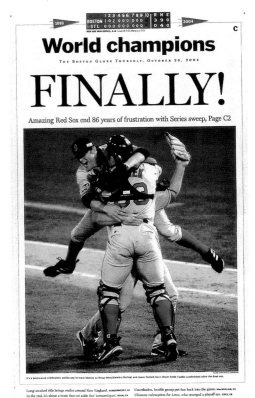

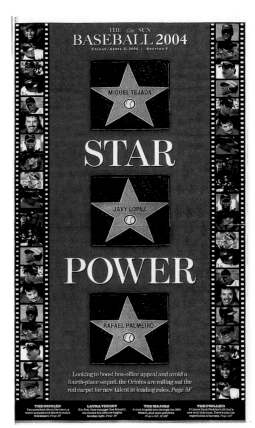

The Baltimore Sun
Baltimore, Md.

Sports page design/175,000 and over

Michael Workman, Sports Design Editor

Milwaukee Journal Sentinel
Milwaukee, Wis.

Sports page design/175,000 and over

Sam Manchester, Assistant Sports Editor

The State
Columbia, S.C.

Sports page design/50,000-174,999

Merry Eccles, Sports Designer

The Seattle Times
Seattle, Wash.

Sports page design/175,000 and over

Mark McTyre, Sports Designer; **Rod Mar,** Photographer; **Angela Gottschalk,** Photo Editor; **Rick Lund,** Presentation Editor; **Harley Soltes,** Photographer

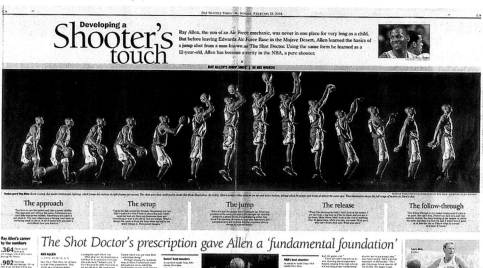

Developing a Shooter's touch

Ray Allen, the son of an Air Force mechanic, was never in one place for very long as a child. But before leaving Edwards Air Force Base in the Mojave Desert, Allen learned the basics of a jump shot from a man known as The Shot Doctor. Using the same form he learned as a 12-year-old, Allen has become a rarity in the NBA, a pure shooter.

RAY ALLEN'S JUMP SHOT | IN HIS WORDS

| The approach | The setup | The jump | The release | The follow-through |

The Shot Doctor's prescription gave Allen a 'fundamental foundation'

Sunday Herald
Glasgow, Scotland

Sports page design/50,000-174,999

David Dick, Deputy Editor

CANCELLED

sundayherald
29 February 2004

sport
www.sundayherald.com

SKI SPECIAL

YOU'RE HISTORY: HAWKS ARE FIRST GLASGOW TEAM TO LIFT TITLE, PAGE 13

The start of a monthly Wild Weekend series Pages 20-21

Premiership chairmen put brakes on British Cup final

EXCLUSIVE BY STEWART FISHER

AOHNA 2004

LES CÉRÉMONIES D'OUVERTURE PAGES A1, A2 ET A3

LE QUÉBEC
QUI GAGNE

La vraie victoire olympique, ne l'oublions pas, consiste à participer aux Jeux, tout simplement. Oubliez les médailles, les honneurs et découvrez aujourd'hui tous les athlètes qui nous représentent à Athènes.

À SURVEILLER
LES QUÉBÉCOIS AUJOURD'HUI
PAGE 2

PRÉDICTIONS
LA PLUS FORTE ÉQUIPE CANADIENNE DE L'HISTOIRE?
PAGE 5

PROGRAMME
LE CALENDRIER COMPLET DES ÉPREUVES ET LA GRILLE TÉLÉ DES JEUX
PAGE 13

TOUTE L'ACTUALITÉ DES JEUX EN DIRECT SUR
www.cyberpresse.ca/jeux

LES SPORTS
PAGES 15 ET 16

GOLF
WOODS ÉVITE L'ÉLIMINATION
PAGE 16

L'AUTO LE LUNDI

La Presse
Montréal, Quebec, Canada

Sports page design/175,000 and over

Francis Leveillee, Designer; **Benoit Giguere,** Art Director; **Alexandre Pratt,** Sports Editor; **Mickel Maruis,** A.M.E./Sports

---

ATHÈNES JUNIOR

JEUX DE MAINS

Il y a plusieurs façons de jauger ses connaissances en matière de Jeux olympiques: avec des questions générales sur les villes hôtes, les records et performances d'athlètes bien connus ou encore, les objets associés à certains sports. Aujourd'hui, nous vous proposons... un jeu de mains. Si l'entraînement des athlètes sollicite tous les muscles de leur corps, c'est bien souvent leurs mains qui les mènent à la victoire.

ANDRÉ DUCHESNE

À QUELLES DISCIPLINES OLYMPIQUES ASSOCIEZ-VOUS LES MAINS SUIVANTES?

RÉPONSES

LE COIN DE L'ANTIQUAIRE

QUIZ
Quels furent les premiers Jeux télédiffusés?

A) Berlin 1936
B) Londres 1948
C) Rome 1960
D) Mexico 1968

La Presse
Montréal, Quebec, Canada

Sports page design/175,000 and over

Francis Leveillee, Designer; **Benoit Giguere,** Art Director; **Alexandre Pratt,** Sports Editor; **Mickel Maruis,** A.M.E./Sports; **Andre Duchesne,** Journalist

---

TOUR DE LANCE

ARMSTRONG **RACES** INTO HISTORY WITH RECORD **SIXTH** TITLE

REPEAT WINNERS

ARMSTRONG'S STANDING THROUGH THE RACE

THE COURSE: STAGE-BY-STAGE

Seattle Post-Intelligencer
Seattle, Wash.

Sports page design/50,000-174,999

Guillermo Munro, Designer

The Virginian-Pilot
Norfolk, Va.

Sports page design/175,000 and over

Buddy Moore, Designer; **Steve Dandy,** Olympics Editor; **Chic Riebel,**
Sports Editor

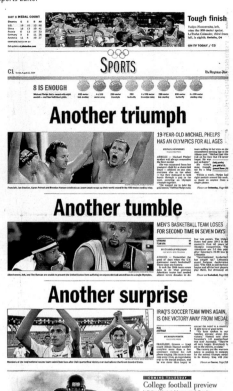

Orlando Sentinel
Orlando, Fla.

Sports page design/175,000 and over

Adam Shiver, Designer; **Joan Andrews,** Sports Design Chief

News & Record
Greensboro, N.C.

Sports page design/50,000-174,999

Doug Harris, Sports Designer

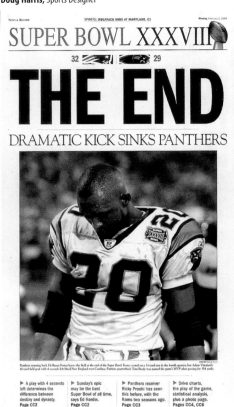

The Boston Globe
Boston, Mass.

Sports page design/175,000 and over

Grant Staublin, Designer; **Lane Turner,** Photographer; **Reid
Laymance,** Assistant Sports Editor; **Dan Zedek,** Design Director

The Seattle Times
Seattle, Wash.

Sports page design/175,000 and over

Mark McTyre, Sports Designer

Fort Worth Star-Telegram
Fort Worth, Texas

Sports page design/175,000 and over

Cody Bailey, Senior Deputy Sports Editor; **Linda Meyer,** Design Editor

Fort Worth Star-Telegram
Fort Worth, Texas

Sports page design/175,000 and over

Cody Bailey, Senior Deputy Sports Editor; **Seth Schrock,** Design Editor; **Michael Currie,** Assistant Sports Editor; **Charean Williams,** Writer

La Presse
Montréal, Quebec, Canada

Sports page design/175,000 and over

Francis Leveillee, Designer; **Benoit Giguere,** Art Director; **Alexandre Pratt,** Sports Editor; **Michel Marois,** A.M.E./Sports

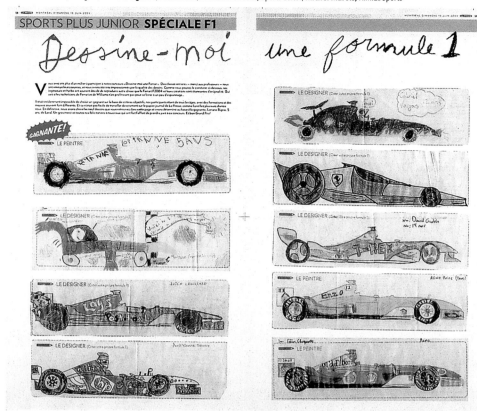

The Indianapolis Star
Indianapolis, Ind.

Sports page design/175,000 and over

Tim Ball, Designer; **Frank Espich,** Picture Editor; **Tim Wheatley,** A.M.E. Sports; **Scott Goldman,** A.M.E./Visuals; **Matt Dial,** Online Editor

Calgary Herald
Calgary, Alberta, Canada

Business page design/50,000-174,999

Travis Reynolds, Graphic Designer

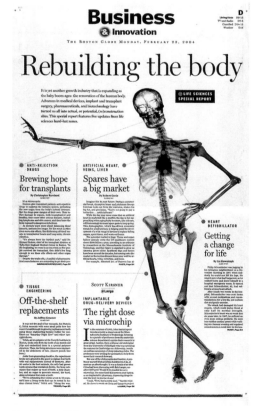

The Boston Globe
Boston, Mass.

Business page design/175,000 and over

Vic DeRobertis, Art Director & Designer; **D.C. Denison,** Editor; **Dan Zedek,** Design Director

Ny Teknik
Stockholm, Sweden

Business page design/50,000-174,999

Elisabeth Vene, Page Designer; **Jonas Askergren,** Graphic Artist; **Pontus Tideman,** Photographer

Die Welt/Berliner Morgen Post
Berlin, Germany

Business page design/175,000 and over

Michael Klocke, Page Designer; **Michael Dilger,** Photo Editor; **Dirk Nolde,** Editor

Hartford Courant
Hartford, Conn.

Business page design/175,000 and over

Ryan C. Healy, Business Designer; **Suzette Moyer,** Design Director; **Richard Borge,** Illustrator

Hartford Courant
Hartford, Conn.

Business page design/175,000 and over

Vada Crosby, Designer; **Suzette Moyer,** Director of Design & Graphics; **Tim Reck,** Designer; **Mel Shaffer,** Assistant Director of Design/Graphics; **Thom McGuire,** A.M.E. Graphics/Photo

Toronto Star
Toronto, Ontario, Canada

Business page design/175,000 and over

Catherine Pike, Designer; **Alfred Holden,** Design Editor; **Neil Cochrane,** Designer; **Carl Neustaedter,** A.M.E. Design; **Ken Kidd,** Senior Editor; **Raffi Anderian,** Illustrator

The Boston Globe
Boston, Mass.

Business page design/175,000 and over

David Schultz, Assistant Director/Design and News; **Christine Murphy**, Designer; **Shirley Leung**, Asstistant Business Editor; **Dan Zedek**, Design Director

Die Zeit
Hamburg, Germany

Business page design/175,000 and over

Staff

The Boston Globe
Boston, Mass.

Business page design/175,000 and over

Vic DeRobertis, Art Director & Designer; **D.C. Denison**, Editor; **Dan Zedek**, Design Director

The Bakersfield Californian
Bakersfield, Calif.

Business page design/50,000-174,999

Michael Borjon, Page Designer

La Presse
Montréal, Quebec, Canada

Business page design/175,000 and over

Andre Rivest, Designer; **Benoit Giguere**, Art Director; **Rene Lewandowski**, Journalist; **Stephane Lavallee**, A.M.E. Business

Die Welt/Berliner Morgen Post
Berlin, Germany

Business page design/175,000 and over

Barbara Krämer, Page Designer; **Beate Nowak,** Graphic Artist; **Dirk Nolde,** Editor

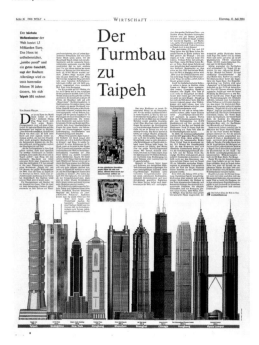

The New York Times
New York, N.Y.

Business page design/175,000 and over

Daniel Adel, Illustrator; **Fred Norgaard,** Art Director

The Star-Ledger
Newark, N.J.

Business page design/175,000 and over

Drew Sheneman, Writer/Illustrator; **Peter Ambush,** Illustrator; **Mike Scott,** Colorist; **Amy Nutt,** Reporter; **George Frederick,** Art Director; **Frank Cecala,** Lettering; **Beverly Reid,** Researcher; **Andre Malok,** Graphic Artist

Hartford Courant
Hartford, Conn.

Business page design/175,000 and over

Ryan C. Healy, Business Designer; **Suzette Moyer,** Design Director

The Boston Globe
Boston, Mass.

Business page design/175,000 and over

Vic DeRobertis, Art Director & Designer; **D.C. Denison,** Editor

The Orange County Register
Santa Ana, Calif.

Inside news page design/175,000 and over

Patty Pitts, Designer; **Larry Nista,** Art Director; **Neil C. Pinchin,** Design Director; **Brenda Shoun,** Deputy Editor/Visuals

Reforma
México City, México

Inside news page design/50,000-174,999

Xóchitl González, Designer; **Ricardo Del Castillo,** Art Director; **Jorge Peñaloza,** Infographic Artist; **Silvia I. Gámez,** Editor; **René Delgado,** Managing Director; **Lázaro Ríos,** General Managing Director; **Homero Fernández,** Section Designer

CUAUHTÉMOC, DE VUELTA AL ORIGEN

Simboliza la grandeza de la patria

Tachan de hazaña cambio de estatua

A fond farewell

The Spokesman-Review
Spokane, Wash.

Inside news page design/50,000-174,999

Geoff Pinnock, Design Director; **Bart Rayniak,** Photo Editor; **Dan Pelle,** Assistant Photo Editor

WAR WITH IRAQ: ONE YEAR LATER

Simple numbers, complex feelings

As a result of U.S. military action against Iraq, do you think the U.S. is more safe from terrorism?

42%

51%

43%

41%

58%

Chicago Tribune
Chicago, Ill.

Inside news page design/175,000 and over

Mike Miner, Art Director; **Charles M. Madigan,** Editor

D-DAY MEMORIAL: 60 YEARS LATER

ALLIED TRIBUTE
Ceremonies in France honor heroes of Normandy invasion

San Jose Mercury News
San Jose, Calif.

Inside news page design/175,000 and over

Kevin Wendt, News Design Director; **Matt Mansfield,** Deputy M.E.; **Shraddha Swaroop,** News Designer; **Akili Ramsess,** Picture Editor

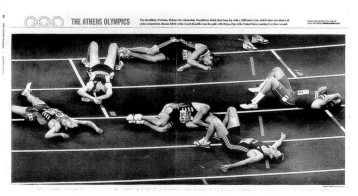

THE ATHENS OLYMPICS

The Palm Beach Post
West Palm Beach, Fla.

Inside news page design/50,000-174,999

Mark Edelson, Presentation Editor; **Roberto Schmidt,** Photographer; **Tim Burke,** A.M.E./Sports

St. Louis Post-Dispatch
St. Louis, Mo.

Inside news page design/175,000 and over

Reagan Branham, Designer

This page is a special idea that forces the reader to participate. What a fun concept for sports fans and non-sports fans alike. The clean design and typography make the colorful letters pop, and they create a neat experience for readers.

Esta página es una idea especial que fuerza al lector a tomar parte de ella. Qué entretenida idea tanto para un hincha deportivo como para quienes no lo son. El diseño y la tipografía limpios hacen que las coloridas letras resalten y creen una genial experiencia para los lectores.

Name that team

Think you know sports? We have compiled an alphabet of logos — or parts of logos — from the four major sports (MLB, NHL, NFL and NBA) and college teams. See if you can identify the teams. Answers are at the bottom of the page. No peeking!

Answers: **A:** Anaheim Angels **B:** Boston Red Sox **C:** Chicago Bears **D:** Detroit Tigers **E:** Edmonton Oilers **F:** Florida Marlins **G:** Green Bay Packers **H:** New Orleans Hornets **I:** Indiana University **J:** New York Jets **K:** Kansas City Chiefs **L:** Los Angeles Lakers **M:** Montreal Expos **N:** Nebraska Cornhuskers **O:** Baltimore Orioles **P:** Pittsburgh Pirates **Q:** Queens College in New York **R:** Houston Rockets **S:** Seattle Mariners **T:** Texas Rangers **U:** San Antonio Spurs **V:** Virginia Tech **W:** Golden State Warriors **X:** Xavier University **Y:** New York Mets **Z:** Utah Jazz

20-26 You are a sports genius. But it's about time to get up off the couch!

15-19 Not bad, but you might consider spending more quality time in front of the TV.

below 15 You call yourself a sports fan? Think again!

Heraldo de Aragón
Zaragoza, Spain

Inside news page design/50,000-174,999

Javier Errea, Art Director; **Ana Perez,** Designer; **Kristina Urresti,** Designer; **Asier Barrio,** Designer; **Pilar Ostale,** Design Editor; **Carmelo Roy,** Designer; **Cristina Salvador,** Designer

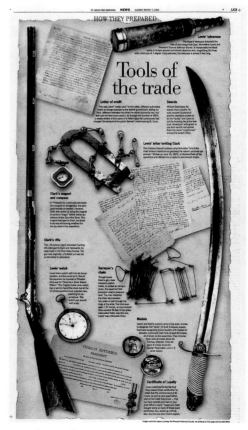

St. Louis Post-Dispatch
St. Louis, Mo.

Inside news page design/175,000 and over

Birgit Dralle, Designer; **Tom Borgman,** Features Design Director; **Wade Wilson,** Design & Graphics Editor

---

National Post
Toronto, Ontario, Canada

Inside news page design/175,000 and over

Gayle Grin, A.M.E./Visuals; **Matthew Fraser,** Editor-in-Chief; **Laura Koot,** News Presentation Editor; **Jeff Wasserman,** Photo Editor; **Ben Errett,** Avenue Editor

NATIONAL LEAGUE CHAMPIONSHIP SERIES

GAME 1	CARDINALS 10, ASTROS 7	GAME 2	CARDINALS 6, ASTROS 4	GAME 3	ASTROS 5, CARDINALS 2	GAME 4	ASTROS 6, CARDINALS 5	GAME 5	ASTROS 3, CARDINALS 0	GAME 6	CARDINALS 6, ASTROS 4
One in the hand	**Swingin' in the rain**	**Astros strike back**	**Fit to be tied**	**Kent crushes Cards**	**Go crazy!**

St. Louis Post-Dispatch
St. Louis, Mo.

Inside news page design/175,000 and over

Chris Snider, News Design Director; **Huy Richard Mach,** Photographer; **Wade Wilson,** Design & Graphics Editor

---

Himmel, so blond

Die Welt/Berliner Morgen Post
Berlin, Germany

Inside news page design/ 175,000 and over

Barbara Krämer, Page Designer; **Michael Dilger,** Photo Editor; **Wolfgang Büscher,** Editor

---

Invisible people

The Dominican Republic's Elias Piña province is 'the poorest province in the whole country and is probably the most forgotten, on the national and international level.'

The Palm Beach Post
West Palm Beach, Fla.

Inside news page design/50,000-174,999

Mark Edelson, Presentation Editor; **Benjamin Rusnak,** Photographer

---

AVENUE
Arts, Culture & Society

All the Queen's men

National Post
Toronto, Ontario, Canada

Inside news page design/175,000 and over

Gayle Grin, A.M.E./Visuals; **Matthew Fraser,** Editor-in-Chief; **Donna MacMullin,** Features Presentations Editor; **Jeff Wasserman,** Photo Editor

---

THE BEST OF NEWSPAPER DESIGN 26 | NEWS | **105**

El Universal
México City, México

Inside news page design/50,000-174,999

Damián Martínez, Design Coordinator; **Héctor Baca,** Co-Editor; **Ernesto Galván,** Editor; **Óscar Santiago,** Art and Design Director; **Raymundo Rivapalacio,** International Coordinator; **Francisco Santiago,** Edition Director; **Roberto Rock,** General Editorial Director; **Rubén Álvarez,** Information Director; **Design Staff; Staff Photographers**

San Jose Mercury News
San Jose, Calif.

Inside news page design/175,000 and over

Kevin Wendt, News Design Director; **Matt Mansfield,** Deputy M.E.; **Susanna Frohman,** Photographer; **Anne-Marie McReynolds,** Photographer; **Geri Migliecz,** Director/Photography

Die Welt/Berliner Morgen Post
Berlin, Germany

Inside news page design/175,000 and over

Robby Lorenz, Page Designer; **Michael Dilger,** Photo Editor; **Wolfgang Büscher,** Editor

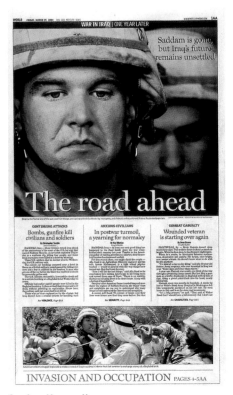

San Jose Mercury News
San Jose, Calif.

Inside news page design/175,000 and over

Caroline Couig, Picture Editor; **Kevin Wendt,** News Design Director; **Matt Mansfield,** Deputy M.E.

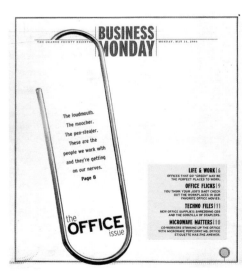

The Orange County Register
Santa Ana, Calif.

Inside news page design/175,000 and over

Kristin Lenz, Designer; **Karen Kelso,** Art Director; **Neil C. Pinchin,** Design Director; **Brenda Shoun,** Deputy Editor/Visuals

Los Angeles Times
Los Angeles, Calif.

Inside news page design/175,000 and over

Joseph Hutchinson, Deputy M.E.; **Michael Whitley,** Deputy Design Director; **Richard Nelson,** Copy Editor

The Star-Ledger
Newark, N.J.

News design/Page(s)/Other 175,000 and over

George Frederick, Graphics Editor; **Andre Malok,** Graphic Artist; **Andrew Garcia Phillips,** Graphics Editor; **Angela Porter,** Graphic Artist

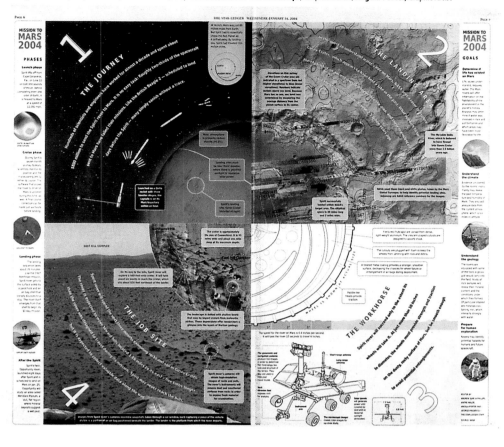

San Francisco Chronicle
San Francisco, Calif.

News design/Page(s)/Other 175,000 and over

Nanette Bisher, Creative Director; **Rick Nobles,** Designer; **James Finefrock,** Insight Editor

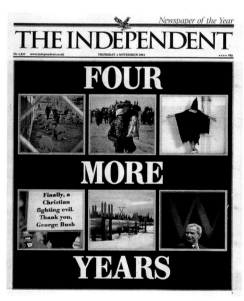

Folha de São Paulo
São Paulo, Brazil

News design/Page(s)/Other 175,000 and over

Massimo Gentile, Art Editor; **Fabio Maria,** Art Sub-Editor; **Jair de Oliveira,** Page Designer

Die Welt/Berliner Morgen Post
Berlin, Germany

News design/Page(s)/Other 175,000 and over

Michael Klocke, Page Designer; **Michel Dilger,** Photo Editor; **Wolfgang Büscher,** Editor

The Independent
London, England

Breaking news topics/Elections

Kevin Bayliss, Art Director

National Post
Toronto, Ontario, Canada

Breaking news topics/Elections

Gayle Grin, A.M.E./Visuals; **Matthew Fraser,** Editor-in-Chief; **Steve Meurice,** Deputy M.E.; **Doug Kelly,** Deputy Director; **Angela Murphy,** Page 1 Editor; **Jeff Wasserman,** Photo Editor

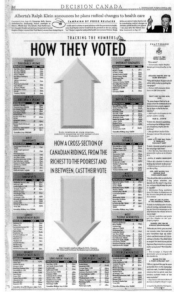

SILVER

Hartford Courant
Hartford, Conn.

Breaking news topics/Elections

Greg Harmel, Designer; **Suzette Moyer,** Director/Design & Graphics; **Dave Grewe,** Photo Editor; **John Scanlan,** Director/Photography; **Thom McGuire,** A.M.E. Graphics/Photography

This page captures the tension of the evening by taking an emotional approach. The editors revved the energy on the page within their stylistic voice — and without screaming. This page stretches the limits of the craft by showing the brain power that went into the publication's election coverage.

Esta página captura la tensión de la noche a través de un enfoque emocional. Los editores acrecentaron la energía de la página con una voz de estilo, pero sin gritar. Esta página expande los límites de la profesión al mostrar el alcance de la inteligencia que llevó la cobertura de las elecciones de esta publicación.

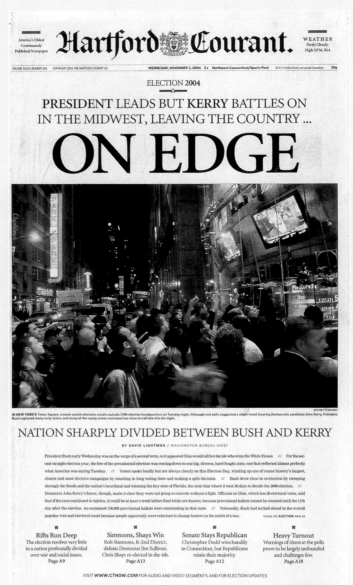

The New York Times
New York, N.Y.

Breaking news topics/Elections

Tom Bodkin, Design Director

Hartford Courant
Hartford, Conn.

Breaking news topics/Elections

Greg Harmel, Designer; **Suzette Moyer,** Director/Design & Graphics; **Dave Grewe,** Photo Editor; **John Scanlan,** Director/Photography; **Thom McGuire,** A.M.E. Graphics/Photography

El Correo
Bilbao, Spain

Breaking news topics/Terrorist attacks

Diego Zúñiga, Art Director; **Alberto Torregrosa,** Editorial Art & Design Consultant; **María del Carmen Navarro,** Design Editor; **Mikel García Macías,** Designer; **Ana Espligares,** Designer; **Aurelio Garrote,** Designer; **Laura Piedra,** Designer; **Rafael Marañón,** Designer; **Pacho Igartua,** Designer; **Virginia López,** Designer

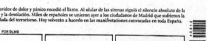

España llora

Masacre en Madrid

192 muertos en atentados contra cuatro trenes

Diario de Sevilla
Sevilla, Spain

Breaking news topics/Terrorist attacks

Jaun Carlos Zambrano, Design Editor; **Rafael Avilés,** Design Editor Assistant

Sur
Malaga, Spain

Breaking news topics/Terrorist attacks

Rafael Ruiz, Section Designer; **M. Dolores de la Vega,** Designer; **Fernando González,** Director/Photography; **Francisco Sánchez Ruano,** Art Director; **Alberto Torregrosa,** Editorial Design Consultant

En by merket for livet

Bergens Tidende
Bergen, Norway

Breaking news topics/Terrorist attacks

Arne Edvardsen, Editor; **Walter Jensen,** Chief of Presentation; **Tore Sehl,** Page Coordinator; **Anne Hovden,** Page Editor; **Anne Britt Kilvik,** Page Editor; **Oddmund Holmelid,** Page Designer

"Sonaban los móviles de los muertos"

Expansión
Madrid, Spain

Breaking news topics/Terrorist attacks

Pablo MaRamírez, Graphics Editor; **Agusto Gonzales Besada,** Design Editor-in-Chief; **Manuel Del Pozo,** Subdirector; **Staff**

Heraldo de Aragón
Zaragoza, Spain

Breaking news topics/Terrorist attacks

Javier Errea, Art Director; **Ana Perez,** Designer; **Kristina Urresti,** Designer; **Asier Barrio,** Designer; **Pilar Ostale,** Design Editor; **Carmelo Roy,** Designer; **Cristina Salvador,** Designer

The Washington Post
Washington, D.C.

Breaking news topics/Obituaries

Ed Thiede, A.M.E./News; **Vince Bzdek,** Deputy A.M.E./News; **Beth Broadwater,** Assistant News Editor; **Tan Ly,** Assistant News Editor; **News Desk Staff**

The Washington Post
Washington, D.C.

Breaking news topics/Obituaries

Ed Thiede, A.M.E./News; **Vince Bzdek,** Deputy A.M.E./News; **Beth Broadwater,** Assistant News Editor; **Tan Ly,** Assistant News Editor; **News Desk Staff**

O Dia
Rio de Janeiro, Brazil

Breaking news topics/Obituaries

André Hippertt, Art Director; **Luisa Bousada,** Designer; **Joao Pedroso,** Editor

Diário de Notícias
Lisbon, Portugal

Breaking news topics/Obituaries

Fabio Sales, Design Consultant; **José Maria Ribeirinho,** A.M.E./Visuals; **Rui Coutinho,** Photo Editor; **Jose Manoel Barroso,** Newsroom Director

The Times-Picayune
New Orleans, La.

Breaking news topics/Natural Disasters

Adrianna Garcia, Designer; **Daniel Swenson,** Graphic Artist; **Ted Jackson,** Photographer; **George Berke,** Design Director; **Doug Parker,** Photo Editor; **Alex Brandon,** Photographer; **Dan Shea,** M.E.; **Angela Hill,** Graphics Editor; **Richard Russell,** Sunday Editor

The Palm Beach Post
West Palm Beach, Fla.

Breaking news topics/Natural Disasters
Staff

HURRICANE JEANNE
Follow the storm's track at PalmBeachPost.com

'You reach a point where you're not surprised by anything. But seeing this, I am disappointed and saddened.'
TED ANDRELLI, Hutchinson Island resident

Hutchinson Island battered

Jeanne erases cleanup, recovery from Frances

INTERSTATE 95
Winds topple furniture truck near 45th Street

VERO BEACH
Ravaging floods test resiliency

LIFE GOES ON

THE BIG DAY | A RUSH TO WED BEFORE STORM

SALON TIME | KEEPING HER DATE

SURF TIME | SEEKING WAVES

Orlando Sentinel
Orlando, Fla.

Breaking news topics/Natural Disasters
Bonita Burton, A.M.E./Visuals; **Staff**

National Post
Toronto, Ontario, Canada

Breaking news topics/Natural Disasters

Gayle Grin, A.M.E./Visuals; **Les Pyette,** Publisher; **Jeff Wasserman,** Photo Editor; **Steve Meurice,** Deputy M.E.

Yushchenko's Orange Revolution verges on victory in Ukraine. A10

NATIONAL POST
VOL.7 NO.53 MONDAY, DECEMBER 27, 2004 www.nationalpost.com

WAVES OF TRAGEDY

12,300 die in quake fallout

Walls of water sweep people away

FIRST > FOR YOU

National Post
Toronto, Ontario, Canada

Breaking news topics/Natural Disasters

Gayle Grin, A.M.E./Visuals/Designer; **Les Pyette,** Publisher; **Jeff Wasserman,** Photo Editor; **Steve Meurice,** Deputy M.E.

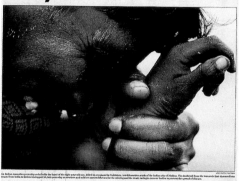

JUNIORS 2-0: Canada crushes Sweden in an 8-1 romp, S1, plus Cam Cole on the Crosby kerfuffle, S8

NATIONAL POST
VOL.7 NO.54 TUESDAY, DECEMBER 28, 2004 www.nationalpost.com

■ Many could have been saved: Canadian scientist
■ Officials fear flooding, bodies will spread disease

25,000 DEAD

TENS OF THOUSANDS STILL MISSING AT SEA

Rescuers looking for the dead in treetops

MORE COVERAGE

'You could see a wall of water four storeys high'

bodareal el banquete

El Rey recuerda a los novios sus obligaciones

El menú del banquete reflejó la gastronomía de las 17 comunidades autónomas y se sirvió en el Patio del Príncipe del Palacio Real

Un ofrenda sencilla y un beso a las puertas de la Basílica de Atocha

Sur
Malaga, Spain

Breaking news topics/Editor's choice, national

M. Dolores de la Vega, Section Designer; **Rafael Ruiz,** Designer; **Baldomero Villanueva,** Designer; **Fernando González,** Director/Photography; **Francisco Sánches Ruano,** Art Director; **Alberto Torregrosa,** Editorial Design Consultant

---

Clarín

Horror en el aula

Clarín
Buenos Aires, Argentina

Breaking news topics/Editor's choice, local/regional

Gustavo Lo Valvo, Art Director; **Staff**

Apple Daily
Taipei, Taiwan

Breaking news topics/Editor's choice, local/regional

Ben Wong Kam Wa, Art Director; **Bob Chen Bo Jain,** Deputy Art Director; **Charles Wang Shih Chuan,** Senior Assistant Art Director; **Polo Fu Ta Hsiu,** Senior Designer; **Tsai Chun Neng,** Senior Designer; **Chang I. Chung,** Senior Designer; **Lena Huang Yi Huand,** Assistant Art Director

Hartford Courant
Hartford, Conn.

Breaking news topics/Editor's choice, local/regional

Greg Harmel, Designer; **Suzette Moyer,** Director/Design & Graphics; **John Scanlan,** Director/Photography; **Thom McGuire,** A.M.E. Graphics/Photography; **Mark Mirko,** Photographer; **Dave Grewe,** Photo Editor

GUILTY

Harford Courant
Hartford, Conn.

Breaking news topics/Editor's choice, local/regional

Greg Harmel, Designer; **Suzette Moyer,** Director/Design & Graphics; **Tony Bacewicz,** Photo Editor; **John Scanlan,** Director/Photography; **Thom McGuire,** A.M.E. Graphics/Photography

RESIGNATION

ABC
Madrid, Spain

Breaking news topics/Editor's choice, national

Staff

Sur
Malaga, Spain

Breaking news topics/Editor's choice, national

Rafael Ruiz, Designer; **M. Dolores de la Vega,** Section Designer; **Fernando González,** Director/Photography; **Francisco Sánchez Ruano,** Art Director; **Alberto Torregrosa,** Editorial Design Consultant; **Baldomero Villanueva,** Designer; **P. Velasco,** Graphic Artist; **Fernando Rubio,** Graphic Artist

El Diario de Hoy
San Salvador, El Salvador

Breaking news topics/Editor's choice, international

Juan Durán, Art Director & Designer; **Teodoro Lira,** Graphics Editor; **Jorge Castillo,** Infographic Editor; **Veronica Ferrufino,** Entertainment Editor; **Remberto Rodriguez,** Graphics Co-Editor/Designer; **Hugo Rodriguez,** Designer; **Ricardo Saravia,** Designer

Aftonbladet
Stokholm, Sweden

Breaking news topics/Editor's choice, international

Staff

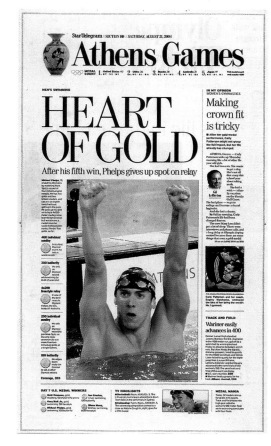

Fort Worth Star-Telegram
Fort Worth, Texas

Breaking news topics/Editor's choice, sports

Celeste Williams, Sports Editor; **Michael Currie,** Assistant Sports Editor; **Terry Bigham,** Copy Editor

Fort Worth Star-Telegram
Fort Worth, Texas

Breaking news topics/Editor's choice, sports

Celeste Williams, Sports Editor; **Michael Currie,** Assistant Sports Editor; **Terry Bigham,** Copy Editor; **Seth Schrock,** Design Editor

The San Diego Union-Tribune
San Diego, Calif.

Special news topics/The Athens Olympics

Greg Manifold, Sports Designer; **Joshua Penrod,** Sports Designer; **Dave Wilson,** Page Designer; **Christopher Meighan,** Page Designer; **Sean M. Huffy,** Photographer; **Bruce Huff,** Sports Photo Editor; **Doug Williams,** Deputy Sports Editor; **Chris Ross,** News Design Editor; **Michael Franklin,** Photo Editor; **Staff**

National Post
Toronto, Ontario, Canada

Special news topics/The Athens Olympics

Gayle Grin, A.M.E./Visuals; **Matthew Fraser,** Editor-in-Chief; **Donna MacMullin,** Features Presentations Editor

Estado de Minas
Belo Horizonte, Brazil

Special news topics/The Athens Olympics

Eduardo Barros, Illustrator; **Marcelo Monteiro,** Graphic Artist; **Ary Moraes,** Illustrator/Graphic Director; **Álvaro Duarte,** Art Director; **Ivan Drummond,** Researcher; **Claudio Arreguy,** Sports Editor; **Josemar Gimenez,** Editor-in-Chief

Los Angeles Times
Los Angeles, Calif.

Special news topics/Ronald Reagan's death and funeral

Joseph Hutchinson, Deputy M.E.; **Michael Whitley,** Deputy Design Director; **Lorraine Wang,** Designer; **David Campbell,** Designer; **Dan Santos,** Designer; **Colin Crawford,** A.M.E./Design & Photo; **Calvin Hom,** Photo Editor; **Mary Cooney,** Photo Editor; **Alan Hagman,** Photo Editor; **Rob St. John,** Photo Editor

El Correo
Bilbao, Spain

Special news topics/The Athens Olympics

Diego Zúñiga, Art Director; **Alberto Torregrosa,** Editorial Art & Design Consultant; **María del Carmen Navarro,** Design Editor; **Mikel García Macías,** Designer; **Ana Espligares,** Designer; **Aurelio Garrote,** Designer; **Laura Piedra,** Designer; **Rafael Marañón,** Designer; **Pacho Igartua,** Designer; **Virginia López,** Designert

Chicago Tribune
Chicago, Ill.

Special news topics/The Athens Olympics

Staff

SILVER

Los Angeles Times
Los Angeles, Calif.

Special news topics/Editor's choice, local/regional

Joseph Hutchinson, Deputy M.E.; **Michael Whitley,** Deputy Design Director; **Richard Nelson,** Copy Editor

This is a great example of a hard-to-tell story done with grace and elegance. The grid system is consistent and subtle, with a European feel. The old pictures, old newspapers and documents, as well as smart secondary elements, propel the reader through the pages.

Éste es un buen ejemplo de un artículo difícil de vender que fue realizado con gracia y elegancia. El sistema de grilla es consistente y sutil, con un aire europeo. Las fotos antiguas, los diarios y documentos viejos, y los inteligentes elementos secundarios empujan al lector a través de las páginas.

IVAN WAS THE GREAT LEVELER

South Florida Sun-Sentinel
Fort Lauderdale, Fla.

Special news topics/Natural Disasters

Denise M. Reagan, Designer; **Angel Valentin,** Photographer; **Mary Vignoles,** Photo Editor; **Tom Peyton,** Design Director

Sing Tao Daily
Hong Kong, China

Special news topics/Natural Disasters

Danny Wong Shu Wai, Creative Director; **Daniel Wong Chi Yung,** Art Director; **Art Staff**

The Spokesman-Review
Spokane, Wash.

Special news topics/ Editor's choice, local/ regional

Ralph Walter, Page Designer; **Bart Rayniak,** Photo Editor; **Brian Plonka,** Photographer; **Geoff Pinnock,** Design Director

St. Louis Post-Dispatch
St. Louis, Mo.

Special news topics/Editor's choice, local/ regional

Chris Lee, Photographer; **Wade Wilson,** Director/Design & Graphics; **Carlos Ayulo,** Sports Design Coordinator; **Chris Stanfield,** Night Photo Editor; **Larry Coyne,** Director/ Photography

Los Angeles Times
Los Angeles, Calif.

Special news topics/Editor's choice, local/ regional

Michael Whitley, Deputy Design Director; **Bill Gaspard,** News Design Director; **Damon Winter,** Photographer; **Colin Crawford,** A.M.E./Photo

Chicago Sun-Times
Chicago, Ill.

Special news topics/ Editor's choice, local/ regional

Robb Montgomery, News Design Editor; **Eric White,** Design Editor; **Nancy Stuenkel,** Photo Editor; **Greg Good,** Graphic Artist; **Don Hayner,** M.E./News; **John Barron,** Executive Managing Editor; **Michael Cooke,** Editor-in-Chief

The Seattle Times
Seattle, Wash.

Special news topics/ Editor's choice, local/ regional

Carol Nakagawa, Pacific Magazine Art Director; **Denise Clifton,** News Designer; **Ted Basladynski,** News Designer; **Benjamin Benschneider,** Photographer; **Mark Nowlin,** Graphic Artist; **Kristopher Lee,** Graphic Artist; **Whitney Stensrud,** Assistant Art Director/Graphics; **Fred Nelson,** Photo Editor; **Heather McKinnon,** Features Designer; **Steve Ringman,** Photographer

SILVER

La Presse
Montréal, Quebec, Canada

Special news topics/Editor's choice, international

Genevieve Dinel, Designer; **Benoit Giguere,** Art Director; **Bob Skinner,** Photographer; **Alain-Pierre Hovasse,** Photo Editor; **Michele Ouimet,** Journalist; **Agnes Gruda,** A.M.E./News

This is a great piece. The typography, secondary elements, white space and color use are handled nicely. It all feels just right.

Éste es un gran artículo. La tipografía, los elementos secundarios, el espacio en blanco y el uso del color están bien ejecutados. Todo se siente en su lugar.

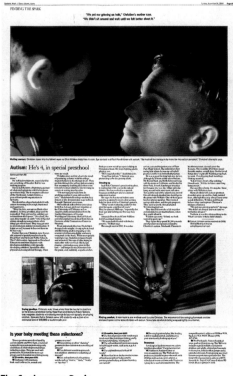

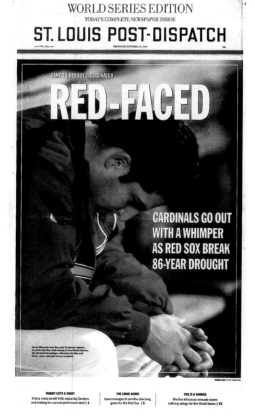

The Spokesman-Review
Spokane, Wash.

Special news topics/Editor's choice, local/regional

Geoff Pinnock, Design Director; **Bart Rayniak,** Photo Editor; **Brian Plonka,** Photographer

The Spokesman-Review
Spokane, Wash.

Special news topics/Editor's choice, local/regional

Geoff Pinnock, Design Director; **Bart Rayniak,** Photo Editor; **Jed Conklin,** Photographer

St. Louis Post-Dispatch
St. Louis, Mo.

Special news topics/Editor's choice, national

Chris Snider, News Design Director; **Wade Wilson,** Director/Design & Graphics; **Carlos Ayulo,** Sports Design Coordinator; **Chris Stanfield,** Night Photo Editor; **Larry Coyne,** Director/Photography; **Sid Hastings,** Assistant Director of Photography; **J.B. Forbes,** Photographer; **Chris Lee,** Photographer

Scotland on Sunday
Edinburgh, Scotland

Special news topics/Editor's choice, international

John McLellan, Editor; **Tom Little,** Deputy Editor; **Mark Grayson,** Art Director; **Angela McKean,** Deputy Art Director; **Iain Donnachie,** Senior Designer; **Tony Marsh,** Executive Picture Editor; **Peter Laing,** News Editor; **Chris Dry,** Production & Systems Editor; **Palmer Watson Ltd.,** Consultants

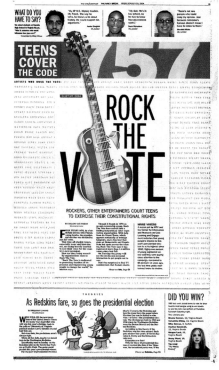

Stunned aftermath | of siege bloodbath

Terror gives way to anger, bewilderment and inconsolable grief as the horrific nature of the ordeal suffered by Beslan's hostages begins to emerge

Russia mourns victims of massacre

The horror of second 9/11 with more suicide bombing to come

The Virginian-Pilot
Norfolk, Va.

Special news topics/Editor's choice, national

Jim Haag, Designer; **Robert Suhay,** Designer; **Judy Le,** Designer; **Stacy Addison,** Designer; **Lori Kelley,** Designer; **Gretchen Hager,** Designer; **Paul Nelson,** News Editor; **Deborah Withey,** Deputy M.E./Presentation; **Julie Elman,** Designer

---

NBA FINALS
GAME 9

LAKERS 99   DETROIT 91

Rising to the Moment

Bryant's clutch three-pointer sends game into OT, where Lakers get even

BILL PLASCHKE
Era's Biggest Shot Is Numb Kind of Wonderful for L.A.

After Nearly Facing an 0-2 Deficit, L.A. Has Some Momentum for Motown

■ For baseball, hockey, track and all other sports news, see Section D

Los Angeles Times
Los Angeles, Calif.

Special news topics/Editor's choice, local/regional

Michael Whitley, Deputy Design Director; **Vic Seper,** Designer; **Calvin Hom,** Photo Editor; **Alex Gallardo,** Photo Editor; **George Wilhelm,** Photo Editor; **Wally Skalij,** Photographer

---

The San Diego Union-Tribune

OPENING DAY
EXTRA

PETCO PARK | APRIL 8, 2004 | STADIUM EDITION | 50¢

A complete guide to the park and a look beneath the surface at what fans don't see. /2, 5

Special delivery

It's been a long time coming, but a new era dawns downtown

THE FIRST PITCH
Padres' David Wells, facing San Francisco's Ray Durham

THE NIGHT
Attendance: Sell-out, seating capacity 42,500

HE SAID IT

The San Diego Union-Tribune
San Diego, Calif.

Special news topics/Editor's choice, sports

Staff

KURT BUSCH RULES NASCAR
GREG BIFFLE WINS FORD 400, SPORTS

SEAHAWKS BEAT DOLPHINS 24-17
NFL, MONDAY

South Florida Sun-Sentinel

MONDAY | NOVEMBER 22, 2004

SOUTH COUNTY EDITION

PALESTINIAN CHILDREN

Jan. 30 election date set in Iraq

Unrest, threats hamper voter registration

'I never would have brought a child into this world to suffer this'

A daunting challenge for post-Arafat peacemakers will be coping with the fury and frustration of young people in Gaza and the West Bank for whom violence, death and destruction have become part of daily life.

Graham won't stop focusing on security

Daily Digest

GAME OVER

GAME OVER

INDEX

South Florida Sun-Sentinel
Fort Lauderdale, Fla.

Special news topics/Editor's choice, international

Denise M. Reagan, Designer; **Mike Stocker,** Photographer; **Mary Vignoles,** Photo Editor; **Tom Peyton,** Design Director

SILVER

The Plain Dealer
Cleveland, Ohio

Special news topics/Editor's choice, sports

Emmet Smith, Designer; **David Campbell,** Associate
Sports Editor; **Stephen Beard,** Illustrator; **Bob Keim,**
Assistant Sports Editor/Night; **Roy Hewitt,** Sports Editor;
David Kordalski, A.M.E./Visuals

The designer took a pretty standard sports event – the biggest
game of the year – and told stories in a different format, taking the
art to the next level. None of the pages were done in traditional
narrative form, and no traditional photos were used. These pages
were a treat for someone who is really into the game, and they
captured the event's emotion.

El diseñador tomó un evento deportivo bastante estándar – el
principal partido del año – y relató historias en un formato
diferente, llevando el arte al nivel superior. Ninguna de estas
páginas fue realizada bajo un formato de narración tradicional,
y tampoco se usaron fotos tradicionales. Estas páginas fueron un
gusto para alguien que se apasiona por el partido, y lograron captar
la emoción del evento.

El Gráfico
Antiguo Cuscatlan, El Salvador

Special news topics/Editor's choice, sports

Agustin Palacios, Coordinator of Design; **José Jaén,** Designer; **Alexander Rivera,** Designer; **Gabriel
Orellana,** Designer; **Carlos Realegeno,** Designer; **Cristian Villalta,** Editor-in-Chief

The Dallas Morning News
Dallas, Texas

Special news topics/Editor's choice, sports

Jason Dugger, Designer; **Chris Velez,** Graphic
Artist; **Rob Schneider,** Design Editor/Sports;
Michael Hogue, Illustrator; **Damon Marx,**
Designer; **Carl Ellis,** Designer; **Mike Kondracki,**
Sunday Sports Editor; **Roxanna Pellin-Scott,**
Assistant Sports Editor; **Andrew P. Scott,** Photo
Editor; **Chris Wilkins,** Photo Editor

The New York Times
New York, N.Y.

Special news topics/Editor's choice, sports

Wayne Kamidoi, Art Director; **Joe Zeff,** Illustrator; **Staff**

FEATURES & MAGAZINES

chapter 5

The photography blew us away. The back-page illustrations are striking. This section has crackle and snap, but it is consistent and very tasteful. We appreciate the nuances in the use of space and typography. It uses restraint. It is not overly designed. It is easy to navigate and read.

La fotografía nos impresionó. Las ilustraciones de la última página son impresionantes. Esta sección tiene relieve y vigor, pero es consistente y tiene mucho gusto. Nos gustan las variaciones en el uso del espacio y la tipografía. Es controlada y no está sobrediseñada. Es fácil de navegar por ella y leerla.

SILVER

Die Welt
Berlin, Germany

Lifestyle/Features section design/ 50,000-174,999

Barbara Krämer, Page Designer; **Sandra Garbers,** Editor; **Jan Draeger,** Editor

South Florida Sun-Sentinel
Fort Lauderdale, Fla.

Opinion section design/175,000 and over

Staff

The Independent on Sunday
London, England

Lifestyle/Features section design/175,000 and over

Carolyn Roberts, Art Director; **Sophie Batterbury,** Picture Editor; **Tristan Davies,** Editor; **Michael Whitty,** Deputy Picture Editor; **Keith Howitt,** Production Editor

Sunday Morning Post
Hong Kong, China

Entertainment section design/50,000-174,999

Troy Dunkley, Features Art Director

SILVER

Die Zeit
Hamburg, Germany

Lifestyle/Features section design/175,000 and over

Staff

The art direction is so well planned that the long stories don't overwhelm you. The visual communication is so strong that you don't need to read the language. The longer cover story is nicely counter-balanced by shorter pieces. Very sophisticated visuals really speak to you.

La dirección de arte está tan bien planificada que los artículos largos no son agobiantes. La comunicación visual es tan poderosa que no se necesita leer el idioma. El largo artículo de tapa está bien contrapesado con artículos más cortos. Los elementos visuales muy sofisticados realmente comunican.

DOSSIER

Unter Verdacht

The New York Times
New York, N.Y.

Entertainment section design/175,000 and over

Nita Kalish, Art Director

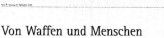

Von Waffen und Menschen

Die Welt/ Berliner Morgen Post
Berlin, Germany

Lifestyle/Features section design/50,000-174,999

Ralf Jacob, Page Designer/ Photo Editor; **Michael Dilger,** Photo Editor; **Jan Draeger,** Editor; **Sandra Garbers,** Editor

Berliner Illustrirte Zeitung

Meine Waffe und ich

Los Angeles Times
Los Angeles, Calif.

*Food section
design/175,000 and over*

Christian Potter Drury,
Features Design Director;
Wes Bausmith, Design
Editor; **Nick Cuccia,**
Design Editor; **Jan Molen,**
Design Editor; **Joseph
Hutchinson,** Deputy
M.E.; **Richard Dirk,** Photo
Editor

Göteborgs-Posten
Goteborg, Sweden

*Other feature section
design/175,000 and over*

Mikael Hjerpe, Designer;
Roger Olsson, Designer;
Stefan Renström,
Designer; **Albert
Rosander,** Designer;
Beatrice Lind, Designer;
**Karin Teghammar
Arell,** Designer; **Gunilla
Wernhamn,** Designer

The Boston Globe
Boston, Mass.

*Opinion page
design/175,000 and over*

Jennifer Schuessler,
Editor; **Gregory Klee,**
Designer; **Dan Zedek,**
Design Director

SILVER

Dagens Nyheter
Stockholm, Sweden

*Lifestyle/Features page design/175,000
and over*

Markus Edin, Art Director; **Jesper
Waldersten,** Illustrator

You don't need to know
what this winner says. You
can feel the fear. It agitates
you, makes your heart beat
faster when you see it. It's
strong, steady and anchored.
Many great decisions were
made, especially in the use
of white space.

No es necesario saber lo que
dice este ganador. Se puede
sentir el miedo. Te agita y
acelera tu corazón cuando lo ves. Es poderoso,
estable y está bien anclado. Se tomaron muchas
buenas decisiones, especialmente en el uso del
espacio blanco.

Dagens Nyheter
Stockholm, Sweden

*Lifestyle/Features section
design/175,000 and over*

Johan Rutherhagen, Art
Director; **Pelle Asplund,**
Art Director; **Ebba Bonde,**
Art Director; **Lotta Ek,** Art
Director

O SACO DE PLÁSTICO
A FRASE MAIS LOUCA
O CANTINHO XENÓFOBO
AS JOKEMAILS MAIS
INDECENTES

indígena

SEXTA-FEIRA 1 OUTUBRO 2004

Os humores de Ana Bola   Easy Rider especial em DVD

Graham Greene em Portugal Cats O novo disco dos R.E.M.

O Gang dos Tubarões   A Regra de Quatro

This is a gutsy cover – simple and brilliant. The page comes alive with the black cat, built only with color and type. The designer just lays out the idea and lets the reader fill in the blanks.

Ésta es una tapa al grano – simple y brillante. La página tiene vida gracias al gato negro construido solo con color y tipografía. El diseñador simplemente diseña la idea y deja que el lector llene los espacios vacíos.

SILVER

O Independente
Lisbon, Portugal

Entertainment page design/49,999 and under

Sónia Matos, Art Director & Designer;
Inés Serra Lopes, Editor-in-Chief;
Leonardo Ralha, Editor

Hartford Courant
Hartford, Conn.

Entertainment page design/175,000 and over

Chris Moore, Assistant Director/ Design

Chicago Tribune
Chicago, Ill.

Entertainment page design/ 175,000 and over

Jason McKean, Art Director; **Mike Miner,** Associate Design Editor; **Daniel Bejar,** Illustrator; **Heidi Stevens,** Assistant Editor; **Scott Powers,** Editor

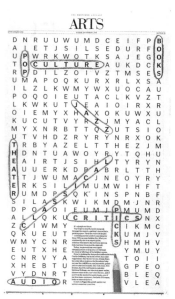

Hartford Courant
Hartford, Conn.

Entertainment page design/ 175,000 and over

Chris Moore, Assistant Director/Design

San Jose Mercury News
San Jose, Calif.

Entertainment page design/ 175,000 and over

Stephanie Grace Lim, Designer

Frankfurter Allgemeine Sonntagszeitung
Frankfurt am Main, Germany

Science/Technology page/175,000 and over

Thomas Heumann, Infographics Director;
Karl-Heinz Döring, Infographics Artist; **Doris Oberneder**, Layout; **Andreas Kuther**, Photo Editor; **Ulf von Rauchhaupt**, Science Editor

It took a lot of planning to pull this off. The information has some timeliness and urgency, and it creates a 3-D shape that is satisfying and has real meaning.

Llevar esto acabo tomó mucha planificación. La información tiene una eternidad y una urgencia, y crea una forma tridimensional que es satisfactoria y tiene real significado.

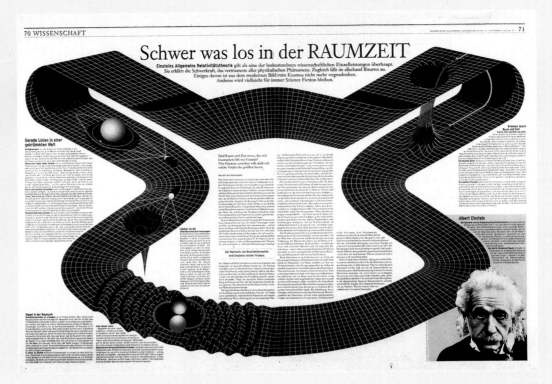

San Jose Mercury News
San Jose, Calif.

Science/Technology page/175,000 and over

Tracy Cox, Designer/Illustrator; **Bonita Burton**, Business Design Director; **Kris Viesselman**, Creative Director; **Matt Mansfield**, Deputy M.E.

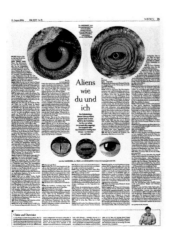

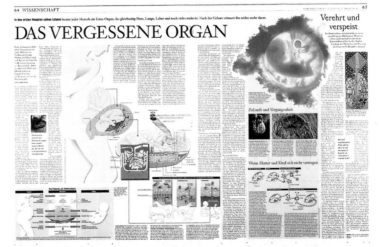

Frankfurter Allgemeine Sonntagszeitung
Frankfurt am Main, Germany

Science/Technology page/175,000 and over

Thomas Heumann, Infographics Director; **Karl-Heinz Döring**, Infographics Artist; **Anja Horn**, Layout; **Andreas Kuther**, Photo Editor; **Richard Friebe**, Science Editor

---

Die Zeit
Hamburg, Germany

Science/Technology page/175,000 and over

Staff

Frankfurter Allgemeine Sonntagszeitung
Frankfurt am Main, Germany

Science/Technology page/175,000 and over

Thomas Heumann, Infographics Director; **Karl-Heinz Döring**, Infographics Artist; **Anja Horn**, Layout; **Andreas Kuther**, Photo Editor; **Irene Meichsner**, Science Author; **Volker Stollorz**, Science Author

El Mundo Metropoli
Madrid, Spain

Magazines/Cover design

Rodrigo Sanchez, Art Director &
Designer; **Maria Gonzalez,** Designer;
Carmelo Caderot, Design Director

The New York Times Magazine
New York, N.Y.

Magazines/Cover design

Janet Froelich, Creative Director; **Arem
Duplessis,** Art Director; **Kristina DiMatteo,**
Designer; **Michael Ian Kaye,** Illustrator

¿ P a s i ó n   o   t o r t u r a ?

La película de Mel Gibson

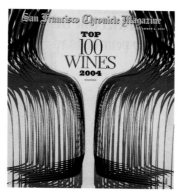

San Francisco Chronicle
San Francisco, Calif.

Magazines/Cover design

Nanette Bisher, Creative Director; **Joey
Riggs,** Art Director; **George Russell,**
Associate Art Director; **Alison Biggar,**
Editor; **Laura Compton,** Senior Editor;
Kathleen Hennessy, Photo Editor; **Lance
Jackson,** Illustrator; **Jerry Telfer,** Color
Prepresser

Conceptually this cover goes above
and beyond the obvious. It uses
the form of cover design in a fresh
way, shoving the barbed wire to
the top in tense way, so you feel the
emptiness beneath.

Conceptualmente, esta tapa va por
encima y más allá de lo evidente.
Usa el formato de diseño de tapa
de manera fresca, empujando el
alambre púa hacia arriba de forma
tensa, con el fin de que uno pueda
sentir el vacío debajo.

SILVER

El Mundo Metropoli
Madrid, Spain

*Magazines/Cover
design*

Rodrigo Sanchez, Art
Director & Designer;
Maria Gonzalez,
Designer; **Carmelo
Caderot,** Design
Director; **Angel
Becerril,** Photographer

El Mundo Magazine
Madrid, Spain

Magazines/Special sections

Rodrigo Sanchez, Art Director & Designer; **Maria Gonzalez,** Designer;
Natalia Buño, Designer; **Javier Sanz,** Designer; **Carmelo Caderot,**
Design Director

El Mundo Metropoli
Madrid, Spain

Magazines/Cover design

Rodrigo Sanchez, Art Director & Designer; **Maria
Gonzalez,** Designer; **Carmelo Caderot,** Design
Director

El Mundo Metropoli
Madrid, Spain

Magazines/Cover design

Rodrigo Sanchez, Art Director & Designer;
Maria Gonzalez, Designer; **Carmelo
Caderot,** Design Director; **Raul Arias,**
Illustrator

Dagens Nyheter
Stockholm, Sweden

Magazines/Cover design

Ebba Bonde, Art Director; **Fredrik Funch,** Photographer; **Pär Biörkman,** Photo Editor

El Mundo Metropoli
Madrid, Spain

Magazines/Cover design

Rodrigo Sanchez, Art Director & Designer; **Maria Gonzalez,** Designer; **Carmelo Caderot,** Design Director

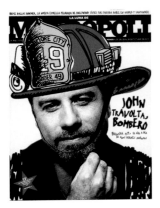

El Mundo Metropoli
Madrid, Spain

Magazines/Cover design

Rodrigo Sanchez, Art Director & Designer; **Maria Gonzalez,** Designer; **Carmelo Caderot,** Design Director; **Natalia Buño,** Illustrator

El Mundo Metropoli
Madrid, Spain

Magazines/Cover design

Rodrigo Sanchez, Art Director & Designer; **Maria Gonzalez,** Designer; **Carmelo Caderot,** Design Director

San Francisco Chronicle
San Francisco, Calif.

Magazines/Cover design

Nanette Bisher, Creative Director; **Joey Riggs,** Art Director; **George Russell,** Associate Art Director; **Alision Biggar,** Editor; **Laura Compton,** Senior Editor; **Kathleen Hennessy,** Photo Editor; **Christian Northeast,** Illustrator; **Jerry Telfer,** Color Prepresser

The Globe and Mail
Toronto, Ontario, Canada

Opinion page design/175,000 and over

Cinders McLeod, Design Editor; **David Pratt,** Executive Art Editor; **David Woodside,** Weekend Design Editor; **Steve Adams,** Illustrator; **Jerry Johnson,** Focus Editor; **Cathrin Bradbury,** Weekend Editor

SILVER

The New York Times Magazine
New York, N.Y.

Magazines/Cover design

Janet Froelich, Creative Director; **Arem Duplessis,** Art Director; **Kristina Dimatteo,** Designer; **Zachary Scott,** Photographer; **Kathy Ryan,** Photo Editor

You almost sense that the blackboard is an extension of the child's imagination, as big as the universe. You can spend a lot of time looking at the subtle details, such as the chalk wiped on the back of his pants and the areas of chalkboard where the drawing has been erased and redrawn.

Casi se siente que la pizarra es la extensión de la imaginación infantil, tan grande como el universo entero. Se puede pasar un buen rato mirando los sutiles detalles, como la tiza borrada en el dorso de sus pantalones y las áreas de la pizarra donde el dibujo se ha borrado y vuelto a dibujar.

The New York Times Magazine
New York, N.Y.

Magazines/ Special sections

Janet Froelich, Creative Director; **Arem Duplessis,** Art Director; **Jeff Glendenning,** Designer; **Kathy Ryan,** Photo Editor

Zaman
Istanbul, Turkey

Opinion page design/175,000 and over

Fevzi Yazici, Art Director; **Ekrem Dumanli**, Editor-in-Chief; **Mustafa Saglam**, Design Director; **Osman Turhan**, Illustrator; **Yasemin Alay**, Designer

The New York Times
New York, N.Y.

Opinion page design/175,000 and over

Nicholas Blechman, Art Director; **M.K. Mabry**, Illustrator

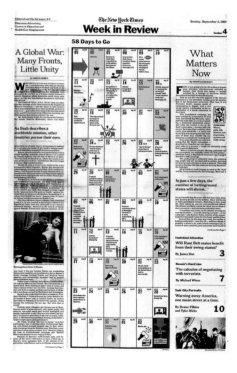

Toronto Star
Toronto, Ontario, Canada

Opinion page design/175,000 and over

Spencer Wynn, Designer; **Patrick McCormick**, Editor; **Catherine Pike**, Art Director; **Carl Neustaedter**, A.M.E. Design; **Bill Schiller**, Section Editor; **Raffi Anderian**, Illustrator

Heraldo de Aragón
Zaragoza, Spain

Lifestyle/Features section design/50,000-174,999

Javier Errea, Art Director; **Ana Perez**, Designer; **Kristina Urresti**, Designer; **Asier Barrio**, Designer; **Pilar Ostale**, Designer Manager; **Carmelo Roy**, Designer

The New York Times Magazine
New York, N.Y.

Magazines/Inside page design

Janet Froelich, Creative Director; **Arem Duplessis**, Art Director; **Nancy Harris**, Designer; **Kathy Ryan**, Photo Editor

The Boston Globe
Boston, Mass.

Opinion page design/175,000 and over

Jennifer Schuessler, Editor; **Gregory Klee,** Designer; **Dan Zedek,** Design Director

Chicago Tribune
Chicago, Ill.

Opinion page design/175,000 and over

Mike Miner, Art Director; **Charles M. Madigan,** Editor

Die Zeit
Hamburg, Germany

Opinion page design/175,000 and over

Staff

China Times
Taipei, Taiwan

Lifestyle/Features page design/175,000 and over

Tang Ai Feng, Graphic Designer

Los Angeles Times
Los Angeles, Calif.

Lifestyle/Features section design/175,000 and over

Judy Pryor, Design Editor; **Carrie Barber,** Design Editor; **Hal Wells,** Photo Editor; **Kelli Sullivan,** Deputy Design Director; **Joseph Hutchinson,** Deputy M.E.; **Staff**

Los Angeles Times
Los Angeles, Calif.

Home/Real estate section design/175,000 and over

Joseph Hutchinson, Deputy M.E.; **Christian Potter Drury,** Features Design Director; **Kelli Sullivan,** Deputy Design Director; **Jan Molen,** Design Editor; **Iris Schneider,** Photo Editor

Chicago Tribune
Chicago, Ill.

Opinion page design/175,000 and over

Mike Miner, Art
Director; **Charles M.
Madigan,** Editor

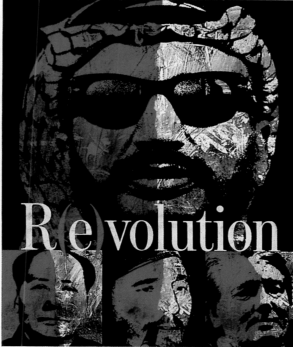

R(e)volution

Arafat: Great figure, even greater enigma
By Ron Grossman

For Castro, survival is guiding principle
By Patrick Rucker

Ukraine: A rebellion turns to rule of law
By Yohanan Petrovsky-Shtern

Chicago Tribune
Chicago, Ill.

Opinion page design/175,000 and over

Mike Miner, Art
Director; **Charles M.
Madigan,** Editor; **Rick
Tuma,** Illustrator

THE AMERICAN PRESIDENT AT WAR

**The
Boston Globe**
Boston, Mass.

Opinion page design/175,000 and over

Jennifer Schuessler,
Editor; **Gregory Klee,**
Designer; **Dan Zedek,**
Design Director

Ideas & Books

LOCKED IN

War stories

Iraq, Then and Now

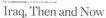

Another kind of fear

Canadian photographer Farah Nosh has felt Iraqis' despair, before and after the war
'The fear remains,' she writes of everyday life, 'it just has different causes now'

**San Francisco
Chronicle**
San Francisco, Calif.

Opinion page design/175,000 and over

Nanette Bisher,
Creative Director; **Lois
Kazakoff,** Deputy
Editorial Page Editor;
John Sullivan, Editorial
Page Editor; **Lance
Jackson,** Illustrator &
Designer

7d5!
111110
10101!
2005!

Toronto Star
Toronto, Ontario, Canada

Opinion page design/175,000 and over

Spencer Wynn, Designer; **Patrick McCormick,** Editor; **Catherine Pike,** Art Director; **Carl
Neustaedter,** A.M.E. Design; **Bill Schiller,** Section Editor; **Farah Nosh,** Photographer

El Mundo
Madrid, Spain

Opinion page design/175,000 and over

Carmelo Caderot, Design Director; **Manuel De Miguel,** Art Director & Designer; **Ricardo Martinez,** Illustrator

South Florida Sun-Sentinel
Fort Lauderdale, Fla.

Opinion page design/175,000 and over

Robyn Wishna, Designer; **Michael Laughlin,** Photographer; **Tim Rasmussen,** Photo Director

The Boston Globe
Boston, Mass.

Opinion page design/175,000 and over

Jennifer Schuessler, Editor; **Gregory Klee,** Designer; **Dan Zedek,** Design Director

San Jose Mercury News
San Jose, Calif.

Opinion page design/175,000 and over

Kevin Wendt, News Design Director; **Matt Mansfield,** Deputy M.E.; **Doug Griswold,** Artist; **Kim Fararo,** Perspective Editor

The Baltimore Sun
Baltimore, Md.

Opinion page design/175,000 and over

Michael Workman, Sports Design Editor

San Francisco Chronicle
San Francisco, Calif.

Opinion page design/175,000 and over

Nanette Bisher, Creative Director; **Lois Kazakoff,** Deputy Editorial Page Editor; **John Sullivan,** Editorial Page Editor; **Lance Jackson,** Illustrator & Designer

Chicago Tribune
Chicago, Ill.

Opinion page design/175,000 and over

Mike Miner, Art Director; **Charles M. Madigan,** Editor

Reading Eagle
Reading, Pa.

Opinion page design/50,000-174,999

Charles M. Gallagher, M.E.; **Grant Mahon,** Design Editor

The Boston Globe
Boston, Mass.

Opinion page design/175,000 and over

Jennifer Schuessler, Editor; **Gregory Klee,** Designer; **Dan Zedek,** Design Director

Chicago Tribune
Chicago, Ill.

Opinion page design/175,000 and over

Mike Miner, Art Director; **Charles M. Madigan,** Editor

Svenska Dagbladet
Stockholm, Sweden

Lifestyle/Features page design/175,000 and over

Jurek Holzer, Photographer; **Staff**

The Independent
London, England

Lifestyle/Features page design/175,000 and over

Adam Leigh, Review Editor; **Dan Barber,** Deputy Art Director; **Olyn Blair,** Artworker

Arizona Daily Star
Tucson, Ariz.

Lifestyle/Features page design/50,000-174,999

Hugo Torres, Page Designer; **José Merino,** Design Director

Arizona Daily Star
Tucson, Ariz.

Lifestyle/ Features page design/50,000- 174,999

Maria Camou de Toledo, Page Designer; **Chiara Bautista,** Graphic Artist; **José Merino,** Design Director

Accent

COLOR COMPLEX
Skin-tone debate raises awareness of a continuing bias

Loft offers one-time screening of film that censures Bush's Iraq war policies

Politiken
Copenhagen, Denmark

Lifestyle/ Features page design/50,000- 174,999

Søren Nyeland, Design Editor; **Jesper Friis,** Editor; **Mai-Britt Bernt Jensen,** Designer; **Søren Hansen,** Copy Editor

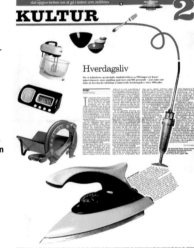

KULTUR 2

Hverdagsliv

Arizona Daily Star
Tucson, Ariz.

Lifestyle/ Features page design/50,000- 174,999

Sid Steketee, Page Designer; **José Merino,** Design Director

SundayAccent

SIMPLE SYMBOL

It's not the design but the beliefs attached to it that are so complex

San Francisco Chronicle
San Francisco, Calif.

Lifestyle/Features page design/175,000 and over

Rico Mendez, Page Designer; **Matt Petty,** Art Director; **Nanette Bisher,** Creative Director; **Art Rogers,** Photographer; **Paul Wilner,** Editor

TIME LAPSE

Dagens Nyheter
Stockholm, Sweden

Lifestyle/Features page design/175,000 and over

Johan Rutherhagen, Art Director; **Nina Andén,** Page Designer; **Åse Bengtsson,** Photo Editor; **Elin Berge,** Photographer

El Norte
Monterrey, México

Lifestyle/ Features page design/50,000- 174,999

Edgar García Rodríguez, Designer; **Fernando Santiago,** Illustrator; **Guillermo Reyes Aguilar,** A.M.E.; **Carlos Martínez Salas,** Section Editor; **Martha Treviño,** Editor

Arte
Dos clásicos en busca de lectores

The Seattle Times
Seattle, Wash.

Lifestyle/Features page design/175,000 and over

Boo Davis, Designer/Illustrator

NORTHWEST LIFE

The rule of COOL

The Sacramento Bee
Sacramento, Calif.

Lifestyle/Features page design/175,000 and over

Margaret Spengler, Designer;
Howard Shintaku, Design
Director; **Barbara Stubbs,**
Assistant Director/Design; **Pam
Dinsmore,** A.M.E. Features/
Design

VARIETY

TUESDAY
November 2, 2004

CAST YOUR BALLOT in the nation's 55th presidential election. On a lighter note for Decision Tuesday, we take a look back at colorful campaigns of years past, from a squeaky-close state race to a rhinoceros that led its party. E2.

Who needs a defibrillator at home?

ABCs aflutter

Alphabet captures beauty, variety of butterflies

The Columbus Dispatch
Columbus, Ohio

*Lifestyle/
Features page
design/175,000
and over*

Todd Bayha, Page
Designer; **Scott
Minister,** Art
Director

Star Tribune
Minneapolis, Minn.

*Lifestyle/Features page
design/175,000 and over*

Tippi Thole, Features Designer;
Lisa Clausen, Features Design
Director; **Joel Koyama,**
Photographer; **Randy Miranda,**
Variety Editor

Politiken
Copenhagen, Denmark

Lifestyle/Features page design/175,000 and over

Søren Nyeland, Design Editor; **Christian Ilsøe,** Editor; **Mai-
Britt Bernt Jensen,** Designer

The Independent
London, England

Lifestyle/Features page design/175,000 and over

Adam Leigh, Review Editor; **Dan Barber,** Deputy Art
Director; **Olyn Blair,** Artworker

The Holiday Issue

The Independent
London, England

Lifestyle/Features page design/175,000 and over

Adam Leigh, Review Editor; **Dan Barber,** Deputy Art Director; **Max Ellis,**
Illustrator

Star Tribune
Minneapolis,
Minn.

*Lifestyle/
Features page
design/175,000
and over*

Tippi Thole,
Features Designer;
Lisa Clausen,
Features Design
Director; **Mark
Boswell,**
Illustrator; **Randy
Miranda,** Variety
Editor

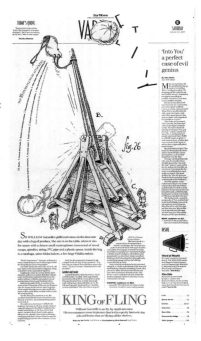

KING OF FLING

**Dagens
Nyheter**
Stockholm,
Sweden

*Lifestyle/Features
page design/
175,000 and over*

Lotta Ek, Art
Director; **Nina
Andén,** Page
Designer; **Pär
Björkman,**
Photo Editor;
Auette Nantell,
Photographer

CIRKUSLIV

Hartford Courant
Hartford, Conn.

Lifestyle/Features page design/175,000 and over

Chris Moore, Assistant Director/Design

**Hartford
Courant**
Hartford, Conn.

*Lifestyle/
Features page
design/175,000
and over*

**Jennifer
Rochette,**
Features Designer;
Suzette Moyer,
Director/Design
& Graphics; **Chris
Moore,** Assistant
Director/Design;
**Richard
Messina,**
Photographer

CAN-DO ATTITUDE

Images Of High School Manners

Bringing Your Spirit To Work

LIEBERMAN AND THE JEWISH MEDIA

'Do It Yourself'
Trend Builds To A Whole New Level:
Phenomenon

MTV Returns To Roots

Networks Loaded For Sweeps
With New Episodes, Specials

Hartford Courant
Hartford, Conn.

*Lifestyle/Features
page design/
175,000 and over*

Jennifer Rochette,
Features Designer;
Suzette Moyer,
Director/Design
& Graphics; **Chris
Moore,** Assistant
Director/Design

'Wedding Gifts' for 'Cathy' Will Help Homeless Pets

Los Angeles Times
Los Angeles, Calif.

*Lifestyle/Features page
design/175,000 and over*

Judy Pryor, Design
Editor; **Joseph
Hutchinson,** Deputy
M.E.; **Kelli Sullivan,**
Deputy Design Director;
Jack Unruh, Illustrator

THE COLLECTOR'S EDITION
OUTDOORS

All about trout

Komm
zurück,
Pop

Die Welt/Berliner Morgen Post
Berlin, Germany

Lifestyle/Features page design/50,000-174,999

Barbara Krämer, Page Designer & Photo Editor; **Tom
Uecker,** Digital Imaging; **Sandra Garbers,** Editor; **Jan
Draeger,** Editor

Dagens Nyheter
Stockholm, Sweden

Lifestyle/Features page design/175,000 and over

Pelle Asplund, Art Director; **Anne-Li Karlsson,** Illustrator

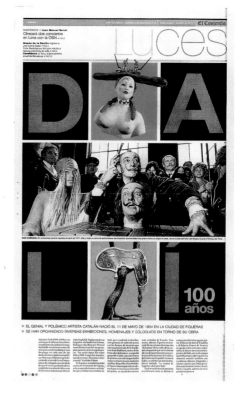

El Comercio
Lima, Peru

*Lifestyle/
Features page
design/175,000
and over*

**Xabier Diaz
de Cerio,** Art
Director; **Paola
Damonte,**
Design Editor;
**Verónica
Salem,** Graphics
Editor; **Milagros
Valenzuela,**
Graphic
Designer; **Rosa
Romero,**
Designer

CLUTCH ME!

LOVE ME, SQUEEZE ME, NEVER LEAVE ME

POLITICAL FOOD FIGHT

**Hartford
Courant**
Hartford, Conn.

*Lifestyle/
Features page
design/175,000
and over*

Chris Moore,
Assistant
Director/Design;
Mark Mirko,
Photographer

National Post
Toronto, Ontario, Canada

Lifestyle/Features page design/175,000 and over

Gayle Grin, A.M.E./Visuals; **Matthew Fraser,** Editor-in-Chief; **Sarah Murdoch,** M.E./Features; **Shielagh McEvenue,** Saturday Post Editor; **Christine Dewairy,** Saturday Post Art Dir./Designer

National Post
Toronto, Ontario,
Canada

*Lifestyle/
Features page
design/175,000
and over*

Gayle Grin, A.M.E./
Visuals/Designer;
Matthew Fraser,
Editor-in-Chief;
Ben Errett, Avenue
Editor

Teresa, Interrupted

The Boston Globe
Boston, Mass.

Magazines/Inside page design

Erin Jang, Assistant Art Director/Designer

Die Zeit
Hamburg, Germany

Lifestyle/Features page design/175,000 and over

Staff

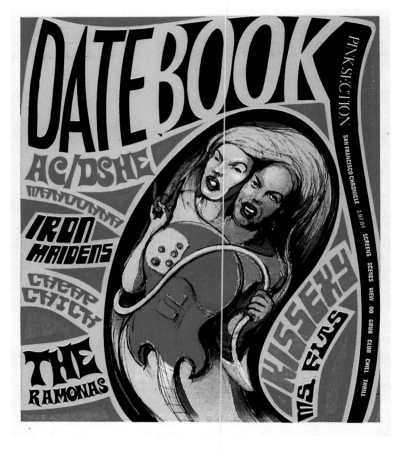

San Francisco Chronicle
San Francisco, Calif.

Entertainment page design/175,000 and over

Joe Brown, Pink Editor; **Matt Petty,** Art Director; **Nanette Bisher,** Creative Director; **Lance Jackson,** Illustrator

---

The Plain Dealer
Cleveland, Ohio

Lifestyle/ Features page design/175,000 and over

Andrea Levy, Illustrator; **Adrian Johnson,** Designer

Chicago Tribune
Chicago, Ill.

Entertainment page design/175,000 and over

Stephen Ravenscraft, Art Director; **Linda Bergstrom,** Editor; **Pablo,** Illustrator

Chicago Tribune
Chicago, Ill.

Entertainment page design/175,000 and over

Jason McKean, Art Director; **Heidi Stevens,** Assistant Editor

---

La Revista
México City, México

Magazines/Inside page design

Ignacio Rodriguez Reyna, Director; **Margela Rivas,** Graphics Editor; **Adrian Mealand,** Photo Editor; **Roberto Canseco,** Designer

Detroit Free Press
Detroit, Mich.

Other feature page design/175,000 and over

Pat Sedlar, Designer; **Mauricio Gutierrez,** Deputy Design Director/ Features; **Steve Dorsey,** Design & Graphics Director

The Orange County Register
Santa Ana, Calif.

Entertainment page design/175,000 and over

Rick Ngoc Ho, Designer

Chicago Tribune
Chicago, Ill.

Entertainment page design/175,000 and over

Jason McKean, Art Director; **Travis Coburn,** Illustrator;
Heidi Stevens, Assistant Editor

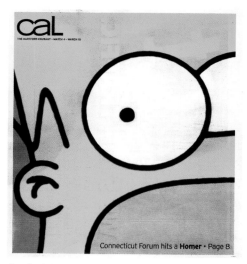

Hartford Courant
Hartford, Conn.

Entertainment page design/175,000 and over

Chris Moore, Assistant Director/Design

The Seattle Times
Seattle, Wash.

Entertainment page design/175,000 and over

Boo Davis,
Designer/Illustrator

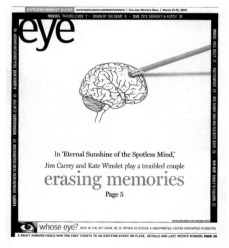

San Jose Mercury News
San Jose, Calif.

Entertainment page design/175,000 and over

Stephanie Grace Lim, Designer/Illustrator

Göteborgs-Posten
Goteborg, Sweden

Entertainment page design/175,000 and over

Magnus Nilsson, Designer; **Cissi Welin,** Illustrator

El Mundo
Madrid, Spain

Magazines/ Inside page design

Carmelo Caderot, Design Director;
Manuel De Miguel, Art Director & Designer

San Jose Mercury News
San Jose, Calif.

Entertainment page design/175,000 and over

Stephanie Grace Lim, Designer/ Illustrator

Hartford Courant
Hartford, Conn.

Entertainment page design/175,000 and over

Chris Moore, Assistant Director/Design; **Tim Reck,** Designer; **Felix Sockwell,** Illustrator; **Suzette Moyer,** Director/Design & Graphics

Público
Lisbon, Portugal

Entertainment page design/50,000-174,999

Isabel Coutinho, Editor; **Jorge Guimarães,** Designer; **Fernanda Fragateiro,** Illustrator

Público
Lisbon, Portugal

Entertainment page design/50,000-174,999

Isabel Coutinho, Editor; **Jorge Guimarães,** Designer; **Cristina Sampaio,** Illustrator

Hartford Courant
Hartford, Conn.

Food page design/175,000 and over

Chris Moore, Assistant Director/Design; **Sherry Peters,** Photographer; **Allison Corbett,** Photo Editor

Göteborgs-Posten
Goteborg, Sweden

Food page design/175,000 and over

Gunilla Wernhamn, Designer; **Thomas Yeh,** Photographer/Illustrator

San Francisco Chronicle
San Francisco, Calif.

Entertainment page design/175,000 and over

Joe Brown, Pink Editor; **Matt Petty,** Art Director; **Nanette Bisher,** Creative Director; **Patrick McDonnell,** Illustrator

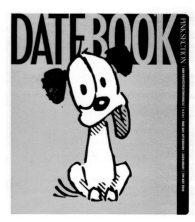

Die Rache der Hamster

VON SUSANNE FRÖMEL

Die Stadt Mainz will einen Gewerbepark bauen. Doch auf dem Baugelände leben seltene Feldhamster. Sobald sie aus dem Winterschlaf erwachen, sollen sie in eine andere Gegend gelockt werden. Das wird nicht ganz einfach

Die Zeit
Hamburg, Germany

*Home/Real estate
page design/175,000
and over*

Staff

Los Angeles Times

FOOD

Wednesday, December 15, 2004

SPECIAL HOLIDAY ISSUE

THE FLAVORS OF CHRISTMAS

Oriental spices, essential fruits, soulful brandy: These little luxuries all come together for the holiday.

By Regina Schrambling

Dark and silky
Chocolate makes the ultimate holiday confections. Page 2

Divisive spirit
Which is the world's best brandy, Cognac or Armagnac? Page 9

Santa, please?
The dreams of a flavor of his own: let's just say it's from Piedmont. Page 9

Los Angeles Times
Los Angeles, Calif.

Food page design/175,000 and over

Joseph Hutchinson, Deputy M.E.; **Christian Potter Drury,** Features Design Director; **Wes Bausmith,** Design Editor; **Ricardo DeAratanha,** Photographer; **Richard Derk,** Photo Editor

---

Chicago Tribune

7 GOOD EATING WEDNESDAY SEPTEMBER 1, 2004

A growing crop of new flavors brings culinary opportunities—and new questions

Oil boom

WALNUT RICE BRAN GRAPESEED HAZELNUT ALMOND AVOCADO

By Judith Weinraub / Tribune staff reporter

Tribune photo by Bob Fila

INSIDE GOOD EATING

Chicago Tribune
Chicago, Ill.

Food page design/175,000 and over

Catherine Nichols, Art Director; **Bob Fila,** Photographer; **Carol Haddix,** Editor

---

Science & Health

EXPLORING THE RED PLANET

FROM PANORAMAS TO CLOSE-UPS, CAMERAS SURVEY LANDSCAPE

Identifying landmarks at Gusev Crater

Viewing the crater: The Spirit Rover

Exploring sites at Meridiani Planum

Hitting bedrock: The Opportunity Rover

Finding Mars' true colors

Placing new eyes on Mars

San Jose Mercury News
San Jose, Calif.

Science/Technology page/175,000 and over

Javier Zarracina, Deputy Graphics Director; **Andrea Maschietto,** Graphic Artist; **Kris Viesselman,** Creative Director; **HyunJu Chappell-Hine,** Designer; **Glennda Chui,** Reporter

---

7 GOOD EATING WEDNESDAY

Bean boom

Chicago's roasters help fuel the growing demand for gourmet coffees

INSIDE GOOD EATING

Chicago Tribune
Chicago, Ill.

Food page design/175,000 and over

Catherine Nichols, Art Director; **Bob Fila,** Photographer; **Carol Haddix,** Editor; **Joe Gray,** Assistant Editor

Los Angeles Times
Los Angeles, Calif.

Food page design/175,000 and over

Joseph Hutchinson, Deputy M.E.; **Christian Potter Drury**, Features Design Director; **Wes Bausmith**, Design Editor; **Judy Pryor**, Design Editor; **Richard Derk**, Photo Editor; **Ken Hively**, Photographer

Arizona Daily Star
Tucson, Ariz.

Food page design/ 50,000-174,999

Hugo Torres,
Page Designer;
José Merino,
Design Director

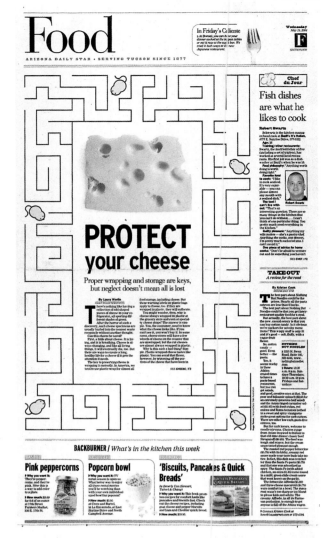

Chicago Tribune
Chicago, Ill.

Food page design/175,000 and over

Catherine Nichols, Art Director; **Carol Haddix**, Editor; **Serge Bloch**, Illustrator

Star Tribune
Minneapolis; Minn.

Food page design/175,000 and over

Rhonda Prast, Assistant Design Director/News; **Lee Dean**, Taste Editor; **Rick Sennott**, Photographer

Chicago Tribune
Chicago, Ill.

Food page design/175,000 and over

Catherine Nichols, Art Director; **Bob Fila**, Photographer; **Carol Haddix**, Editor; **Joe Gray**, Assistant Editor

Los Angeles Times
Los Angeles, Calif.

Food page design/175,000 and over

Joseph Hutchinson, Deputy M.E.; **Christian Potter Drury**, Features Design Director; **Wes Bausmith**, Design Editor; **Ken Hively**, Photographer; **Richard Derk**, Photo Editor

Hartford Courant
Hartford, Conn.

Food page design/175,000 and over

Chris Moore, Assistant Director/Design; **Suzette Moyer**, Director/Design & Graphics

The Plain Dealer
Cleveland, Ohio

Home/Real estate page design/175,000 and over

Amanda Hamann, Lead Features Designer

South Florida Sun-Sentinel
Fort Lauderdale, Fla.

Travel page/175,000 and over

Susana Sanchez, Designer; **Ben Crandell,** Features Art Director; **Tom Peyton,** Visual Editor

Hartford Courant
Hartford, Conn.

Fashion page design/175,000 and over

Jennifer Rochette, Features Page Designer; **Suzette Moyer,** Director/Design & Graphics; **Chris Moore,** Assistant Director/Design

Los Angeles Times
Los Angeles, Calif.

Home/Real estate page design/175,000 and over

Iris Schneider, Photo Editor; **Kelli Sullivan,** Deputy Design Director; **Joseph Hutchinson,** Deputy M.E.; **Christian Potter Drury,** Features Design Director

The Plain Dealer
Cleveland, Ohio

Home/Real estate page design/175,000 and over

Maty Lou Sneyd, Designer

Dagens Nyheter
Stockholm, Sweden

Fashion page design/175,000   and over

Markus Edin, Art Director; **Karin Mårtensson,** Illustrator

Politiken
Copenhagen, Denmark

Fashion page design/175,000 and over

Søren Nyeland, Design Editor; **Christine Cato,** Designer; **Marianne Gram,** Editor; **Sidse Lange,** Designer;

Martin Lehmann, Photographer; **Edel Hildebrandt,** Copy Editor; **Annette Nyvang,** Copy Editor

Los Angeles Times
Los Angeles, Calif.

Home/Real estate page design/175,000 and over

Joseph Hutchinson, Deputy M.E.; **Christian Potter Drury,** Features Design Director; **Kelli Sullivan,** Deputy Design Director; **Iris Schneider,** Photo Editor; **Francine Orr,** Photographer

Los Angeles Times
HOME
Thursday, August 26, 2004

DECORATING
Pamper your walls
What makes a can of paint worth $50 a gallon? The color, of course — and more special effects than a summer blockbuster. There are shades that scream and grand finishes that evoke vistas of windswept sand. Lifting the lid on L.A.'s latest decorating craze. *Page 8*

THE CALIFORNIA GARDEN
Creating beauty, the hard way

BETWEEN US
The ghosts of owners past

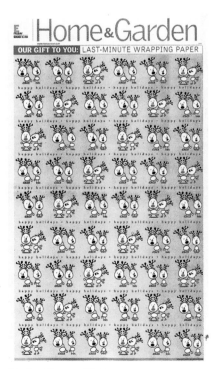

Home&Garden
OUR GIFT TO YOU: LAST-MINUTE WRAPPING PAPER

San Jose Mercury News
San Jose, Calif.

Home/Real estate page design/175,000 and over

Stephanie Grace Lim, Features Design Director; **David Frazier,** Features Design Director

THE HARTFORD COURANT
AT HOME
FRIDAY, OCTOBER 22, 2004

By JENNA CHO
COURANT STAFF WRITER

Just as fashion trends mark an era, so does the way we dress our walls.

Wallpaper, that material our parents and grandparents used to spiff up their homes, is back in style, and it's not just Grandma's wall coverings that are hip again.

Patterns are in. Color is in. And for the very fashionable, there are oversized periods and commas amidst seas of orange.

The sale of wallpaper, which according to the Paint and Decorating Retailers Association was only $1.03 billion last year compared with $4.2 billion in 1963, is being given a big nudge as it attempts to reinvent itself in the modern home.

"I love wallpaper because it can really transform a room, even more than color can," says Thea Davidson of Thea Davidson Design Co. in Avon. "I'm pattern hungry and love being able to introduce pattern, whether it be subtle or elaborate."

PLEASE SEE WALLPAPER, PAGE H8

Swank Wear For Walls

With A Bit Of Bold Here, A Trace Of Traditional There, Patterns Are Back

Hartford Courant
Hartford, Conn.

Home/Real estate page design/175,000 and over

Chris Moore,
Assistant Director/Design

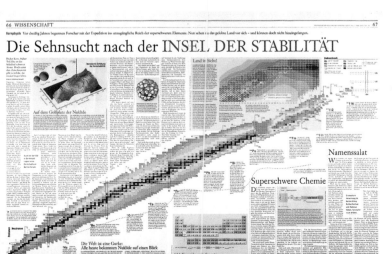

66 WISSENSCHAFT

Kernphysik Vor dreißig Jahren begannen Forscher mit der Expedition ins unzugängliche Reich der superschweren Elemente. Nun scheint's: das gelobte Land vor sich – und können doch nicht hineingelangen.

Die Sehnsucht nach der INSEL DER STABILITÄT

67

Frankfurter Allgemeine Sonntagszeitung
Frankfurt am Main, Germany

Science/Technology page/175,000 and over

Thomas Heumann, Infographics Director; **Karl-Heinz Döring,** Infographics Artist; **Anja Horn,** Layouter; **Karsten Middeldorf,** Layouter; **Ulf von Rauchhaupt,** Science Editor

San Jose Mercury News
San Jose, Calif.

Science/Technology page/175,000 and over

Tracy Cox, Designer; **Javier Zarracina,** Deputy Graphics Director; **Kris Viesselman,** Creative Director; **Matt Mansfield,** Deputy M.E.

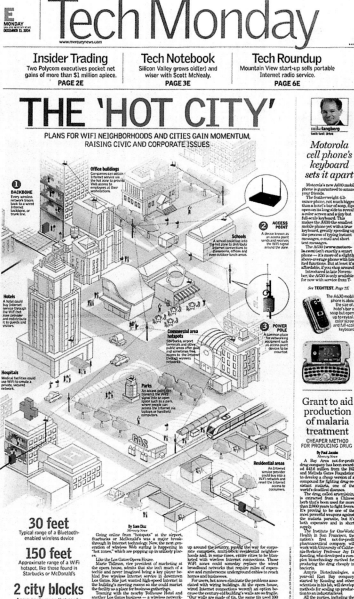

The New York Times
New York, N.Y.

Travel page/175,000 and over

Barbara Richer, Art Director;
Edwin Fotheringham, Illustrator

The Spokesman-Review
Spokane, Wash.

Travel page/50,000-174,999

Ralph Walter, Page Designer;
Brian Plonka, Photographer;
Geoff Pinnock, Design Director;
Bart Rayniak, Photo Editor

SonntagsZeitung
Zürich, Switzerland

Science/Technology page/175,000 and over

Stefan Semrau, Art Director;
Andrea Müller, Designer; **Edith Huwiler,** Infographic Artist; **Tobias Peier,** Infographic Artist

Göteborgs-Posten
Goteborg, Sweden

Other feature page design/175,000 and over

Gunilla Wernhamn, Designer/Illustrator;
Thord Eriksson, Photographer

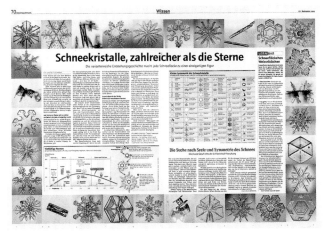

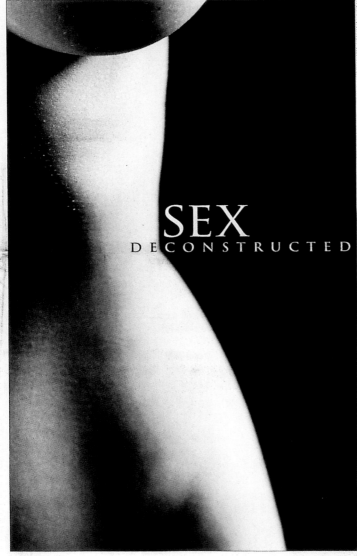

THE SUNDAY MAGAZINE OF THE HARTFORD COURANT | FEBRUARY 8, 2004

NORTHEAST

SEX DECONSTRUCTED

A THERAPIST TALKS ABOUT WOMEN, SEXUALITY AND WHAT "IT" IS. PLUS: AN ARRANGED MARRIAGE, TRUE LOVE ONLINE, EIGHT-MINUTE DATES, HOOKING UP ON CAMPUS, THE ACCESSORY PARTY AND THE FOOD OF LOVE

A SPECIAL ISSUE

Hartford Courant
Hartford, Conn.

Magazines/Cover design

Melanie Shaffer, Assistant Director/Design; **Bruce Moyer,** Photo Editor; **Sherry Peters,** Photographer; **Suzette Moyer,** Design Director; **Thom McGuire,** A.M.E. Graphics/Photo

Die Zeit
Hamburg, Germany

Science/Technology page/175,000 and over

Staff

Frankfurter Allgemeine Sonntagszeitung
Frankfurt am Main, Germany

Science/Technology page/175,000 and over

Thomas Heumann, Infographics Director; **Karl-Heinz Döring,** Infographics Artist; **Doris Oberneder,** Layout; **Andreas Kuther,** Photo Editor; **Georg Rüschemeyer,** Science Author

El Mundo Metropoli
Madrid, Spain

Magazines/Cover design

Rodrigo Sanchez, Art Director & Designer; **Maria Gonzalez,** Designer; **Carmelo Caderot,** Design Director

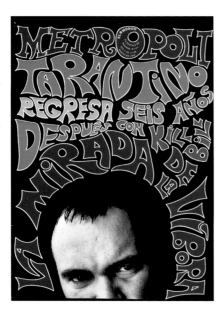

El Mundo Metropoli
Madrid, Spain

Magazines/Cover design

Rodrigo Sanchez, Art Director & Designer; **Maria Gonzalez,** Designer; **Carmelo Caderot,** Design Director; **Ulises Culebro,** Illustrator

El Mundo Metropoli
Madrid, Spain

Magazines/ Cover design

Rodrigo Sanchez, Art Director & Designer; **Maria Gonzalez,** Designer; **Carmelo Caderot,** Design Director

rooms with a view

PHOTOGRAPHS BY LYNN ISCHAY : THE PLAIN DEALER

Berliner Illustrirte Zeitung

Die Null muss stehen

Berlin hat einen Fußballverein. Er heißt Hertha BSC und ist erstklassig. Zumindest noch. Stolze 13 Punkte haben die Herthaner in der Vorrunde der Bundesliga-Saison geholt. Sonnabend geht es ausgerechnet zum Herbstmeister Werder Bremen. Aber all das ist gar nicht so wichtig. Wichtig ist, dass es Hertha vielen Menschen so schwer macht, sie zu lieben. Warum nur?

Wünsche an das Jahr 2005

The Boston Globe
Boston, Mass.

Magazines/Inside page design

Erin Jang, Assistant Art Director; **David Plunkert,** Illustrator; **Headcase Design,** Illustrator; **Marc Boutavant,** Illustrator; **Kent Dayton,** Photographer; **Doug Most,** Editor; **Brendan Stephens,** Art Director; **Dan Zedek,** Design Director

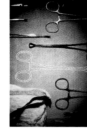

Left Behind

The stories are scary: A patient finds that his surgeon left a sponge or maybe a clamp in his body. But Atul Gawande is trying to write happier endings.

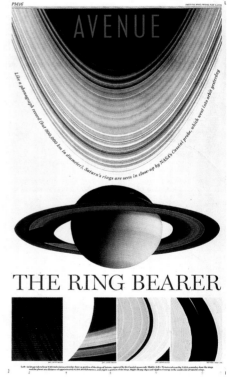

AVENUE

Like a phonograph record (but 300,000 km in diameter), Saturn's rings are seen in close-up by NASA's Cassini probe, which went into orbit yesterday.

THE RING BEARER

National Post
Toronto, Ontario, Canada

Other feature page design/175,000 and over

Gayle Grin, A.M.E./Visuals; **Matthew Fraser,** Editor-in-Chief; **Donna MacMullin,** Features Presentations Editor; **Ben Errett,** Arts and Life Editor; **Tracey Lazos,** Designer

68 WISSENSCHAFT

MIT FÜSSEN GETRETEN

Vom Acker gemacht

Frankfurter Allgemeine Sonntagszeitung
Frankfurt am Main, Germany

Science/Technology page/175,000 and over

Thomas Heumann, Infographics Director; **Karl-Heinz Döring,** Infographics Artist; **Doris Oberneder,** Layout; **Andreas Kuther,** Photo Editor; **Jonas Siehoff,** Text Author

Diário de Notícias
Lisbon, Portugal

Magazines/Inside page design

Jose Maria Ribeirinho, Art Director; Pedro Rolo Duarte, Director; Paulo Barata Corrêa, Art Editor; Nuno Janela, Designer; Hugo Neves, Designer; Sofia Perdigão, Designer

Diário de Notícias
Lisbon, Portugal

Magazines/Inside page design

José Maria Ribeirinho, Art Director; Pedro Rolo Duarte, Director; Paulo Barata Corrêa, Art Editor; Nuno Janela, Designer; Hugo Neves, Designer; Sofia Perdigão, Designer; Augusto Brázio, Photographer

El Mundo
Madrid, Spain

Magazines/Inside page design

Carmelo Caderot, Design Director; Manuel De Miguel, Art Director & Designer

The Boston Globe
Boston, Mass.

Home/Real estate page design/175,000 and over

Chin Wang, Art Director; Serge Bloch, Illustrator; Michael Prager, Editor; Dan Zedek, Design Director

The Washington Post Magazine
Washington, D.C.

Magazines/Cover design

J. Porter, Art Director; Keith Jenkins, Photo Editor; Jennifer Beeson, Assistant Photo Editor; Carla Fielder, Assistant Art Director; Leslie Garcia, Production Manager

Göteborgs-Posten
Goteborg, Sweden

Other feature page design/175,000 and over

Albert Rosander, Designer; Cissi Welin, Illustrator

El Mundo Metropoli
Madrid, Spain

Magazines/Cover design

Rodrigo Sanchez, Art Director & Designer; **Maria Gonzalez,** Designer; **Carmelo Caderot,** Design Director; **Raul Arias,** Illustrator

El Mundo Metropoli
Madrid, Spain

Magazines/Cover design

Rodrigo Sanchez, Art Director & Designer; **Maria Gonzalez,** Designer; **Carmelo Caderot,** Design Director; **Luis Parejo,** Illustrator

El Mundo Metropoli
Madrid, Spain

Magazines/ Cover design

Rodrigo Sanchez, Art Director & Designer; **Maria Gonzalez,** Designer; **Carmelo Caderot,** Design Director

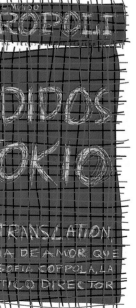

The Boston Globe
Boston, Mass.

Magazines/Inside page design

Josue Evilla, Assistant Art Director; **Webb Chappell,** Photographer; **Doug Most,** Editor; **Brendan Stephens,** Art Director; **Dan Zedek,** Design Director

The New York Times Magazine
New York, N.Y.

Magazines/Inside page design

Janet Froelich, Creative Director; **Joele Cuyler,** Designer; **Kathy Ryan,** Photo Editor; **Jean-Baptiste Mondino,** Photographer

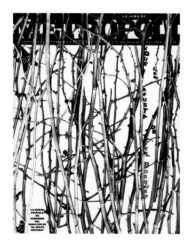

El Mundo Metropoli
Madrid, Spain

Magazines/Cover design

Rodrigo Sanchez, Art Director & Designer; **Maria Gonzalez,** Designer; **Carmelo Caderot,** Design Director

El Mundo Metropoli
Madrid, Spain

Magazines/Cover design

Rodrigo Sanchez, Art Director & Designer; **Maria Gonzalez,** Designer; **Carmelo Caderot,** Design Director

HERBIE'S BLUES
CHICAGO'S GIANT OF THE PIANO COMES HOME IN APRIL FOR A TRIUMPHANT WEEK OF PERFORMANCES.
BUT HE STRIKES A MOURNFUL NOTE IN DISCUSSING THE SHAKY FUTURE OF JAZZ.

BY HOWARD REICH
PHOTO BY JILL GREENBERG

16 | CHICAGO TRIBUNE MAGAZINE

Chicago Tribune Magazine
Chicago, Ill.

Magazines/Inside page design

David Syrek, Art Director;
Joseph Darrow, Art Director;
Jill Greenberg, Photographer;
Elizabeth Taylor, Editor

El Mundo
Madrid, Spain

Magazines/Inside page design

Carmelo Caderot, Design Director; **Manuel De Miguel,** Art Director & Designer

Marca
Madrid, Spain

*Magazines/
Inside page
design*

**Juan Carlos
Fernández,**
Designer/
Illustrator;
**Jose Juan
Gámez,**
Art Director;
**Antonio
Martín
Hervás,**
Design Director;
**Blanca
Serrano,**
Designer

Diário de Notícias
Lisbon, Portugal

Magazines/Inside page design

José Maria Ribeirinho, Art Director; **Pedro Rolo Duarte,** Director;
Paulo Barata Corrêa, Art Editor; **Nuno Janela,** Designer;
Hugo Neves, Designer; **Sofia Perdigão,** Designer

**Hartford
Courant**
Hartford, Conn.

*Magazines/
Overall design*

Vada Crosby,
Designer;
Suzette Moyer,
Director/Design
& Graphics;
Bruce Moyer,
Photo Editor;
Mel Shaffer,
Assistant
Director/Design;
Thom McGuire,
A.M.E. Graphics/
Photo

Changing All the Rules

How the Bush administration quietly — and radically — transformed the nation's clean-air policy.

By Bruce Barcott

Photographs by Mitch Epstein

The New York Times Magazine
New York, N.Y.

Magazines/Inside page design

Janet Froelich, Creative Director; **Arem Duplessis,** Art Director; **Joele Cuyler,** Designer; **Kathy Ryan,** Photo Editor; **Mitch Epstein,** Photographer

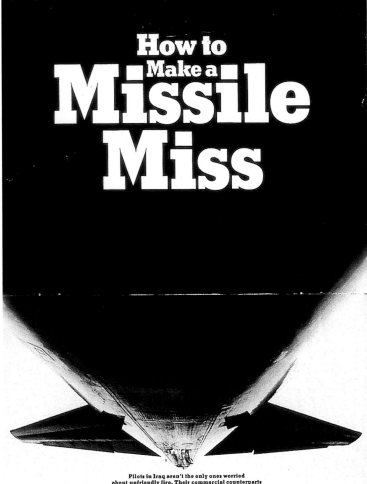

How to Make a Missile Miss

Pilots in Iraq aren't the only ones worried about unfriendly fire. Their commercial counterparts here in the U.S. are also looking for ways to avoid the threat of shoulder-launched rockets.

By Matthew Brzezinski

Photograph by Phillip Toledano

The New York Times Magazine
New York, N.Y.

Magazines/Inside page design

Janet Froelich, Creative Director; **Kathy Ryan,** Photo Editor; **Phillip Toledano,** Photographer

Göteborgs-Posten
Goteborg, Sweden

Other feature page design/175,000 and over

Stefan Renström, Designer; **Kurt M. Lightner,** Illustrator

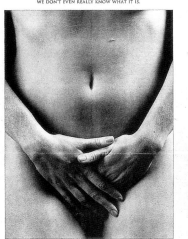

LEONORE TIEFER THINKS WE'RE LOOKING FOR SEX IN ALL THE WRONG PLACES. IN FACT, SHE SAYS, WE DON'T EVEN REALLY KNOW WHAT IT IS.

THE SNOW JOB

INTERVIEW BY DEBORAH PETERSEN SWIFT | PHOTOGRAPHS BY SHERRY PETERS

Hartford Courant
Hartford, Conn.

Magazines/Inside page design

Melanie Shaffer, Assistant Director/Design; **Bruce Moyer,** Photo Editor; **Sherry Peters,** Photographer; **Suzette Moyer,** Director/Design & Graphics; **Thom McGuire,** A.M.E. Graphics/Photo

2004, el año que vivimos

A lo largo de este bisiesto que se marcha han sucedido muchas cosas: la tragedia del 11-M, la victoria de Rodríguez Zapatero en las elecciones, la boda del Príncipe Felipe, la reelección de Bush... Como la memoria es selectiva, hemos pedido a los humoristas Idígoras y Pachi que nos endulcen el repaso final.

El Mundo Magazine
Madrid, Spain

Magazines/Special sections

Rodrigo Sanchez, Art Director & Designer; **Maria Gonzalez,** Designer; **Natalia Buño,** Designer; **Javier Sanz,** Designer; **Carmelo Caderot,** Design Director

Göteborgs-Posten
Goteborg, Sweden

Other feature page design/175,000 and over

Gunilla Wernhamn, Designer; **Roger Olsson,** Designer; **Stefan Edetoft,** Photographer

The New York Times Magazine
New York, N.Y.

Magazines/Inside page design

Janet Froelich, Creative Director; **Arem Duplessis,** Art Director; **Catherine Gilmore-Barnes,** Designer; **Kathy Ryan,** Photo Editor

The New York Times Magazine
New York, N.Y.

Magazines/Inside page design

Janet Froelich, Creative Director; **Arem Duplessis,** Art Director; **Catherine Gilmore-Barnes,** Designer; **Kathy Ryan,** Photo Editor; **Neal Slavin,** Photographer

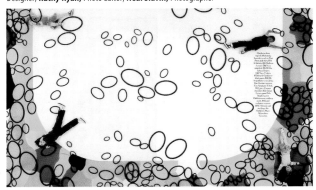

El Mundo Magazine
Madrid, Spain

Magazines/Overall design

Rodrigo Sanchez, Art Director & Designer; **Maria Gonzalez,** Designer; **Natalia Buño,** Designer; **Javier Sanz,** Designer; **Carmelo Caderot,** Design Director

DESIGN FALL 2004

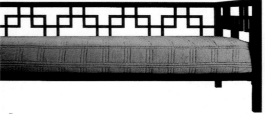

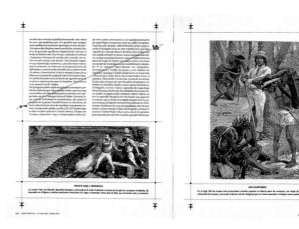

The Home Stretch

DAYBEDS WORTH DREAMING ABOUT. From top: Benson daybed, upholstered in synthetic suede, by Mitchell Gold, $1,295. At Mitchell Gold Showroom at ABC Carpet & Home, 888 Broadway. Parco 94-inch daybed, upholstered in cowhide, $4,350. At Poltrona Frau, 145 Wooster Street. Overlapping Squares daybed (twin mattress not included), by West Elm, $369. Go to www.westelm.com.

The New York Times
New York, N.Y.

Magazines/Overall design

Janet Froelich, Creative Director

Atenas 2004

La última carrera

Cuando los dioses mueren allí donde todo comenzó, en el Olimpo de Atenas

un reportaje de Gérard Rancinan y Virginie Luc

Cómo se hizo

El Mundo Magazine
Madrid, Spain

Magazines/Inside page design

Rodrigo Sanchez, Art Director & Designer; **Maria Gonzalez,** Designer; **Natalia Buño,** Designer; **Javier Sanz,** Designer; **Carmelo Caderot,** Design Director; **Gerard Rancinan,** Photographer

---

El Mundo
Madrid, Spain

Magazines/Inside page design

Carmelo Caderot, Design Director; **Manuel De Miguel,** Art Director & Designer

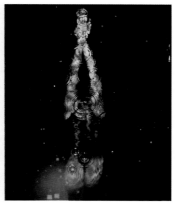

The Strokes

The New York Times Magazine
New York, N.Y.

Magazines/Inside page design

Janet Froelich, Creative Director; **Arem Duplessis,** Art Director; **Nancy Harris,** Designer; **Kathy Ryan,** Photo Editor; **Ryan McGinley,** Photographer

VISUALS

chapter 6

{ A Life in the Balance }

If the CITY,

the COUNTY,

his FAMILY,

his COUNSELORS,

his TEACHERS,

the POLICE,

even BULLETS

can't rescue a kid like

JOE JONES, who can?

Is he, at 16, already doomed

to a cell or a casket?

By Michael Krikorian
PHOTOGRAPH BY ROBERT MAXWELL

LOS ANGELES TIMES MAGAZINE, January 4, 2004 13

GOLD

Los Angeles Times Magazine
Los Angeles, Calif.

Photography/Portrait

Nan Oshin, Art Director; **Robert Maxwell,** Photographer; **Roger Gurbani,** Designer

The touching of hands, the leaning of the head, the closed eyes, the whiskers on the face — all are charged with intimacy and emotion. The crop takes it to a whole new level, breaking boundaries. The extreme contrast of color, depth of detail and rich, bluish tone make this a truly memorable photograph.

La forma en que se tocan las manos, la inclinación de la cabeza, los ojos cerrados, los bigotes en la cara; todo está cargado con intimidad y emoción. El recorte lleva la imagen a otro nivel que rompe los límites. El extremo contraste de color, la profundidad del detalle y el rico tono azuloso hacen que esta foto sea realmente memorable.

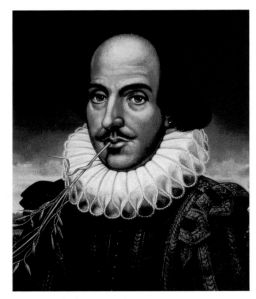

The New York Times Magazine
New York, N.Y.

Illustration/Single

Janet Froelich, Creative Director; **Arem Duplessis,** Art Director; **Todd Albertson,** Designer; **Marco Ventura,** Illustrator

Zaman
Istanbul, Turkey

Illustration/Single

Fevzi Yazici, Art Director; **Osman Turhan,** Illustrator

Illustration by DUGALD STERMER

The Washington Post Magazine
Washington, D.C.

Illustration/Single

J. Porter, Art Director; **Keith Jenkins,** Photo Editor; **Jennifer Beeson,** Assistant Photo Editor; **Carla Fielder,** Assistant Art Director; **Leslie Garcia,** Production Manager; **Dugalo Stermer,** Illustrator

USA Today
McLean, Va.
Illustration/Single
Sam Ward, Artist

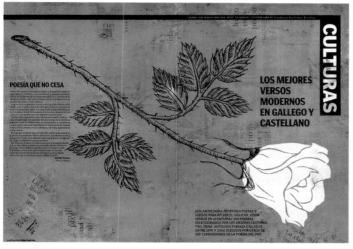

La Voz de Galicia
La Coruna, Spain
Illustration/Single
Alma Larroca, Illustrator; **Manuel Martínez,** Designer; **Antonio González,** Designer; **Jesús Gil Sáenz,** Art Director; **Mabel Rodríguez,** Designer

The Boston Globe
Boston, Mass.
Illustration/Single
Serge Bloch, Illustrator; **Lesley Becker,** Designer; **Dan Zedek,** Design Director

Los Angeles Times
Los Angeles, Calif.
Illustration/Single
Joseph Hutchinson, Deputy M.E.;
Steven E. Banks, Design Director;
Scott Menchin, Illustrator

Chicago Tribune
Chicago, Ill.
Illustration/Single
Hugo Espinoza, Art Director/Ilustrator; **Tim Bannon,** Editor; **Lisa Gutierrez,** Reporter

Los Angeles Times
Los Angeles, Calif.
Illustration/Single
Joseph Hutchinson, Deputy M.E.;
Kelli Sullivan, Deputy Design Director; **Reuben Munoz,** Design Editor; **Sarah Wilkins,** Illustrator

SILVER

The New York Times Magazine
New York, N.Y.

Photography/Portrait

Janet Froelich, Creative Director;
Cathy Gilmore-Barnes,
Designer; **Kathy Ryan,** Photo
Editor; **Robert Maxwell,**
Photographer

This is obviously a portrait, and because this is Norah Jones, we know her. But here, her face grabs your attention. Her eyes have a beautiful expression. The lighting is wonderful. This is a true example of what a portrait should be — straightforward, with no gimmicks. It also illustrates how a photographer can communicate with a subject; there's a connection there, an emotional intensity. The photo has the same emotional connection, the same mystery, as looking at the Mona Lisa.

Obviamente es un retrato, y dado que se trata de Norah Jones, la conocemos. Pero en este caso, su cara logra captar la atención. Sus ojos tiene una linda expresión. La iluminación es maravillosa. Éste es un gran ejemplo de lo que debería ser un retrato; directo y sin trucos. También muestra la forma en que un fotógrafo puede comunicarse con el sujeto; se evidencia una conexión y una intensidad emocional. La foto tiene la misma conexión emocional y el mismo misterio de cuando se mira la Mona Lisa.

Chicago Tribune
Chicago, Ill.

Illustration/Single

Luba Lukova, Illustrator; **Joan Cairney,** Art Director

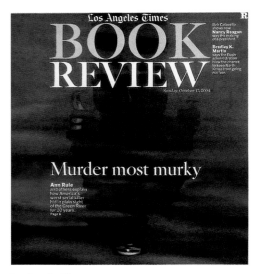

Los Angeles Times
Los Angeles, Calif.

Illustration/Single

Joseph Hutchinson, Deputy M.E.; **Christian Potter Drury,** Feauture Design Director; **Carol Kaufman,** Design Editor; **Mirkoj Ilic,** Illustrator

Los Angeles Times
Los Angeles, Calif.

Illustration/Single

Carol Kaufman, Design Editor; **Kelli Sullivan,** Deputy Design Director; **Joseph Hutchinson,** Deputy M.E.; **Brad Holland,** Illustrator

Los Angeles Times
Los Angeles, Calif.

Illustration/Single

Carol Kaufman, Design Editor; **Kelli Sullivan,** Deputy Design Director; **Joseph Hutchinson,** Deputy M.E.; **Henrik Drescher,** Illustrator

Chicago Tribune Magazine
Chicago, Ill.

Illustration/Single

Christoph Niemann, Illustrator; **David Syrek**, Art Director; **Joseph Darrow**, Art Director; **Elizabeth Taylor**, Editor

San Francisco Chronicle
San Francisco, Calif.

Illustration/Single

Nanette Bisher, Creative Director; **Lance Jackson**, Illustrator & Designer

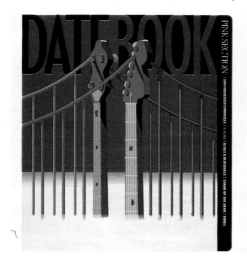

La Voz de Galicia
La Coruna, Spain

Illustration/Single

Julián de Velasco, Illustrator; **Manuel Martínez**, Designer; **Antonio González**, Designer; **Jesús Gil Sáenz**, Art Director; **Mabel Rodríguez**, Designer

Morgenavisen Jyllands-Posten
Viby, Denmark

Illustration/Single

Niels Bo Bojesen, Illustrator

Morgenavisen Jyllands-Posten
Viby, Denmark

Illustration/Single

Thorgerd B. Jensen, News Graphic Artist

The Boston Globe
Boston, Mass.

Illustration/Single

Erin Jang, Assistant Art Director/ Designer; **David Plunkert**, Illustrator; **Doug Most**, Editor; **Brendan Stephens**, Art Director; **Dan Zedek**, Design Director

Chicago Tribune Magazine
Chicago, Ill.

Illustration/Single

David Cowles, Illustrator; **Joe Darrow**, Art Director; **David Syrek**, Art Director; **Elizabeth Taylor**, Editor

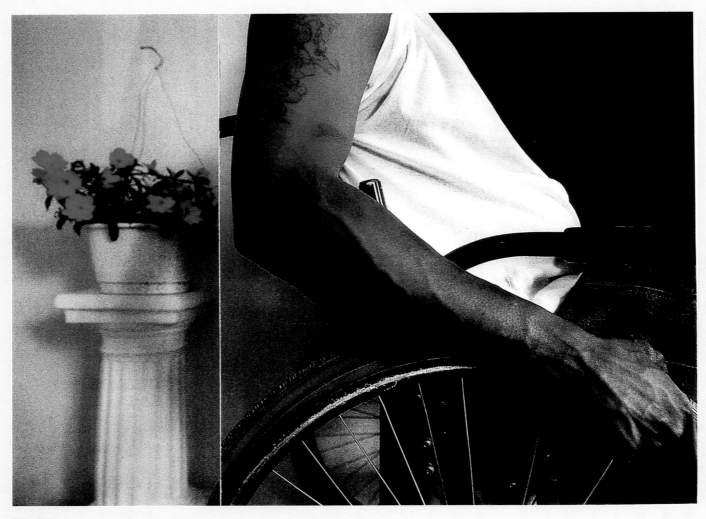

SILVER

The Boston Globe Magazine
Boston, Mass.

Photography/Portrait

Brendan Stephens, Art Director; **Suzanne Kreiter,**
Photographer; **Doug Most,** Editor; **Dan Zedek,** Design Director

You don't have to show
someone's face to make a
portrait, to know about this
man. This image is perfect.
It shines.

No es necesario mostrar la
cara de alguien para hacer
un retrato; para conocer
este hombre. Esta imagen es
perfecta. Se destaca.

The Wall Street Journal
South Brunswick, N.J.

Illustration/Single

Orlie Kraus, Art Director;
Christopher Niemann, Illustrator;
Greg Leeds, Executive Art Director

The Wall Street Journal
South Brunswick, N.J.

Illustration/Single

Orlie Kraus, Art Director; **Guy Billout,**
Illustrator; **Greg Leeds,** Executive Art
Director

Chicago Tribune
Chicago, Ill.
Illustration/Single

Daniel Bejar, Illustrator; **Jason McKean,** Art Director

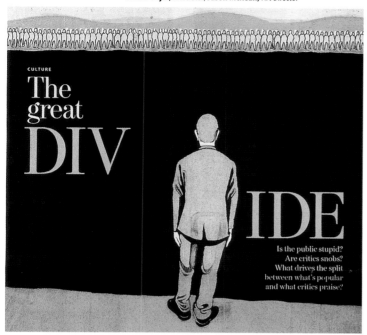

National Post
Toronto, Ontario, Canada
Illustration/Single

Gayle Grin, A.M.E./Visuals;
Matthew Fraser, Editor-in-Chief;
Jason Logan, Illustrator; **Christine
Dewairy,** Saturday Post Art Director/
Designer

The Wall Street Journal
South Brunswick, N.J.
Illustration/Single

Orlie Kraus, Art Director; **Arthur E. Giron,** Illustrator; **Greg Leeds,**
Executive Art Director

The Denver Post
Denver, Colo.
Illustration/Multiple

Jeff Neumann, Illustrator

The New York Times Magazine
New York, N.Y.
Illustration/Single

Janet Froelich, Creative Director; **Arem
Duplessis,** Art Director ; **Jeff Glendenning,**
Designer; **Jason Holley,** Illustrator

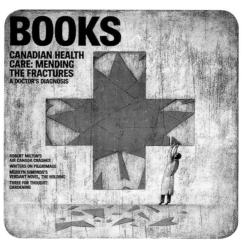

The Globe and Mail
Toronto, Ontario, Canada
Illustration/Single

Cinders McLeod, Design Editor;
David Pratt, Executive Art Director;
Steve Adams, Illustrator; **Martin
Levin,** Book Editor; **Patrick Martin,**
Comment Editor

Seattle Post-Intelligencer
Seattle, Wash.
Illustration/Multiple

Guillermo Munro, Illustrator

SILVER

Los Angeles Times
Los Angeles, Calif.

Photography/Portrait

Damon Winter, Photographer; **Calvin Hom**, Deputy Director Photo; **Kirk McKoy**, Senior Features Photo Editor

This photograph has a beautiful setting — a track runner out of his element. This photographer aimed to show Carl Lewis as a person, not just a runner. The pier beams and water illustrate the strength of subject. The photo is full of Biblical and historical symbolism.

Esta fotografía tiene un lindo escenario; un atleta fuera de su elemento. Este fotógrafo intentó mostrar a Carl Lewis como una persona, y no solo como un corredor. Los pilotes del muelle y el agua ilustran la fuerza del sujeto. La foto está llena de simbolismo bíblico e histórico.

La Voz de Galicia
La Coruna, Spain

Illustration/Multiple

Manuel Martínez, Designer; **Álvaro Valiño**, Infographics/Illustrator; **Antonio González**, Designer; **Jesús Gil Sáenz**, Art Director; **Mabel Rodríguez**, Designer

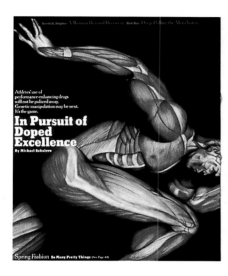

The New York Times Magazine
New York, N.Y.

Illustration/Multiple

Janet Froelich, Creative Director; **Arem Duplessis,** Art Director; **Jeff Glendenning,** Designer; **Elizabeth Peyton,** Illustrator

The New York Times Magazine
New York, N.Y.

Illustration/Multiple

Janet Froelich, Creative Director; **Nancy Harris,** Designer; **Anita Kunz,** Illustrator

El Mundo Magazine
Madrid, Spain

Illustration/Multiple

Rodrigo Sanchez, Art Director & Designer; **Paula Sanz,** Illustrator; **Carmelo Caderot,** Design Director

San Antonio Express-News
San Antonio, Texas

Photography/General news (planned)

Doug Sehres, Director of Photography; **Bob Owen,** Photographer; **Todd Stewart,** Designer

SILVER

The New York Times Magazine
New York, N.Y.

Photography/Project page or spread

Janet Froelich, Creative Director; **Joele Cuyler,** Designer;
Kathy Ryan, Photo Editor; **Inez Van Lamsweerde,**
Photographer; **Vinoodh Matadin,** Photographer

The Palm Beach Post
West Palm Beach, Fla.

Photography/Spot news

Greg Lovett, Photographer

The scale of this project, the sheer volume
and quality of images are mind-blowing.
The rhythm of how it was put together,
with the variety of expressions, scale and
cropping, is wonderful.

La escala de este proyecto, el gran
volumen y la calidad de las imágenes son
impresionantes. El ritmo de la forma
en que fue armado, con la variedad de
las expresiones, la escala y el recorte, es
maravilloso.

Rocky Mountain News
Denver, Colo.

*Photography/General news
(planned)*

Chris Schneider, Photographer

South Florida Sun-Sentinel
Fort Lauderdale, Fla.

Photography/General news (planned)

Anastasia Walsh Infanzon, Photographer

Rocky Mountain News
Denver, Colo.

Photography/General news (planned)

Judy Walgren, Photographer

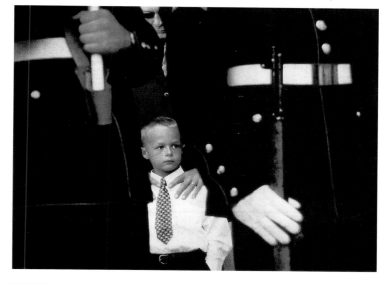

Rocky Mountain News
Denver, Colo.

Photography/General news (planned)

Marc Piscotty, Photographer

Toronto Star
Toronto, Ontario, Canada

Photography/Spot news

Lucas Oleniuk, Photographer

The Plain Dealer
Cleveland, Ohio

Photography/Spot news

John Kuntz, Photographer

Rocky Mountain News
Denver, Colo.

Photography/General news (planned)

Todd Heisler, Photographer

The Baltimore Sun
Baltimore, Md.

Photography/Spot news

Kim Hairston, Photographer

The San Diego Union-Tribune
San Diego, Calif.

Photography/Spot news

Dan Trevan, Staff Photographer

DAY ON THE TRAIL
John Kerry

MORE PHOTOS AT WWW.CONCORDMONITOR.COM

Sen. John Kerry's day in New Hampshire starts when his private jet lands at the Concord Airport and staff members meet him on the tarmac.

Kerry steps from his bus at Concord High and is met by former governor Jeanne Shaheen (right).

After a long speech at Concord High School, as well as filing for the primary, Kerry and his national press secretary, David Wade (center), review his speech while traveling aide Setti Warren (right) makes calls.

A campaign worker adorned with stickers listens from the back of the room as Kerry speaks at the Laconia Fire Station.

Quirks & fancies

• What is your average shut-eye per night? Five hours of dreams for America's future, occasionally interrupted by night-mares of four more years of George W. Bush.

• What is the book you read to your children most often? We ran through the entire Dr. Seuss collection.

• Who is your favorite super hero and why? Superman. I remember watching the shows and reading the comic books as a child. In the last few years, Christopher Reeve has showed real courage worthy of Superman himself.

• Who is your favorite professional athlete? Lance Armstrong. He had the courage to beat cancer and come back even stronger.

• If you gave George Bush a gift, what would it be? How to Make Friends and Influence People by Dale Carnegie. If George Bush took the time to read it, he could learn a thing or two about rebuilding America's alliances and making our country safer in the world.

• What is your guilty pleasure? Hostess cupcakes.

• What's the best vacation you've ever taken? Any time on the Cape and islands off Massachusetts.

• Who is your favorite foreign leader and why? Nelson Mandela. Courage, conviction and extraordinary vision all in one inspirational man.

• What is your favorite thing to cook? Pancakes. When my daughters were young, we would make them in animal shapes on Sunday mornings.

• What CD did you listen to this week? The Rising by Bruce Springsteen.

Kerry puts his feet up and makes calls between fire house meetings.

Photos by Jim Korpi

SILVER

Concord Monitor
Concord, N.H.

Photography/Photo series

Dan Habib, Photo Editor/Photographer; **Preston Gannaway,** Photographer; **Jim Korpi,** Photographer; **Elaine Skylar,** Photographer

This is a wonderful effort in concept and execution. Instead of profiling the candidates, the paper told the story in pictures of strange and delightful moments. The work is consistently good, with work from three different photographers. It's a very creative approach and a real service to readers.

Éste es un maravilloso esfuerzo, tanto en su concepto como en su forma de ejecución. En vez de dar el perfil de los candidatos, este diario contó la historia en fotos de momentos extraños y encantadores. El trabajo de tres fotógrafos es consistentemente bueno. El enfoque es muy creativo y un verdadero servicio a los lectores.

The Plain Dealer
Cleveland, Ohio

Photography/Sports

Roadell Hickman, Photographer

Knoxville News Sentinel
Knoxville, Tenn.

Photography/Sports

Cathy Clarke, Photographer

The Charlotte Observer
Charlotte, N.C.

Photography/Spot news

Patrick Schneider, Photographer;
Pricilla Tsai, Page Designer; **Peter Weinberger,** Photo Editor

ASESINAN A LAVACOCHES EN UN MICRO Y LOS AGRESORES SÓLO LE ROBAN MORRALLA AL CHOFER
PÁG.17

Humberto Reyes fue alcanzado en el cuello por una bala de sus victimarios.

Metro
México City, México

Photography/Spot news

Luis Alberto Vargas, Photographer;
Roberto Paniagua, Graphics Coordinator; **Ricardo Del Castillo,** Art Director; **Ricardo Elizondo,** Managing Director; **Lázaro Rios,** General Managing Director

Richmond Times-Dispatch
Richmond, Va.

Photography/Spot news

Mark Gormus, Photographer

Richmond Times-Dispatch
Richmond, Va.

Photography/Spot news

Dean Hoffmeyer, Photographer

Scripps Treasure Coast Newspapers
Stuart, Fla.

Photography/Spot news

Jason Nuttle, Photojournalist; **Lloyd Young,** Picture Editor; **Michelle Mazzone,** Presentations Editor

A PATCH OF WINNERS

We received dozens of entries in our pumpkin decorating contest, including one featuring the likeness of Charles M. Schulz, creator of "The Great Pumpkin" (right, by Virginia Kolence, 71, of Palo Alto) and a glittery disco pumpkin by San Francisco restaurateur Harry Denton (opposite page). Here are the other winners:

ON THE COVER (clockwise from top left) Katherine J. Hill, 25, San Francisco; Sadie Alan, 7; Elise Prowse, 48, Berkeley; Jessica K. Bodner, San Francisco.

PAGE 20 (left to right) First row: Ed Yarnell, San Bruno; Jan Molen, 60, St. Helena. Second row: "Jackie O Lantern" by C. Paxton, San Francisco; Carmalitha M. Person, 45, San Francisco; Jeanette Conley, San Francisco; Debbie Wilson, "Harvest Your Love" by Florence Wisemann, Napa. Third row: Megan Maloch, San Francisco; Helen Ludwig, 95, San Francisco; Sarah Cain, 7, Walnut Creek; Rob Lowrey, San Francisco; Sandra Mortimore, Walnut Creek.

PAGE 21 First row: Rowena Witchie, 34, and Lil' Mumkin, 21 weeks, San Francisco; Talbot Adamson, San Francisco. Second row: Angelica Lee, 4, San Francisco; Paul Holtz. Third row: Flory Ney-Clement, Benicia; Karen Hamm, San Francisco. Fourth row: Dan Holland, San Francisco; Gail Gandolfi, Belmont; "The Anti-Jack LaLanne-tern" by Ellen W. Leroe, San Francisco; Tylia Bruno, 10, Pacifica; group project, Crest Adult Center class. Fifth row: Lillian Cim Lee, San Francisco; Breffni Mathews, 51, San Francisco; Teena Miller, Vallejo; Terry Englehart, 55, Oakland; William Aiken, San Francisco.

SILVER

San Francisco Chronicle
San Francisco, Calif.

Miscellaneous

Matt Petty, Art Director; **Nanette Bisher,** Creative Director; **Joe Brown,** Pink Section Editor; **David Bridges,** Scanning Technicial; **Sue Adolphson,** Deputy Pink Editor; **Carolyn White,** A.M.E. Features

The concept is perfect. Asking readers to create designs from the original cover is very interactive, alive and full of life. It's more than graphic design — it's trying to connect with readers.

El concepto es perfecto. Pedir que los lectores creen diseños a partir de la tapa original es muy interactivo, vivaz y lleno de vitalidad. Es más que diseño gráfico; es una forma de tratar de conectarse con los lectores.

San Antonio Express-News
San Antonio, Texas

Photography/Sports

Doug Sehres, Director of Photography; **William Luther,** Photographer; **Chuck Blount,** Designer

Los Angeles Times
Los Angeles, Calif.

Photography/Sports

Wally Skalij, Photographer

POSEIDON ADVENTURE
Like the ancient Greek god, Michael Phelps seeks to rule the waters of Athens

The Baltimore Sun
Baltimore, Md.

Photography/Sports

Karl Merton Ferron, Photographer; **Monty Cook,** Designer

Toronto Star
Toronto, Ontario, Canada
Photography/Feature
Steve Russell, Photographer

The New York Times
New York, N.Y.
Photography/Feature
Joao Silva, Photographer

Los Angeles Times
Los Angeles, Calif.
Photography/Feature
Brian Vander Brug, Staff Photographer; **Hal Wells,** Photo Editor;
Kirk McKoy, Senior Features Photo Editor; **Judy Pryor,** Designer

**Tempting
the trolls**

Guide Harley Klemme sees
opportunity in the hidden cracks that
cleave his ancestral land. But to make
money showing off these slot
canyons, he has to wriggle past
bureaucrats, Wind People and
other unsympathetic beings.

Detroit Free Press
Detroit, Mich.
Photography/Sports
Mandi Wright, Staff Photographer; **Diane Weiss,** Picture Editor;
Christoph Fuhrmans, Designer; **Nancy Andrews,** Director of
Photography; **Steve Dorsey,** Design & Graphics Director

The News & Observer
Raleigh, N.C.
Photography/Feature
Sher Stoneman, Photojournalist; **John Hansen,** Picture Editor; **Andrea
Jones,** Designer

The News & Observer
Raleigh, N.C.

Photography/Feature

Travis Long, Photojournalist; **John Hansen,** Picture Editor; **Andrea Jones,** Designer

Reforma
México City, México

Photography/Feature

Roberto Paniagua, Designer/Graphics Coordinator; **Ricardo Del Castillo,** Art Director; **Agustín Márquez,** Photographer; **Ricardo Elizondo,** Section Director; **René Delgado,** Managing Director; **Lázaro Ríos,** General Managing Director; **Pedro Terán,** Editor

Récord
México City, México

Photography/Sports

Juan Ramón Rodríguez, Photographer; **Alejo Nájera,** Design Editor/Designer; **Alejandro Belman,** Design Editor; **Alberto Nava,** Art Director; **Alejandro Gómez,** Editorial Director; **José Luis Barros,** Graphics Editor

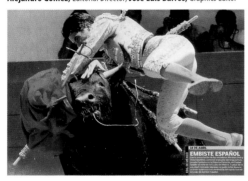

Knoxville News Sentinel
Knoxville, Tenn.

Photography/ Feature

Joe Howell, Photographer

Toronto Star
Toronto, Ontario, Canada

Photography/Feature

Steve Russell, Photographer

Rocky Mountain News
Denver, Colo.

Photography/Feature

Todd Heisler, Photographer

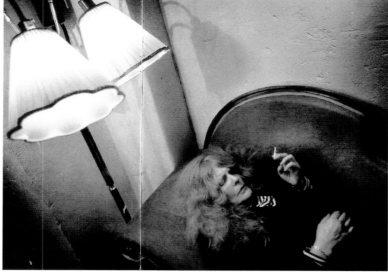

Dagens Nyheter
Stockholm, Sweden

Photography/ Portrait

Linus Meyer, Photographer; **Pär Björkman,** Picture Editor; **Pelle Asplund,** Art Director; **Sasha Johansson,** Page Designer

The Record
Kitchener, Ontario, Canada

Photography/Portrait

Mathew McCarthy, Staff Photographer

The San Diego Union-Tribune
San Diego, Calif.

Photography/Portrait

K.C. Alfred, Photographer

Star Tribune
Minneapolis, Minn.

Photography/ Feature

Brian Peterson, Photographer

Seattle Post-Intelligencer
Seattle, Wash.

Photography/Feature

Karen Ducey, Photographer

Rocky Mountain News
Denver, Colo.

Photography/Portrait

Judy Walgren, Photographer

Los Angeles Times
Los Angeles, Calif.

Photography/ Portrait

Anacleto Rapping, Photographer; **Cindy Hively,** Photo Editor; **Kirk McKoy,** Senior Features Photo Editor; **Paul Gonzales,** Design Editor

The Denver Post
Denver, Colo.

Photography/ Portrait

Glenn Asakawa, Staff Photography

Toronto Star
Toronto, Ontario, Canada
Photography/Portrait
Lucas Oleniuk, Photographer

The Record
Kitchener, Ontario, Canada
Photography/Portrait
Mirko Petricevic, Photographer

Los Angeles Times
Los Angeles, Calif.

Photography/ Portrait

Damon Winter, Photographer; **Cindy Hively,** Photo Editor; **Kirk McKoy,** Senior Features Photo Editor; **Paul Gonzales,** Design Editor

Los Angeles Times
Los Angeles, Calif.

Photography/ Portrait

Genaro Molina, Photographer; **Cindy Hively,** Photo Editor; **Kirk McKoy,** Senior Features Photo Editor; **Paul Gonzales,** Design Editor

The Boston Globe
Boston, Mass.

Photography/Portrait

Brendan Stephens, Art Director; **Mark Ostow,** Photographer; **Doug Most,** Editor; **Dan Zedek,** Design Director

Los Angeles Times
Los Angeles, Calif.

Photography/Portrait

Damon Winter, Staff Photographer; **Calvin Hom,** Deputy Director of Photography; **Kirk McKoy,** Senior Features Photo Editor

The Plain Dealer
Cleveland, Ohio

Photography/Portrait

Mike Levy, Photographer

The Washington Post Magazine
Washington, D.C.

Photography/Illustration

J. Porter, Art Director; **Keith Jenkins,** Photo Editor; **Jennifer Beeson,** Assistant Photo Editor; **Carla Fielder,** Assistant Art Director; **Leslie Garcia,** Production Manager; **Randy Mays,** Photo Illustrator

Morgenavisen Jyllands-Posten
Viby, Denmark

Photography/Illustration

Lars Pryds, Page Designer

Los Angeles Times
Los Angeles, Calif.

Photography/Portrait

Wally Skalij, Staff Photographer; **Cindy Hively,** Photo Editor; **Kirk McKoy,** Senior Features Photo Editor; **Paul Gonzales,** Design Editor

The Plain Dealer
Cleveland, Ohio

Photography/Illustration

Andrea Levy, Photo Illustrator

The Plain Dealer
Cleveland, Ohio

Photography/Illustration

Dale Omori, Photographer

Toronto Star
Toronto, Ontario, Canada

Photography/Illustration

Keith Beaty, Photographer

The Oregonian
Portland, Ore.

Photography/Illustration

Jonathan Barkat, Illustrator; **Reed Darmon,** Designer; **Nancy Casey,** Features Art Director

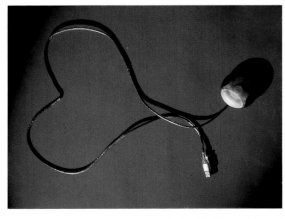

The Washington Post Magazine
Washington, D.C.

Photography/Illustration

J. Porter, Art Director; **Keith Jenkins,** Photo Editor; **Jennifer Beeson,** Assistant Photo Editor; **Carla Fielder,** Assistant Art Director; **Leslie Garcia,** Production Manager; **Doug Mindell,** Photo Illustrator

The Gazette
Montreal, Quebec, Canada

Photography/Project page or spread

Jeanine Lee, Design Editor; **Roland-Yves Carignan,** Design Director; **Phil Carpenter,** Photographer; **Stu Cowan,** Sports Editor; **Lynn Farrell,** Photo Editor

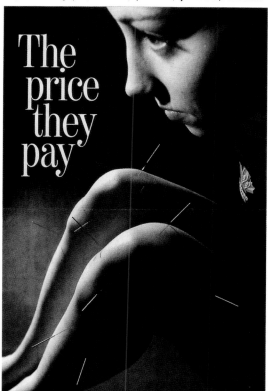

The Washington Post Magazine
Washington, D.C.

Photography/Project page or spread

J. Porter, Art Director; **Keith W. Jenkins,** Photo Editor; **Jennifer Beeson,** Assistant Photo Editor; **Carla Fielder,** Assistant Art Director; **Carol Guzy,** Photographer; **Leslie A. Garcia,** Editorial Production Manager; **Kyoko Hamada,** Photographer; **David Deal,** Photographer; **Other Staff Photographers**

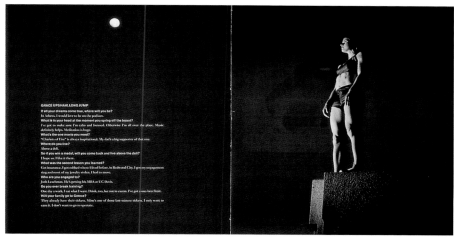

San Francisco Chronicle
San Francisco, Calif.

Photography/Project page or spread

Nanette Bisher, Creative Director; **Carlos Avila Gonzalez,** Photographer; **Kathleen Hennessy,** Picture Editor; **Susan Gilbert,** Deputy M.E.; **Randy Greenwell,** Deputy Director of Photography; **Joey Rigg,** Art Director; **George Russell,** Associate Art Director

San Jose Mercury News
San Jose, Calif.

Photography/Project page or spread

Jim Gensheimer, Photographer

Detroit Free Press
Detroit, Mich.

Photography/Project page or spread

Chip Somodevilla, Staff Photographer; **Jessica Trevino,** Picture Editor; **Steve Dorsey,** Design & Graphics Director; **Nancy Andrews,** Director of Photography

When war is routine
Scenes of danger and destruction become ordinary after a couple of months in Iraq

The New York Times Magazine
New York, N.Y.

Photography/Project page or spread

Janet Froelich, Creative Director; **Jeff Glendenning,** Designer; **Kathy Ryan,** Photo Editor; **Annabel Clark,** Photographer

Our Journal
A mother and daughter chronicle a recovery from cancer together.

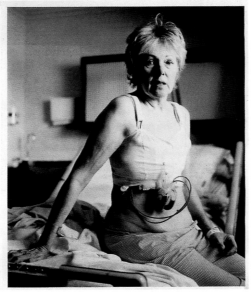

The Plain Dealer
Cleveland, Ohio

Photography/Project page or spread

Eustacio Humphrey, Photographer; **Bill Gugliotta,** Director of Photography; **Jeff Greene,** Picture Editor; **Sharon Yemich,** Designer; **Ellen Stein Burbach,** Magazine Editor

DATEBOOK

From the Ferry Building to the Castro district, with U.N. Plaza in the middle, Market Street serves as the backbone of a city that's crossroads to the world

San Francisco Chronicle
San Francisco, Calif.

Photography/Project page or spread

Nanette Bisher, Creative Director; **Christina Koci Hernandez,** Photographer; **Kathleen Hennessy,** Picture Editor; **Susan Gilbert,** Deputy M.E.; **Randy Greenwell,** Deputy Director of Photography; **Frank Mina,** Senior Art Director/News; **Matt Petty,** Senior Art Director/Design

Seattle Post-Intelligencer
Seattle, Wash.

Photography/Project page or spread

Scott Eklund, Photographer

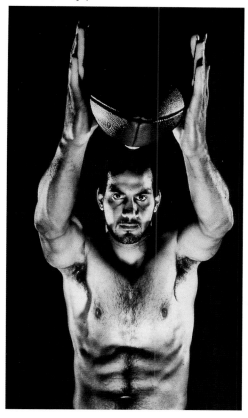

El Mundo Del Siglo XXI
Madrid, Spain

Photography/Project page or spread

Angel Casaña, Photography Chief; **Staff Photographers; Contributing Photographers**

Army Times
Springfield, Va.

Photography/Page design

Rob Curtis, Photographer; **John Bretschneider,** Graphic Artist; **Mark Fondersmith,** Art Director; **Steve Elfers,** Director/Photography

South Florida Sun-Sentinel
Fort Lauderdale, Fla.

Photography/Project page or spread

Michael Laughlin, Photographer

South Florida Sun-Sentinel
Fort Lauderdale, Fla.

Photography/Photo series

Photography Staff

The New York Times Magazine
New York, N.Y.

Photography/Project page or spread

Janet Froelich, Creative Director; **Arem Duplessis,** Art Director;
Kristina Dimatteo, Designer; **Kathy Ryan,** Photo Editor; **Paolo
Pellegin,** Photographer

The Press Democrat
Santa Rosa, Calif.

Photography/Project page or spread

John Burgess, Photographer

The Press Democrat
Santa Rosa, Calif.

Photography/Project page or spread

John Burgess, Photographer

**The New York Times
Magazine**
New York, N.Y.

Photography/Project page or spread

Janet Froelich, Creative Director;
Arem Duplessis, Art Director &
Designer; **Matthew Pillsbury,**
Photographer; **Kathy Ryan,** Photo
Editor

The New York Times Magazine
New York, N.Y.

Photography/Illustration

Janet Froelich, Creative Director; **Nancy Harris**, Designer; **Kathy Ryan**, Photo Editor; **Dan Winters**, Photographer

It's not that the Democrats don't have
sensible, sophisticated plans to deal with Iraq, terrorism and homeland security.
It's that their past — and their activist base — speaks so loud and so clear.

The Things They Carry
By James Traub

Photograph by Dan Winters

A NEW WAY OF LIFE
HMONG REFUGEE FAMILY GETS MORE FAMILIAR WITH ITS ADOPTED HOMELAND

San Jose Mercury News
San Jose, Calif.

Photography/Photo series

Dai Sugano, Photographer

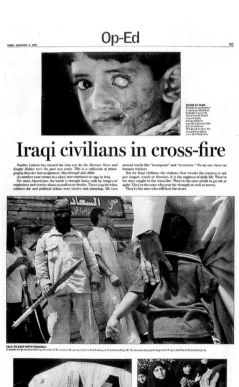

Op-Ed

Iraqi civilians in cross-fire

War zone revisited

San Jose Mercury News
San Jose, Calif.

Photography/Photo series

Pauline Lubens, Photographer

Rocky Mountain News
Denver, Colo.

Photography/Photo series

Ken Papaleo

Star Tribune
Minneapolis, Minn.

Photography/Photo series

Stormi Greener, Photographer; **Vickie Kettlewell**, Photo Editor; **Peter Koeleman**, Director/Photography; **Rhonda Prast**, Assistant Director of Design/News

Hartford Courant
Hartford, Conn.

Photography/Photo series

Cloe Poisson, Photographer; **Richard Messina**, Photographer; **Michael McAndrews**, Photographer; **Stephen Dunn**, Photographer; **John Scanlan**, Director/Photography; **Thom McGuire**, A.M.E. Graphics/Photography; **Suzette Moyer**, Design Director

The Wenatchee World
Wenatchee, Wash.

Photography/Photo series

Don Seabrook, Photo Editor

The State
Columbia, S.C.

Photography/Photo series

Renee Ittner-McManus, Photographer; **Kelly Cobb,** Designer; **David Montesino,** Design Director

Hartford Courant
Hartford, Conn.

Photography/Page design

Jennifer Rochette, Features Designer/Illustrator; **Suzette Moyer,** Director/Design & Graphics; **Chris Moore,** Assistant Director/Design; **Richard Messina,** Photographer; **Allison Corbett,** Photo Editor; **John Scanlan,** Director/Photography

'Mistakes are unacceptable'

'This is an incredible accomplishment'

AUTUMN HUES

Photos By RICHARD MESSINA | The Hartford Courant

Overwhelming Beauty Marks The Transition To Another Year's End

Afghanistan's AGONY

"(I'm) thankful that we have such a strong leader like George Bush to fight terror. I believe it's almost a holy war. The more I see, I just keep thinking, 'Wake up America.'"

Rocky Mountain News
Denver, Colo.

Photography/Photo series

Todd Heisler, Photographer

Arkansas Democrat-Gazette
Little Rock, Ark.

Photography/Photo series

Ben Krain, Staff Photographer

The New York Times
New York, N.Y.

Photography/Page design

Doug Mills, Photographer; **Stephen Crowley,** Photographer

Star Tribune
Minneapolis, Minn.

Photography/Page design

Jim Gehrz, Photographer; **Vickie Kettlewell,** Photo Editor; **Peter Koeleman,** Director/Photography; **Rhonda Prast,** Assistant Director/Design

On the Trail, The Hands, Too, Can Speak Volumes

Kerry on the Campaign Trail: Soccer, Hugs, Ferry Rides and More

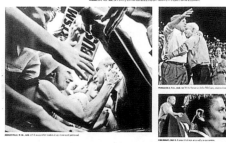

National Post
Toronto, Ontario, Canada

Photography/Page design

Gayle Grin, A.M.E./Visuals;
Matthew Fraser, Editor-in-Chief;
Laura Koot, News Presentation Editor; **Jim Bray,** Sports Editor

MEMORABLE MOMENTS
Highlights from the 2004 Games

Hartford Courant
Hartford, Conn.

Photography/Page design

Melanie Shaffer, Assistant Director/Design; **Bruce Moyer,** Photo Editor; **Michael McAndrews,** Photographer; **Suzette Moyer,** Design Director; **Thom McGuire,** A.M.E. Graphics/Photo

Hartford Courant
Hartford, Conn.

Photography/Page design

Shana Sureck, Photographer; **Stephanie Heisler,** Photo Editor; **John Scanlan,** Director/Photography; **Suzette Moyer,** Design Director; **Thom McGuire,** A.M.E. Graphics/Photo

Detroit Free Press
Detroit, Mich.

Photography/Page design

Amy Leang, Staff Photographer; **Diane Weiss,** Picture Editor; **Robert Huschka,** News Designer; **Nancy Andrews,** Director of Photography; **Steve Dorsey,** Design & Graphics Director; **Romain Blanquart,** Staff Photographer

ADRIAEN'S RISING

Life Pauses In Elizabeth Park's Woods And Dirt Trails, Meadows And Wide-Open Lawns

AMONG THE ROSES

Lasting images from Athens

Sixteen days of competition lead to countless memories

The Dallas Morning News
Dallas, Texas

Photography/Page design

John Hancock, Designer; **Anne Farrar,** Photo Editor; **Rob Schneider,** Design Editor/Sports; **Chris Wilkins,** Photo Editor

The Palm Beach Post
West Palm Beach, Fla.

Photography/Page design

Mark Edelson, Presentation Editor; **Bruce R. Bennett,** Photographer; **Jenna Lehtola,** Features Designer

PASIÓN + EL ARTE

El Gráfico
Antiguo Cuscatlán, El Salvador

Photography/Staff use of photography

Staff

Chicago Tribune
Chicago, Ill.

Information graphics, breaking news/175,000 and over

Phil Geib, Artist; **Chris Soprych,** Artist; **Keith Claxton,** Artist; **Adam Zoll,** Coordinator; **Steve Layton,** Editor

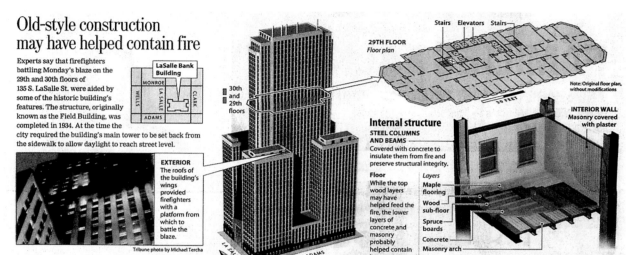

Old-style construction may have helped contain fire

Experts say that firefighters battling Monday's blaze on the 29th and 30th floors of 135 S. LaSalle St. were aided by some of the historic building's features. The structure, originally known as the Field Building, was completed in 1934. At the time the city required the building's main tower to be set back from the sidewalk to allow daylight to reach street level.

LaSalle Bank Building
MONROE
WELLS
LA SALLE
CLARK
ADAMS

30th and 29th floors

29TH FLOOR
Floor plan

Stairs Elevators Stairs

Note: Original floor plan, without modifications

30 FEET

EXTERIOR
The roofs of the building's wings provided firefighters with a platform from which to battle the blaze.

Tribune photo by Michael Tercha

LA SALLE

ADAMS

INTERIOR WALL
Masonry covered with plaster

Internal structure
STEEL COLUMNS AND BEAMS
Covered with concrete to insulate them from fire and preserve structural integrity.

Floor
While the top wood layers may have helped feed the fire, the lower layers of concrete and masonry probably helped contain it, experts say.

Layers
Maple flooring
Wood sub-floor
Spruce boards
Concrete
Masonry arch

Sources: Chicago Fire Department; Graham, Anderson, Probst & White; Tribune reporting

Chicago Tribune/Adam Zoll, Keith Claxton, Chris Soprych and Phil Geib

Fort Worth Star-Telegram
Fort Worth, Texas

Photography/Page design

Kate Gorman, Sunday Coordinator; **Jill Johnson,** Staff Photographer; **Sarah Huffstetler,** Executive Design Director/News; **Gregg Ellman,** Director of Photography/Arlington; **Paul Moseley,** Senior Staff Photographer; **Max Faulkner,** Director of Photography/Fort Worth

InSight A photo gallery of who we are and where we live

A timeless sense of community

PHOTOS BY JILL JOHNSON · STAR-TELEGRAM STAFF

The Palm Beach Post
West Palm Beach, Fla.

Photography/Page design

Mark Edelson, Presentation Editor; **Stuart Franklin,** Photographer; **Paula Bronstein,** Photographer; **Jeff Horner,** Photographer; **Bill Ingram,** Photographer; **Jennifer Podis,** Photographer

As the rainy season approaches, step back for a moment, look past the inconvenience of afternoon downpours and appreciate the magical beauty of water.

WATER
E p h e m e r a l   a r t

St. Petersburg Times
St. Petersburg, Fla.

Information graphics, breaking news/175,000 and over

Jeff Goertzen, Senior Artist; **Amanda Raymond,** News Artist

El Correo
Bilbao, Spain

Information graphics, breaking news/50,000-174,999

Fernando G. Baptista, Editor

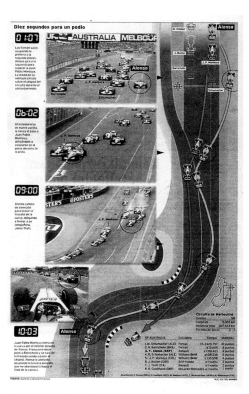

El Mundo Del Siglo XXI
Madrid, Spain

Information graphics, breaking news/175,000 and over

Juantxo Cruz, Graphics Chief Editor; **Modesto J. Carrasco,** Infographic Artist; **Isabel González,** Infographic Artist; **Graphics Staff**; **Research Staff**

El Correo
Bilbao, Spain

Information graphics, breaking news/50,000-174,999

Fernando G. Baptista, Editor; **Gonzalo De Las Heras,** Infographic Artist

Clarín
Buenos Aires, Argentina

Information graphics, breaking news/175,000 and over

Gustavo Lo Valvo, Art Director; **Alejandro Tumas,** Graphic Director; **Pablo Loscri,** Graphics Editor; **Staff Artists**

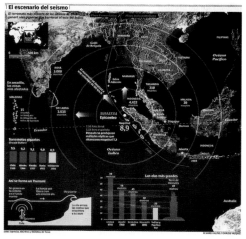

La Voz de Galicia
La Coruna, Spain

Information graphics, breaking news/50,000-174,999

Carlos Vázquez, Infographic Artist; **Álvaro Valiño,** Infographic Artist; **Xoan González,** Infographics Director; **Jesús Gil Sáenz,** Art Director

El Correo
Bilbao, Spain

Information graphics, breaking news/50,000-174,999

Fernando G. Baptista, Editor de Infografía

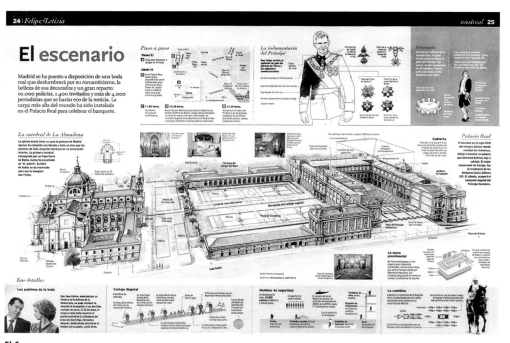

El Correo
Bilbao, Spain

Information graphics, breaking news/50,000-174,999

Fernando G. Baptista, Editor

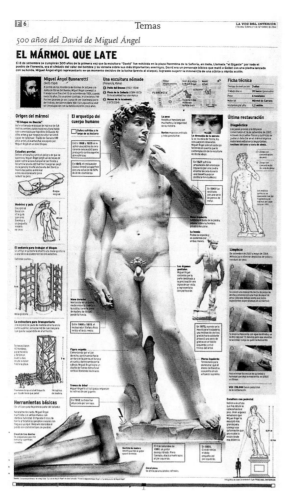

500 años del David de Miguel Ángel

EL MÁRMOL QUE LATE

La Voz del Interior
Cordoba, Argentina

Information graphics, Non-breaking/50,000-174,999

Juan Colombato, Graphic Artist; **Jorge Londero,** Editor; **Miguel De Lorenzi,** Art Director

The News Journal
Wilmington, Del.

Information graphics, Non-breaking/50,000-174,999

Dan Garrow, Graphics Editor

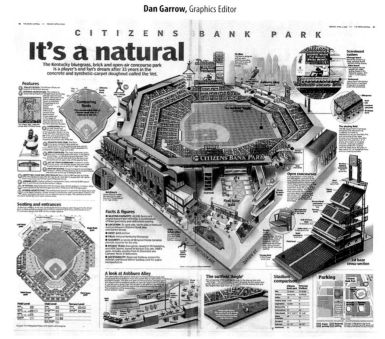

It's a natural

CITIZENS BANK PARK

The Kentucky bluegrass, brick and open-air concourse park is a player's and fan's dream after 33 years in the concrete and synthetic-carpet doughnut called the Vet.

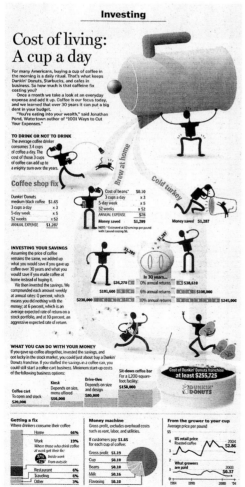

Investing

Cost of living: A cup a day

For many Americans, buying a cup of coffee in the morning is a daily ritual. That's what keeps Dunkin' Donuts, Starbucks, and cafes in business. So how much is that caffeine fix costing you?

Once a month we take a look at an everyday expense and add it up. Coffee is our focus today, and we learned that if over 30 years it can put a big dent in your budget.

"You're eating into your wealth," said Jonathan Pond, Watertown author of "1001 Ways to Cut Your Expenses."

The Boston Globe
Boston, Mass.

Information graphics, Non-breaking/175,000 and over

Hwei Wen Foo, Infographic Artist; **Kathleen Hennrikus,** Researcher; **Shirley Leung,** Editor

"The X Prize competition, more than anything else on this Earth, has the ability to help make private spaceflight and space tourism a reality."
— Burt Rutan, founder of Scaled Composites and builder of SpaceShipOne

So you want to be an Astronaut?

Burt Rutan and his SpaceShipOne aim to give you a chance as he and his team at Scaled Composites go for the record books and a $10 million Ansari X Prize

The Bakersfield Californian
Bakersfield, Calif.

Information graphics, Non-breaking/50,000-174,999

Michael Borjon, Page Designer

San Jose Mercury News

San Jose, Calif.

Information graphics, breaking news/175,000 and over

Javier Zarracina, Deputy Graphics Director; **Karl Kahler,** Graphics Coordinator

Martha Stewart goes to prison

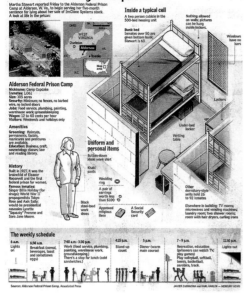

Seattle Post-Intelligencer

Seattle, Wash.

Information graphics, Non-breaking/50,000-174,999

David Badders, Graphic Artist

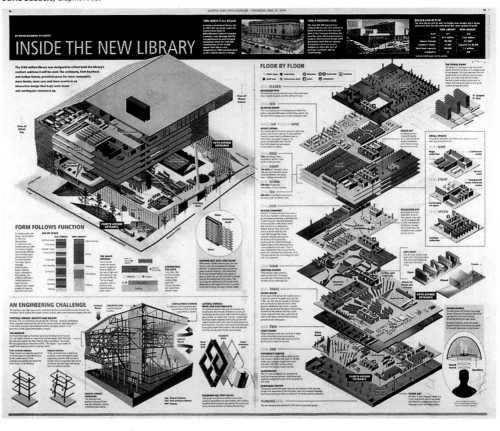

INSIDE THE NEW LIBRARY

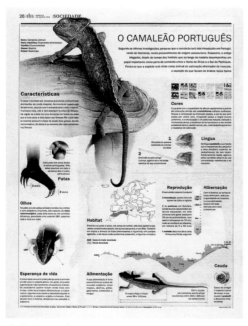

Diário de Notícias

Lisbon, Portugal

Information graphics, Non-breaking/50,000-174,999

Jose Maria Ribeirinho, Art Director; **Cristina Santos,** Infographic Editor; **Paulo Oliveira,** Infographics Artist

O CAMALEÃO PORTUGUÊS

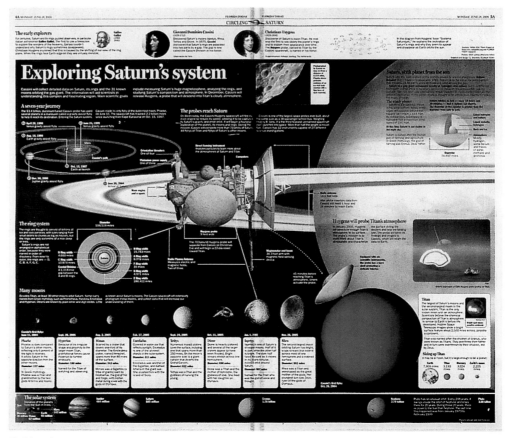

Exploring Saturn's system

Florida Today

Melbourne, Fla.

Information graphics, Non-breaking/50,000-174,999

Tim Standish, Graphic Artist; **Tom Clifford,** A.M.E. Presentation; **Jeff Meesey,** Design Editor

Chicago Tribune
Chicago, Ill.

Information graphics, Non-breaking/175,000 and over

Phil Geib, Graphic Artist; **Chris Soprych,** Graphic Artist; **Haeyoun Park,** Graphics Coordinator; **David Constantine,** Graphics Editor; **Dino Muñoz,** Graphic Artist

The Indianapolis Star
Indianapolis, Ind.

Information graphics, Non-breaking/175,000 and over

Jennifer Imes, Assistant Graphics Editor; **Mark Nichols,** Computer Assisted Reporting Editor; **Robert Dorrell,** Graphics Editor; **Matt Kryger,** Photographer

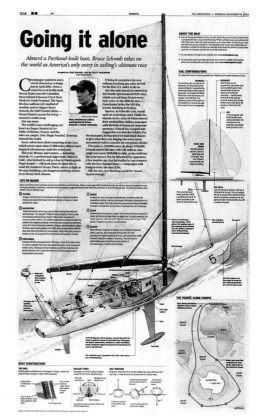

Chicago Tribune
Chicago, Ill.

Information graphics, Non-breaking/175,000 and over

Keith Claxton, Graphic Artist; **Steve Layton,** Graphics Editor

The Oregonian
Portland, Ore.

Information graphics, Non-breaking/175,000 and over

Steve McKinstry, Art Director; **Eric Baker,** Graphic Artist; **Katy Muldoon,** Staff Reporter

The Virginian-Pilot
Norfolk, Va.

Information graphics, Non-breaking/175,000 and over

John Earle, Graphic Artist; **Sam Hundley,** Designer; **Genevieve Ross,** Photographer; **Elizabeth Simpson,** Reporter; **Maria Carrillo,** DME/Projects; **Deborah Withey,** DME/Presentations

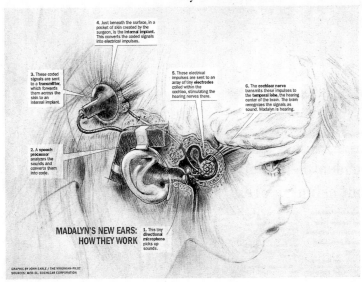

A way out of the silence

MADALYN'S NEW EARS: HOW THEY WORK

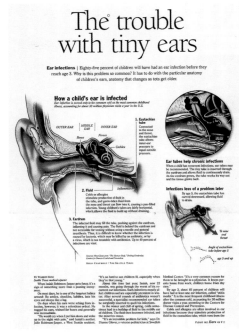

The trouble with tiny ears

The Seattle Times
Seattle, Wash.

Information graphics, Non-breaking/175,000 and over

Kriss Chaumont, News Artist

San Jose Mercury News
San Jose, Calif.

Information graphics, charting/175,000 and over

Javier Zarracina, Deputy Graphics Director; **Andrea Maschietto,** Graphic Artist

South Florida Sun-Sentinel
Fort Lauderdale, Fla.

Information graphics, Non-breaking/175,000 and over

Belinda Long, Graphics Reporter; **Len De Groot,** Assistant Graphics Director; **R. Scott Horner,** Assistant Graphics Director; **Don Wittekind,** Graphics Director

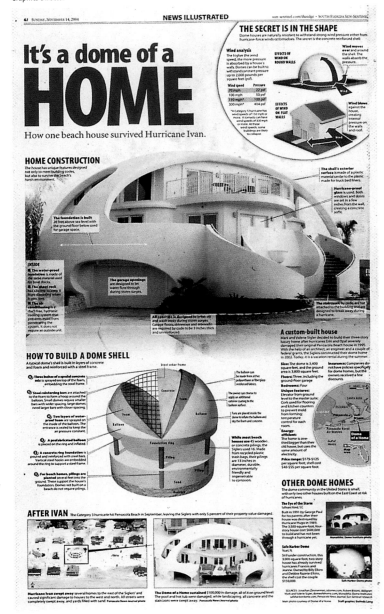

It's a dome of a HOME

How one beach house survived Hurricane Ivan.

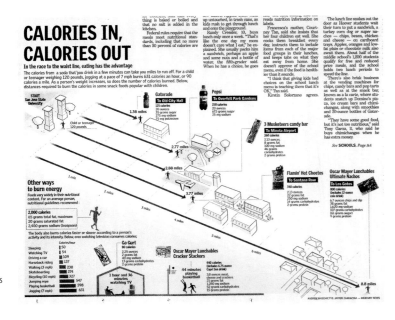

CALORIES IN, CALORIES OUT

In the race to the waist line, eating has the advantage

The Washington Post
Washington, D.C.

Information graphics, charting/175,000 and over

Karen Yourish, Graphics Editor; **Farhana Hossain,** News Artist; **Michael Keegan,** A.M.E./News Art

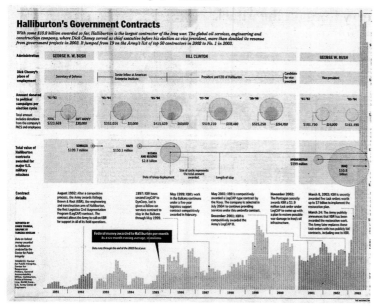

Halliburton's Government Contracts

With some $10.8 billion awarded so far, Halliburton is the largest contractor of the Iraq war. The global oil services, engineering and construction company, where Dick Cheney served as chief executive before his election as vice president, more than doubled its revenue from government projects in 2003. It jumped from 19 on the Army's list of top 50 contractors in 2002 to No. 1 in 2003.

The Credits Just Keep Going and Going and . . .

Below are reproductions of the credits from some notable films; each name mentioned is given its own line.

The Lord of the Rings: The Return of the King
2003

Modern Times
1936

Casablanca
1942

On the Waterfront
1954

The Graduate
1967

Star Wars
1977

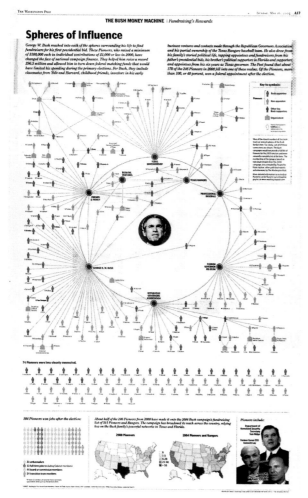

Spheres of Influence

George W. Bush reached into each of the spheres surrounding his life to find fundraisers for his first presidential bid. These Pioneers, who raised a minimum of $100,000 each in individual contributions of $1,000 or less in 2000, have changed the face of national campaign finance. They helped him raise a record $96.3 million and allowed him to turn down federal matching funds that would have limited his spending during the primary elections. For Bush, they include classmates from Yale and Harvard, childhood friends, investors in his early

business ventures and contacts made through the Republican Governors Association and his partial ownership of the Texas Rangers baseball team. He also drew from his family's storied political life, tapping appointees and fundraisers from his father's presidential bid, his brother's political supporters in Florida and supporters and appointees from his six years as Texas governor. The Post found that about 170 of the 246 Pioneers in 2000 fell into one of these realms. Of the Pioneers, more than 100, or 40 percent, won a federal appointment after the election.

The New York Times
New York, N.Y.

Information graphics, charting/175,000 and over

Steve Duenes, Graphics Editor

Chicago's rising property values

While properties in the North Side neighborhoods remain the most expensive, assessed home values in some areas on the West and South Sides have risen by more than 70 percent in the last three years. The recent assessment hikes in the historically poorer areas of Chicago can be attributed to spreading gentrification.

Change in median market values
For residential units between 2000 and 2003, by census block groups

Thriving property values on West Adams Street
The majority of homes on West Adams Street saw more than a 50-percent increase in market values between 2000 and 2003.

Chicago Tribune
Chicago, Ill.

Information graphics, charting/175,000 and over

Phil Geib, Graphic Artist; **Chris Soprych,** Graphic Artist; **Haeyoun Park,** Graphics Coordinator; **David Constantine,** Graphics Editor; **Darnell Little,** Reporter

The Washington Post
Washington, D.C.

Information graphics, charting/175,000 and over

Michael Keegan, Art Director; **Louis Spirito,** News Artist; **Sarah Cohen,** Database Editor; **Alice Crites,** Researcher

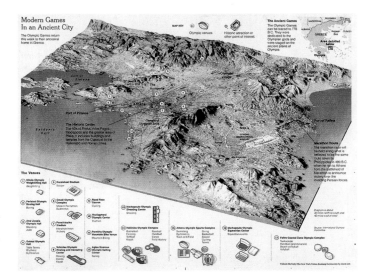

Modern Games In an Ancient City

The Olympic Games return this week to their ancestral home in Greece.

The Ancient Games
The Olympic Games can be traced to 776 B.C. They were dedicated to the Olympian gods and were staged on the ancient plains of Olympia.

The New York Times
New York, N.Y.

Information graphics, mapping/175,000 and over

William McNulty, Graphics Editor

A grand downtown revival

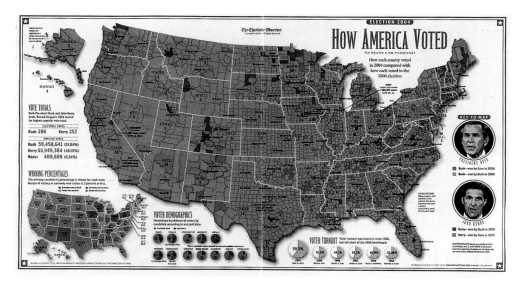

Downtown Springfield's renaissance has grown beyond its entertainment-district roots. The resurgence is continuing, with new apartments, offices and retail spaces moving in, complementing the area's established bars, clubs and restaurants.

Highlights of downtown

① JORDAN VALLEY INNOVATION CENTER (SMS)
② LOFT APARTMENTS
③ FUTURE COLLEGE STATION DEVELOPMENT
④ HEER'S TOWER REDEVELOPMENT
⑤ DISCOVERY CENTER
⑥ SPRINGFIELD EXPO CENTER
⑦ FUTURE ARENA
⑧ HAMMONS FIELD

News-Leader
Springfield, Mo.

Information graphics, mapping/50,000-174,999

Brian McGill, Graphic Artist; **John L. Dengler,** Graphics Editor

---

Bangor Daily News
Bangor, Maine

Information graphics, charting/50,000-174,999

Eric L. Zelz, Director of Graphics and Design; **Jonathan P. Ferland,** Designer

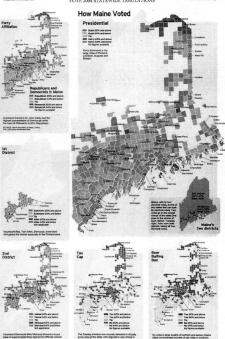

SPECIAL SECTION · Bangor Daily News · NOVEMBER 4, 2004 · D1

VOTER RESULTS
VOTE 2004 STATEWIDE TABULATIONS

How Maine Voted

The 2004 election: How we voted

A look at how Washington voters cast their ballots – and what guided them in their vote for the presidency.

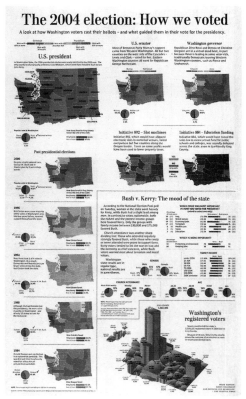

The Seattle Times
Seattle, Wash.

Information graphics, charting/175,000 and over

Kriss Chaumont, News Artist; **Michele Lee McMullen,** News Artist; **Mark Nowlin,** News Artist; **Justin Mayo,** Researcher Reporter

---

HOW AMERICA VOTED

ELECTION 2004

The Charlotte Observer

How each county voted in 2004 compared with how each voted in the 2000 election

VOTE TOTALS
Both President Bush and John Kerry broke President Reagan's 1984 record for highest popular vote total.

ELECTORAL VOTE
Bush 286   Kerry 252

POPULAR VOTE
Bush 59,458,641 (51.04%)
Kerry 55,949,384 (48.03%)
Nader 400,688 (0.34%)

WINNING PERCENTAGES
The winning candidate's percentage is shown for each state. Margin of victory in narrowly won states in 2 percent or less.

VOTER DEMOGRAPHICS
Percentage breakdown of voters by candidate according to exit poll data.

VOTER TURNOUT

The Charlotte Observer
Charlotte, N.C.

Information graphics, mapping/175,000 and over

William Pitzer, News Graphic Editor; **Ted Mellnik,** Database Editor; **Joanne Miller,** Art Director; **Dee Dee Strickland,** Perspective Editor; **Tom Tozer,** Deputy M.E. Presentation

SPECIAL REPORT | PART 1 ✈ OCEANA UNDER PRESSURE

HEMMING IN OCEANA

For the past three decades, the Virginia Beach City Council has failed to heed Navy warnings against allowing homes in high-noise and accident-potential zones around Oceana Naval Air Station. Now, nearly one-third of the city's 439,467 residents live in areas where the Navy views housing as incompatible with the base's mission.

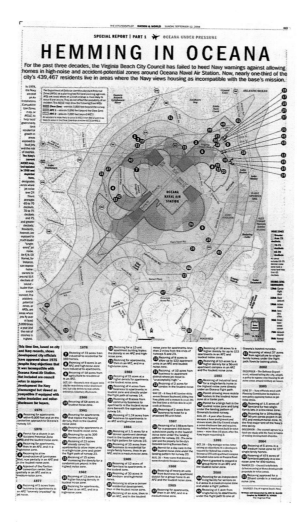

The Virginian-Pilot
Norfolk, Va.

Information graphics, mapping/175,000 and over

The Oregonian
Portland, Ore.

Information graphics, mapping/175,000 and over

Steve McKinstry, Art Director; **Steve Cowden,** Artist

Burglars, driven by meth addiction, are on a binge afflicting Portland.
The Southeast Precinct is hardest hit. Each dot is a burglary reported to police in the first nine months of 2004. With four detectives covering 20 square miles, the cops are overwhelmed. And the crooks know it.

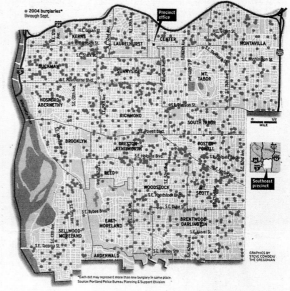

Burglar alarm

URBAN FRONTIER

The Backbone Trail

It's 59½ miles of canyons and ridges stitched together with a few urban seams. And it's not done yet.

Los Angeles Times
Los Angeles, Calif.

Information graphics, mapping/175,000 and over

Leslie Carlson, Staff Artist; **Richard Sanchez,** Graphics Coordinator; **Les Dunseith,** Graphics Editor; **Joseph Hutchinson,** Deputy M.E.

The Washington Post
Washington, D.C.

Information graphics, mapping/175,000 and over

Brenna Maloney, Graphics Editor; **Sarah Cohen,** Database Editor;
Michael Keegan, A.M.E./News Art; **Gene Thorp,** Cartographer

The New York Times
New York, N.Y.

Information graphics, mapping/175,000 and over

Matthew Ericson, Graphics Editor

The Charlotte Observer
Charlotte, N.C.

Information graphics, mapping/175,000 and over

William Pitzer, News Graphic Editor; **John Bordsen,** Travel Editor;
Joanne Miller, Art Director; **Forest Brown,** Copy Editor; **Tom Tozer,**
Deputy M.E. Presentation; **Denise Slaughter,** Designer; **Robin
Johnston,** Deputy Design Director

Results Met With Indifference, Indignation

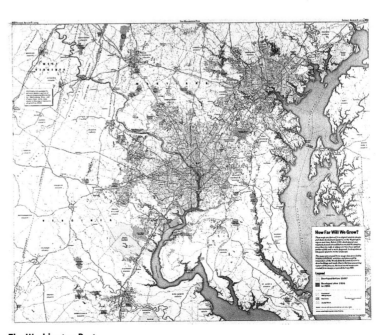

The Washington Post
Washington, D.C.

Information graphics, mapping/175,000 and over

Michael Keegan, A.M.E./News Art; **Gene Thorp,** Cartographer

St. Louis Post-Dispatch
St. Louis, Mo.

Information graphics, mapping/175,000 and over

Jacob Piercy, Graphic Journalist; **Wade Wilson,** Director/Design & Graphics

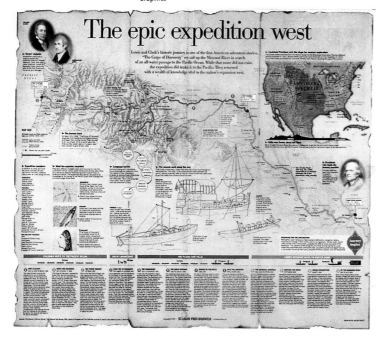

The epic expedition west

St. Petersburg Times
St. Petersburg, Fla.

Information graphics, mapping/175,000 and over

Jeff Goertzen, Senior Graphics Reporter

The battle for the courtyard

On April 4, Sgt. 1st Class Paul R. Smith and his combat engineers were part of a 100-man force sent to the outskirts of Saddam International Airport. Their mission: Set up a roadblock protecting the airport from attack along the main road connecting the airport to Baghdad. About 9 a.m., the roadblock came under fire, and infantrymen set off to find the attackers. The GIs captured some Iraqis and radioed that they needed a place to put them. That set off a sequence of events.

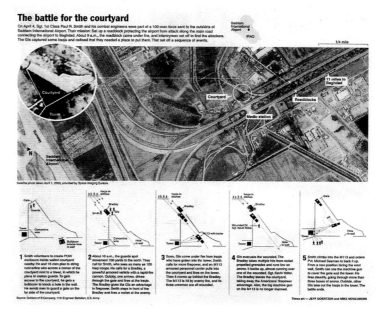

Times art — JEFF GOERTZEN AND MIKE MOSCARDINI

SPECIAL HAWAII ISSUE

Beach bound

What's shaking in design's epicenter

Nose to nose with the Nobel laureate

The Oregonian
Portland, Ore.

Use of graphics

Staff

Sculpting on a grand scale

The forces forming the dome on Mount St. Helens are of the type that have built iconic Cascade peaks.

By MICHAEL MILSTEIN
THE OREGONIAN

Quest for 49

Peyton Manning is poised on Sunday to surpass Dan Marino's 1984 record for TD passes in a season (48) and is on pace for the greatest passing season in history. Here's a comparison between the two seasons.

Manning '04 vs. Marino '84

The Dallas Morning News
Dallas, Texas
Miscellaneous
Rob Schneider, Design Editor/Sports

Houston Chronicle
Houston, Texas
Miscellaneous
Theo Fels

Reforma
México City, México
Miscellaneous
Erika Sosa, Designer; **Miguel Vadillo,** Designer; **Gunther Sahagún,** Photo Editor; **Lázaro Ríos,** General Managing Director; **Homero Fernández,** Editor; **Ricardo Del Castillo,** Art Director; **Luz María Díaz de Leon,** Graphics Editor; **René Delgado,** Managing Director; **Staff Photographers**

El Comercio
Lima, Peru
Miscellaneous
Claudia Burga-Cisneros, Design Editor; **Jose Antonio Mesones,** Designer; **Tiziana Baracco,** Designer; **Cecilia Durand,** Photo Editor

The Star-Ledger
Newark, N.J.

Miscellaneous

Drew Sheneman, Writer/Illustrator; **Peter Ambush,** Illustrator; **Mike Scott,** Colorist; **Amy Nutt,** Reporter; **Andre Malok,** Graphic Artist; **George Frederick,** Art Director; **Frank Cecala,** Lettering; **Beverly Reid,** Researcher

San Francisco Chronicle
San Francisco, Calif.

Miscellaneous

Nanette Bisher, Creative Director; **Don Asmussen,** Cartoonist

Fort Worth Star-Telegram
Fort Worth, Texas

Miscellaneous

Broc Sears, A.M.E. Graphics/Design; **Photo Staff**

Diario de Ibiza
Ibiza, Spain

Miscellaneous

Herminio Javier Fernández, Design Consultant

Arizona Daily Star
Tucson, Ariz.

Miscellaneous

Hugo Torres, Page Designer; **Chiara Bautista**, Graphic Artist; **José Merino,** Design Director; **Staff**

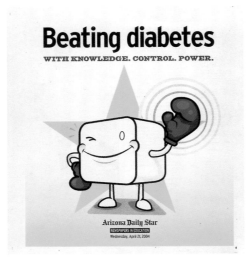

Fort Worth Star-Telegram
Fort Worth, Texas

Miscellaneous

Cody Bailey, Senior Deputy Sports Editor; **Michael Currie,** Assistant Sports Editor

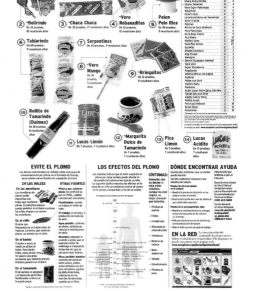

The Orange County Register
Santa Ana, Calif.

Miscellaneous

Neil C. Pinchin, Designer; **Molly Zisk,** Graphic Artist

SMALL NEWSPAPERS

chapter 7

La Palma
West Palm Beach, Fla.

A-section news design

Em Mendez, Editor

Cinco Dias
Madrid, Spain

Business page design

Staff

The Telegraph
Nashua, N.H.

A-section news design

Jocelin Johnson, Assistant News Editor

The Telegraph
Nashua, N.H.

A-section news design

Jocelin Johnson, Assistant News Editor

Santa Barbara News-Press
Santa Barbara, Calif.

A-section news design

Colin Powers, Presentation Editor/News

The Tuscaloosa News
Tuscaloosa, Ala.

A-section news design

Josh Jackson, Copy Editor/Page Designer

Sun Journal
Lewiston, Maine

A-section news design

Paul Wallen, M.E./Visuals; **Keith Hagel**, M.E./Nights; **Pete Phelan**,
Assistant M.E./Nights; **Pete Gorski**, News Artist

Sun Journal
Lewiston, Maine

A-section news design

Paul Wallen, M.E./Visuals; **Daryn Slover**, Photographer

Sun Journal
Lewiston, Maine

A-section news design

Paul Wallen, M.E./Visuals; **Keith Hagel**, M.E./Nights; **Pete Phelan**,
Assistant M.E./Nights

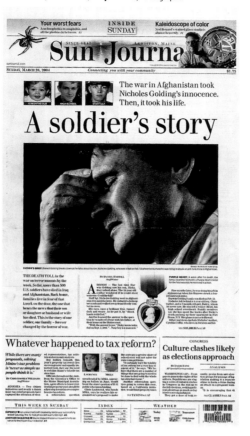

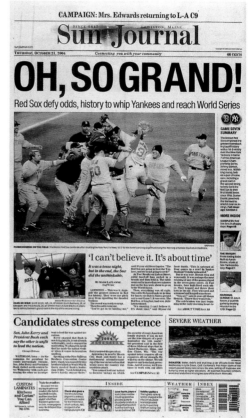

The Ball State Daily News
Muncie, Ind.

A-section news design

Chad Yoder, Illustrator;
Nicole Dudka, Designer;
Shawn Barkdull, M.E.; **Cole McGrath**, Editor-in-Chief

Daily Nebraskan
Lincoln, Neb.

A-section news design

Quentin Lueninghoener,
Design Chief

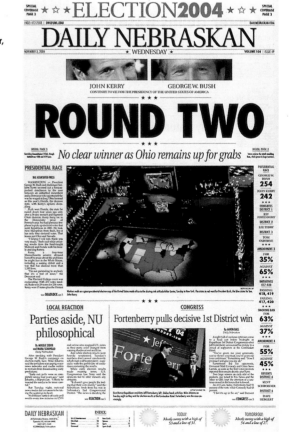

El Caribe
Santo Domingo, Dominican Republic

A-section news design

Victor Manuel Tejada, Director; **María Virgen Gómez,** Sub-Director;
Roberto Severino, Art Director/Designer; **Orlando Ramos,** Photo Editor;
Ricardo Hernández, Photographer; **Carlos Pérez-Díaz,** Consultant;
Montserrat Ortiz Roca, Consultant

Puls Biznesu
Warsaw, Poland

A-section news design

Jacek Utko, Art Director

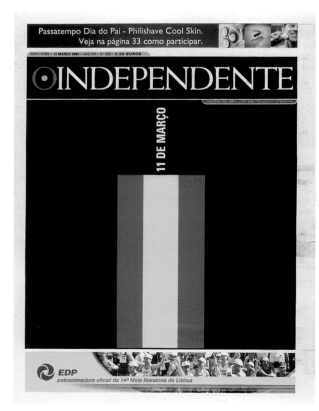

O Independente
Lisbon, Portugal

A-section news design

Sónia Matos, Art Director; **Fernando Barata,** Designer;
Claudia Oliveira, Designer; **José Souto,** Designer; **Inês
Serra Lopes,** Editor-in-Chief

Frontera
Tijuana, México

Local news section design

José Madrigal, Designer; **Raúl Ruiz,** Editor; **Daniel Acuña,** Illustrator/
Photographer; **Julia Ma. Crespo Freijo,** Design Coordinator; **Raül Ruiz
Castillo,** Subdirector Editorial

JOURNAL COURIER

JACKSONVILLE

501 DAILY   TUESDAY, NOVEMBER 2, 2004

CAMPAIGN ★ 2004

Which way will we go?

Bush and Kerry race across crucial states on the final day before America makes up its mind

Confusion over when to count military votes

State seems to leave deadline for receiving certain ballots up to local officials

THAT'S LIFE
For the politician, endorsements not as good as money

Greene clerk ready for showtime

INSIDE TODAY

**Jacksonville
Journal-Courier**
Jacksonville, Ill.

A-section news design

Larry Rowe, Designer; **Steve
Copper,** Design Director

ESPECIAL

BREVES

REVALÚA ONU SU SEGURIDAD

Periodico Provincia
Morelia, México

A-section news design

Arcelia Guadarrama, Editorial
Director; **Gustavo Vega,** Graphics
Editor; **Hamlet Ortiz,** Designer;
Erik Knobl, Designer; **Angel
Muñoz,** Designer; **Julio Ramirez,**
Designer; **Eduardo Estrada,**
Editor; **Juan Carlos Ortega,**
Co-editor

ÉTATS-UNIS
Le nombre d'États indécis rétrécit
Page A 5

MOYEN-ORIENT
Israël craint l'isolement sur la scène internationale
Page A 5

LE DEVOIR

www.ledevoir.com

L'heure du ramadan

Attaques meurtrières dans la zone verte de Bagdad

Deux attentats revendiqués par le groupe d'al-Zarqaoui font dix morts

Charest évite les dossiers épineux

Le gouvernement crée plusieurs équipes de réflexion et s'engage à respecter deux promesses électorales

Forum des générations

Maigre lette visite de Martin à Paris

Le pôle Nord dégèlera avant le passage du Nord-Ouest

CULTURE
Gènesique: 15 nominations pour Fortier et Grande Ourse
À lire en page B 2

À PROPOS DE DIEU

Le Devoir
Montreal, Quebec, Canada

A-section news design

Jules Richer, News Director; **Pierre Beaulieu,** Desk Editor; **Louis
Lapierre,** Desk Editor; **Bernard Descôteaux,** Publisher; **Jean-
Robert Sansfaçon,** M.E.; **Christian Tiffet,** Art Director/Designer

---

Martes
15 de Junio
del 2004
Guadalajara, Jal. México

MURAL

EXPRESIÓN DE JALISCO

Ni agua, ni luz, ni chivas

Trastorna la Ciudad fuerte tormenta con vientos de 85 kilómetros por hora

'Olvidan' a su bebé por el cine

Pedirán priistas frenar Arcediano

CELEBRAN PUMAS CON FOX

Prometen título... sin refuerzos

EL OGRO REVERDECE

Mural
Zapopan, México

A-section news design

Mauricio Rangel Mariscal, Designer/Illustrator; **Enrique Ortiz,**
Photographer; **Fernando Jauregui,** Art Director; **Rosa María Lutz,**
Page Editor; **Jorge Padilla,** Editorial Coordinator; **Guillermo Camacho,**
Editorial Director; **Lázaro Ríos,** General Editorial Director

---

SECCIÓN E
MURAL

COMUNIDAD

LA GACETA DEL CUARTO

TORTURA EN JALISCO

Preposadas y postposadas

DETENCIONES QUE DUELEN

Prometen sancionar robo de material médico

Mural
Zapopan, México

Local news section design

Patricia Maciel Velázquez, Designer/Illustrator; **Mauricio Lozano,**
Photographer; **Felipe Lucero,** Design Manager Editor; **Mauricio
Rangel,** Design Manager Editor; **Fernando Jauregui,** Art Director; **René
Valencia,** Page Editor; **Jaime Barrera,** Editorial Coordinator; **Guillermo
Camacho,** Editorial Director; **Lázaro Ríos,** General Editorial Director

Periodico Provincia
Morelia, México
Sports page design

Arcelia Guadarrama, Director of Editorial; **Gustavo Vega,** Graphics Editor; **Erik Knobl,** Designer; **Angel Muñoz,** Designer; **Julio Ramirez,** Designer; **Hamlet Ortiz,** Designer; **Juan Hurtado,** Editor

Santa Barbara News-Press
Santa Barbara, Calif.
Sports page design

Nick Masuda, Deputy Sports Editor; **Gerry Spratt,** Sports Editor; **Jerry Roberts,** Publisher; **Linda Strean,** M.E.; **Mike Eliason,** Photographer

Mural
Jalisco, México
Sports page design

Jesús González, Designer; **Miguel Angel Tovar,** Photographer; **Felipe Lucero,** Design Manager Editor; **Mauricio Rangel,** Design Manager Editor; **Fernando Jauregui,** Art Director; **Sergio Patiño,** Page Editor; **Francisco Solares,** Editorial Coordinator; **Guillermo Camacho,** Editorial Director; **Lázaro Ríos,** General Editorial Director

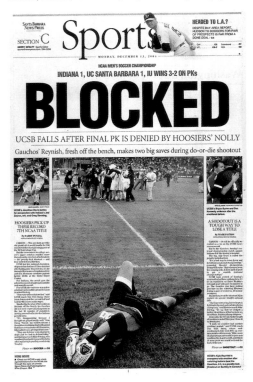

Mural
Jalisco, México
Sports page design

Fernando Jauregui, Art Director; **Felipe Lucero,** Design M.E.; **Mauricio Rangel,** Design M.E.; **Francisco Solares,** Editorial Coordinator Page Editor; **Jesús González,** Designer/Illustrator; **Reuters,** Photographer; **Guillermo Camacho,** Editorial Director; **Lázaro Ríos,** General Editorial Director

Periodico Provincia
Morelia, México
Sports page design

Arcelia Guadarrama, Editorial Director; **Gustavo Vega,** Graphics Editor; **Juan Luis Hurtado,** Editor; **Erik Knobl,** Designer; **Angel Muñoz,** Designer; **Julio Ramirez,** Designer

The Tribune
San Luis Obispo, Calif.
Sports page design

Todd Dybas, Sports Designer; **Eric Branch,** Sports Writer; **Brian Milne,** Sports Writer; **Neil Pascak,** Sports Editor, Presentation Editor

El Gráfico
Antiguo Cuscatlán, El Salvador

Sports page design

José Jaén, Designer; **Jorge Carbajal,** Journalist; **Raúl Gavidia,** Photographer

El Gráfico
Antiguo Cuscatlán, El Salvador

Sports page design

Alexander Rivera, Designer; **Cristian Villalta,** Editor-in-Chief

Conexion
San Antonio, Texas

Sports page design

Dennis Ochoa, Art Director; **Raúl A. Flores,** Editor; **Julie Ann Contreras,** Deputy Editor

Sun Journal
Lewiston, Maine

Sports page design

Ryan Powell, Sports Designer; **Paul Wallen,** M.E./Visuals; **Steve Sherlock,** Sports Editor; **Bill Foley,** Assistant Sports Editor; **Sports Staff**

Aftonbladet
Stokholm, Sweden

Sports page design
Staff

Lördagen 26 juni 2004 kl 23.21 – ett skott till höger och EM-festen är över

" Det är bara att konstatera att vi inte hade turen på vår sida när den här matchen skulle avgöras. Jag tog ingen straff och det måste man göra om man ska vinna när matchen ska avgöras på straffsparksläggning. Det här är helt klart det grymmaste sättet att förlora på.
— *Andreas Isaksson*

Sun Journal
Lewiston, Maine

Sports page design

Ryan Powell, Sports Designer; **Paul Wallen,** M.E./Visuals; **Steve Sherlock,** Sports Editor; **Pete Gorski,** News Artist; **Rex Rhoades,** Executive Editor; **Sports Staff**

O Popular
Goiânia, Brazil

Sports page design

André Rodrigues, Art Director; **Marcelo Roriz,** Page Design Editor; **Christie Queiroz,** Art Editor; **Pollyanna Duarte,** Designer; **William Fernando,** Illustrator; **Luciano Martins,** Section Editor; **Robson Macedo,** Reporter

Torero de mar

Jimmy Rotherham demostró que cualquier surfista salvadoreño puede, con pasión y algo de suerte, saltar al mundo del profesionalismo.

El Gráfico
Antiguo Cuscatlán, El Salvador

Sports page design

Alexander Rivera, Designer; **Gabriel Orellana,** Designer; **Fernando Golscher,** Manager; **Húber Rosales,** Photographer; **Raúl Gavidia,** Photographer; **Mario Amaya,** Photographer

HOLLINGER
Black pourrait confier
ses actions à une fiducie
Page C 3

LIVRES
Une part importante
du marché est québécoise
Page C 8

ÉCONOMIE

Le pétrole franchit la barrière des 50 $US

Inquiétude pour l'économie mondiale

Adtranz: Bombardier règle avec Chrysler

Les provinces se taillent une stratégie du diamant

ALENA: Jim Peterson est ouvert à la discussion

Le Devoir
Montreal, Quebec, Canada

Business page design

Jules Richer, News Director; **Gérard Bérubé,** Business Editor; **Dominique Reny,** Section Editor; **Bernard Descôteaux,** Publisher; **Jean-Robert Sansfaçon,** M.E.; **Christian Tiffet,** Art Director/Designer

---

Expansión
Madrid, Spain

Business page design

Mercedes Suils, Graphic Artist/Designer; **José Juan Gámez,** Art Director; **Amaya Verde,** Graphic Artist/Designer

ENTORNO

El desembarco español en Atenas

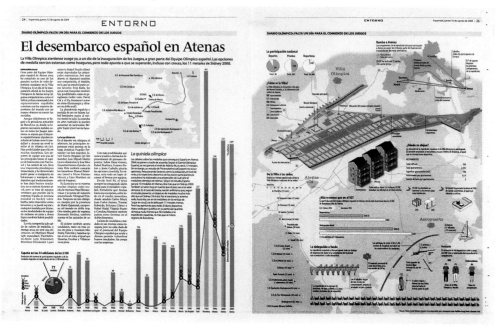

SMART CARS: Even smaller than the Mini Cooper F1   STEPFORD QUIZ: Are you the perfect wife? F3

BUSINESS

50 YEARS AND STILL ON A ROLL

ROLLODROME

For half a century the Larrivee family has run a business that caters to skaters.

Pluck, Onfolio

Plug-ins help sort, store info gathered on Web

Sun Journal
Lewiston, Maine

Business page design

Heather McCarthy, Senior Design Editor; **Daryn Slover,** Photographer

---

Monday, June 21, 2004

MONTEREY COUNTY
AGRICULTURE

Ag 2004

WILL FARMING FOLLOW ITS PRESENT PATTERN?

The Salinas Californian
Salinas, Calif.

Business page design

Anjanette Rieger, News Editor

WORLD'S BEST DESIGNED NEWSPAPER

Poniedziałek

Droga po kapitał
W wersji papierowej i na płycie kompendium wiedzy, jak sięgnąć po miliony miliardy.

chemia

Puls Biznesu

325!
POPULISTÓW

50-proc.
stawka PIT
przegłosowana
Ręce opadają.
Szkoda słów.
STRONY 2-5

CHODZI o to,
aby JEŹDZIĆ

Nissan Micra
za 620 zł
miesięcznie

Puls Biznesu
Warsaw, Poland

Business page design

Jacek Utko, Art Director

El Imparcial
Hermosillo, México

Inside news page design

Hugo Éric Pérez, Designer; **Carlos René Gutiérrez**, Illustrator; **Miyoshi Katsuda**, Art Director; **Jorge Morales**, Editor; **Vicente Gallardo**, Statistics

Palabra
Saltillo, México

Inside news page design/ 49,999 and under

Fabiola A. Pérez Coronado, Graphic Designer; **Javier Fuentes**, Editor; **Pedro Ruiz**, Illustrator; **Delgar Garcia**, Graphics Editor; **David Brondo**, Subdirector Editorial; **Jorge A. Meléndez Ruiz**, Director Editorial

Palabra
Saltillo, México

Inside news page design

Mónica Reyna, Graphic Designer; **Néstor González**, Editor; **Pedro Ruiz**, Illustrator; **Delgar Garcia**, Graphics Editor; **David Brondo**, Editor Director; **Jorge A. Meléndez Ruiz**, Editorial Director

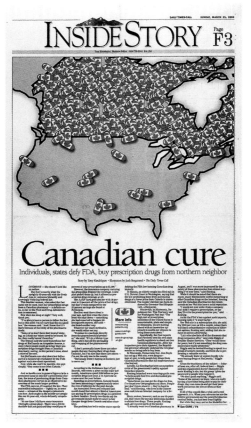

Palabra
Saltillo, México

Inside news page design

Francisco Manuel Sandoval, Graphic Designer; **Néstor González**, Editor; **Pedro Ruiz**, Illustrator; **Delgar Garcia**, Graphics Editor; **David Brondo**, Editor Director; **Jorge A. Meléndez Ruiz**, Editorial Director

Palabra
Saltillo, México

Inside news page design

Francisco Manuel Sandoval, Designer/Graphic Designer; **Néstor González**, Graphic Designer; **Jorge A. Meléndez Ruiz**, Editorial Director; **Delgar Garcia**, Graphics Editor; **David Brondo**, Editor Director

Daily Times-Call
Longmont, Colo.

Inside news page design

Josh Bergstrand, Features Editor

Zeta Weekly
Tijuana, México

News design/Page(s)/Other

Ariel Freaner, Designer/Digital Illustration; **J. Jesus Blancornelas,**
Editor/Co-Director

Zeta Weekly
Tijuana, México

News design/Page(s)/Other

Ariel Freaner, Designer/Digital Illustration; **J. Jesus Blancornelas,**
Editor/Co-Director

Zeta Weekly
Tijuana, México

News design/Page(s)/Other

Ariel Freaner, Designer/Digital Illustration; **J. Jesus Blancornelas,**
Editor/Co-Director

O Independente
Lisbon, Portugal

News design/Page(s)/Other

Sónia Matos, Art Director; **Fernando Barata,** Designer; **Natacha Pereira,** Editor;
Inés Serra Lopes, Editor-in-Chief; **Alain Corbel,** Illustrator

El Imparcial
Hermosillo, México

Inside news page design

Manuel Lizárraga, Designer; **Miyoshi Katsuda,** Art Director; **Carlos
René Gutiérrez,** Illustrator; **Alfredo Zazueta,** Editor

El Caribe
Santo Domingo, Dominican Republic

News design/Page(s)/Other

Victor Manuel Tejada, Director; **María Virgen Gómez,**
Sub-Director; **Roberto Severino,** Art Director/Designer;
Carlos Pérez-Díaz, Innovation Consulting; **Montserrat
Ortiz Roca,** Innovation Consulting

The Tuscaloosa News
Tuscaloosa, Ala.

Lifestyle/Features page design

Janet Sudnik, Copy Editor/Page Designer

El Caribe
Santo Domingo, Dominican Republic

News design/Page(s)/Other

Staff

Mural
Zapopan, México

Lifestyle/Features page design

Fernando Jauregui, Designer/Ilustrator/Photographer; **Felipe Lucero,** Design M.E.; **Mauricio Rangel,** Design M.E.; **Fernando Jauregui,** Art Director; **Karla Garduño,** Page Editor; **Jaun Carlos Garda,** Editorial Coordinator; **Guillermo Camacho,** Editorial Director; **Lázaro Ríos,** General Editorial Director

Taipei Times
Taipei, Taiwan

Lifestyle/Features page design

June Hsu, Designer; **Huei-tse Ho,** Illustrator; **Yi-chun Chen,** Design Editor

O Independente
Lisbon, Portugal

Lifestyle/Features page design

Sónia Matos, Art Director & Designer; **Inés Serra Lopes,** Editor-in-Chief; **Joana Petiz,** Editor

O Independente
Lisbon, Portugal

Entertainment page design

Sónia Matos, Art Director & Designer; **Inés Serra Lopes,** Editor-in-Chief; **Fátima Albuquerque,** Designer; **Leonardo Ralha,** Editor

O Independente
Lisbon, Portugal

Entertainment page design

Sónia Matos, Art Director & Designer; **Leonardo Ralha,** Editor; **Inês Serra Lopes,** Editor-in-Chief

O Independente
Lisbon, Portugal

Entertainment page design

Sónia Matos, Art Director & Designer; **Inés Serra Lopes,** Editor-in-Chief; **Leonardo Ralha,** Editor

O Independente
Lisbon, Portugal

Entertainment page design

Sónia Matos, Art Director & Designer; **Inés Serra Lopes,** Editor-in-Chief; **Fátima Albuquerque,** Designer; **Leonardo Ralha,** Editor

O Independente
Lisbon, Portugal

Entertainment page design

Sónia Matos, Art Director & Designer; **Inés Serra Lopes,** Editor-in-Chief; **Leonardo Ralha,** Editor

O Independente
Lisbon, Portugal

Entertainment page design

Sónia Matos, Art Director; **Fernando Barata,** Designer; **Leonardo Ralha,** Editor; **Inés Serra Lopes,** Editor-in-Chief

O Independente
Lisbon, Portugal

Entertainment page design

Sónia Matos, Art Director & Designer; **Inés Serra Lopes,** Editor-in-Chief; **Leonardo Ralha,** Editor

O Independente
Lisbon, Portugal

News design/Page(s)/Other

Sónia Matos, Art Director & Designer; **Inés Serra Lopes,** Editor-in-Chief; **Fernando Barata,** Designer; **Gonçalvo Viana,** Illustrator; **Natacha Pereira,** Editor

O Independente
Lisbon, Portugal

News design/Page(s)/Other

Sónia Matos, Art Director & Designer; **Inés Serra Lopes,** Editor-in-Chief; **Fernando Barata,** Designer; **Alejandro Gozblau,** Illustrator; **Natacha Pereira,** Editor

Periodico Provincia
Morelia, México

Food page design

Arcelia Guadarrama, Editorial Director; **Gustavo Vega**, Graphics Editor; **Hamlet Ortiz**, Designer; **Erik Knobl**, Designer; **Angel Muñoz**, Designer; **Julio Ramirez**, Designer

ESPECIALES
Domingo
TEQUILA,
UNA BEBIDA CON CARÁCTER

O Independente
Lisbon, Portugal

Home/Real estate page design

Sónia Matos, Art Director; **Fernando Barata**, Designer; **João Fazenda**, Illustrator; **Inés Serra Lopes**, Editor-in-Chief; **Natacha Pereira**, Editor

saúde
Engolidos pelo stresse

CIÊNCIA
Dê-lhes música

ANÁLISE
Dias negros

ALTERNATIVO
Mistério...

Quer combater as suas fobias?

El Imparcial
Hermosillo, México

Science/Technology page design

Luiz H. Cáñez, Designer; **Miyoshi Katsuda**, Art Director; **María del Socorro Arvizu**, Editor

1983 | 1998 | 2002

I SECCIÓN
Informática

1984-2004
20 años
de apple

Objeto de culto

En breve:

1976 | 1984 | 1998 | 2003
1983 | 1988 | 2001

COLLEGE FOOTBALL: Maine loses season opener to Montana, 27-20 C5

SPORTS

SUNDAY, SEPTEMBER 5, 2004 · SunJournal · SECTION C

NO. 54 TEDY BRUSCHI

"This is the team that drafted me, and I've said before that this is the only team I want to play for."

TEAM LEADER

Drafted in 1996, the New England linebacker has helped form the backbone of the Patriots' defense.

BASEBALL
Rangers shut down Boston

Red Sox miss chance to gain ground on Yankees

Hopefully no repeats for Red Sox Nation

Sun Journal
Lewiston, Maine

Sports page designer portfolio/Individual

Ryan Powell, Sports Designer

NCAA BASKETBALL TOURNAMENT: UConn cruises past Vanderbilt C2

SP RTS

FRIDAY, MARCH 26, 2004 · SunJournal · SECTION C

Show time

The Globetrotters bring their slapstick brand of hoops to town for the first time in nearly 40 years.

FLYING HIGH:

Goalies in spotlight

Jimmy Howard leads Maine into today's NCAA East Regional matchup with Harvard.

NCAA hockey
Maine (24-7-3) vs. Harvard (18-14-3), 5 p.m. (MCO9)

One last hurrah?

Punchless B's fall to Leafs

More boxing on tap at Multi-Purpose Center

One that got away

Sun Journal
Lewiston, Maine

Sports page designer portfolio/Individual

Paul Wallen, M.E./Visuals

ATHENS 2004

MONDAY, AUGUST 23, 2004 · SunJournal · SECTION C

THE SUMMER OLYMPICS
DAY 10

STARTING BLOCKS

Mistakes costly for U.S. shooter

WHAT TO WATCH

Today's best

Other highlights

Triumphant

Portland's Wyatt Allen and men's eight team row to gold

MEDAL COUNT

U.S. WOMEN FALL SHORT OF GOLD

HOW MAINE OLYMPIANS FARED

WYATT ALLEN

IAN CROCKER

SLOAN DUROSS

KEVIN EASTLER

INSIDE SPORTS

Mainelacs trade goalie to division rival

TRACK AND FIELD
Gatlin sprints to gold

WORLD'S FASTEST:

Sun Journal
Lewiston, Maine

Sports page designer portfolio/Individual

Ryan Powell, Sports Designer

Conexion
San Antonio, Texas

Features page designer portfolio/Individual

Dennis Ochoa, Art Director

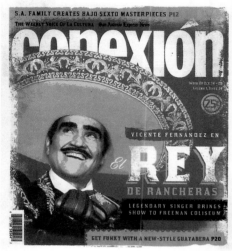

Noticias
Oaxaca, México

Sports page designer portfolio/Individual

Rosalba Morales, Designer

Style Weekly
Richmond, Va.

Features page designer portfolio/Individual

Jeffrey Bland, Art Director

Jacksonville Journal-Courier
Jacksonville, Ill.

Features page designer portfolio/Individual

Guido Strotheide, Designer

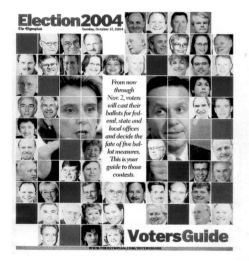

The Olympian
Olympia, Wash.

Combination/Individual

Mark Brunton, Graphic Artist

The Eureka Reporter
Eureka, Calif.

Features page designer portfolio/Individual

Kevin Bell, Graphic Artist

Tabasco Hoy
Villahermosa, México

Information graphics, Non-breaking

Isaac De Coss, Art Director; **Gustavo Alonso Ortiz,** Editor Infographics; **Lizzeth Huerta,** Infographics

Poughkeepsie Journal
Poughkeepsie, N.Y.

Information graphics, Non-breaking

Dean DiMarzo, Director/Design & Graphics

Noticias
Oaxaca, México

Combination/Individual

Teresa Lopez, Designer

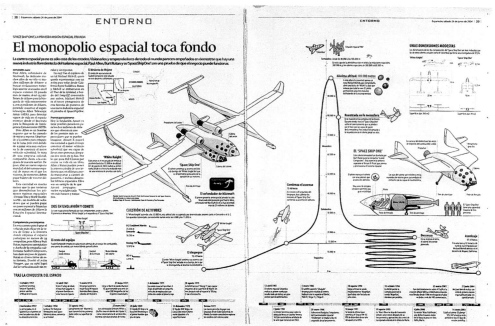

Expansión
Madrid, Spain

Information graphics, Non-breaking

Pablo MaRamírez, Graphics Editor;
José Juan Gámez, Art Director

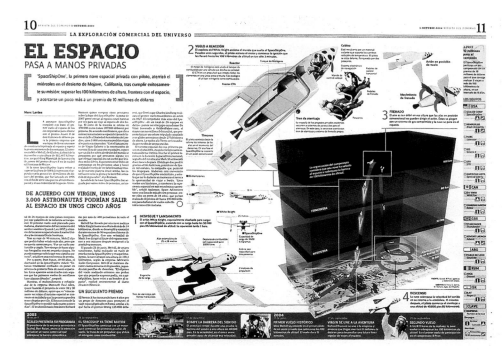

Diario de Sevilla
Seville, Spain

Information graphics, Non-breaking

Manuel Romero Tortosa, Graphics
Editor; **Cristina García Rivera,**
Graphic Artist; **Raquel Feria
Legrand,** Graphic Artist; **Francisco
Barquilla García,** Graphic Artist;
David Uribarri Paguillo, Graphic
Artist

Expansión
Madrid, Spain

Information graphics, Non-breaking

Pablo MaRamírez, Graphics Editor; **José Juan Gámez,** Art
Director; **Rubén Jiménez Lapetra,** Researcher

Expansión
Madrid, Spain

Information graphics/Portfolios/
Non-breaking news (individual)

Pablo MaRamírez, Graphics Editor

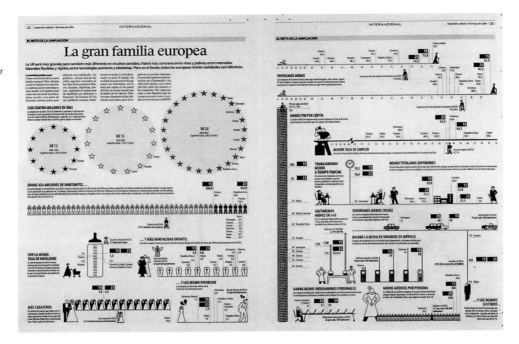

Expansión
Madrid, Spain

Information graphics, charting

Pablo MaRamírez, Graphics
Editor; **José Juan Gámez,** Art
Director; **Rubén Jiménez Lapetra,**
Researcher

Diario de Sevilla
Sevilla, Spain

Information graphics, Non-breaking

Manuel Romero Tortosa, Graphics
Editor; **Cristina García Rivera,**
Graphic Artist; **Francisco Barquilla,**
Graphic Artist; **Antonio Montilla,**
Graphic Artist

BUSINESS
THE FINE ART

SPECIAL COVERAGE

chapter 8

GOLD

The Plain Dealer
Cleveland, Ohio

Special coverage, section pages/Cover only

Terry Chapman, Designer; **Andrea Levy,**
Illustrator; **David Kordalski,** A.M.E./Visuals;
Kristen DelGuzzi, BusinessMonday Editor

This is a brilliantly subtle
way to communicate a
dry story in a beautiful
way. You can almost hear
the page as the pennies
drop. It's a one-two
punch as the letter "A"
is revealed. But, even
if you don't see the "A"
the key information is
still communicated. The
restrained typography
reinforces the message.

Esta es una forma
brillante y sutil de
comunicar una historia
dura de buena forma.
Casi se pueden escuchar
las páginas a medida que
caen los centavos. La
forma en que se revela
la letra "A" es lógica e
inmediata. Pero incluso
si no se ve la "A" igual se
comunica la información
clave. El uso restringido
de la tipografía refuerza el
mensaje.

**Los Angeles
Times**
Los Angeles, Calif.

*Special coverage/
Single subject*

**Joseph
Hutchinson,**
Deputy M.E.;
Wally Skalij,
Photographer;
Paul Gonzales,
Design Editor; **Bill
Gaspard,** News
Design Director;
Genaro Molina,
Photographer;
Kirk McKoy, Photo
Editor; **Cindy
Hively,** Photo
Editor

**The Plain
Dealer**
Cleveland, Ohio

*Special coverage/
Single subject*

**Mary Lou
Sneyd,** Designer;
Dale Omori,
Photographer

Star Tribune
Minneapolis, Minn.

Special coverage/Sections/With ads

Staff

Star Tribune
Minneapolis, Minn.

Special coverage/Single subject

Staff

The Virginian-Pilot
Norfolk, Va.

Special coverage/Sections/With ads

Robert Suhay, Designer; **Denis Finley,** M.E.;
Deborah Withey, Deputy M.E./Presentation;
Erica Smith, Editor; **Bill Bartel,** Editor

FROM RUSSIA
Torrent of Talent Has Emerged From Bourgeois Pastime

Looking to Higher Technology for Drier Courts

The New York Times
New York, N.Y.

Special coverage/Sections/With ads

Wayne Kamidoi, Art Director; **Bob Kessel,** Illustrator; **Chang W. Lee,** Photographer; **Jill Agostino,** Section Editor; **Staff**

Mini or Hummer, power and fashion drive demand

Big and small: some history

my vintage ride

The Boston Globe
Boston, Mass.

Special coverage/Sections/With ads

Tito Bottitta, Art Director & Designer; **Doreen Vigue,** Editor; **Dan Zedek,** Design Director

Söndags
JULBORD

Dagens Nyheter
Stockholm, Sweden

Special coverage/Sections/With ads

Pelle Asplund, Art Director; **Pär Bjorkman,** Photo Editor; **Åse Bengtsson,** Photo Editor; **Anne-Marie Höglund,** Page Designer; **Kajsa Åström,** Page Designer

The illustration is provocative, the placement is marvelous, the photo play is surprising, and the text wraps are beautiful. Swapping the color palette on the stories about mothers and fathers is a witty touch. It's as delightful as it can be, and it represents much information communicated undauntedly.

La ilustración es provocativa, la ubicación en la página es maravillosa, el uso de la fotografía es sorprendente, y las piezas de texto son bonitas. El cambio de la paleta de color en las historias sobre madres y padres es un toque astuto. Es todo lo agradable que puede ser, y entrega mucha información comunicada de forma abierta.

El Panamá América
Panama City, Panama

Special coverage/Single subject

Nelson Fernández, Designer; **Alfredo Lammie,** Illustrator; **Alejandro Ortiz,** Illustrator

The scope and idea of this section is amazing. Elevating this entry are its superb composition, use of color, vertical construction, the grid and its structural underpinning. The level of reporting and commitment to readers is top notch.

El alcance y la idea de esta sección es sorprendente. Enalzan esta pieza su excelente composición, uso del color, construcción vertical, la grilla y el soporte de su estructura. La calidad del reporteo y la dedicación a los lectores es de primer nivel.

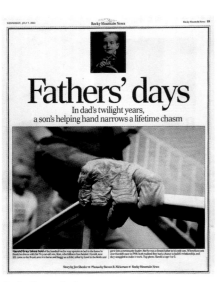

The Seattle Times
Seattle, Wash.

Special coverage/ Single subject

Boo Davis, Designer/ Illustrator

Rocky Mountain News
Denver, Colo.

Special coverage/Sections/Without ads

Chris Schneider, Photographer; **Armando Arrieta,** Designer; **Janet Reeves,** Director/Photography; **Randall K. Roberts,** Presentation Director; **Kathy Bogan,** Design Director

Rocky Mountain News
Denver, Colo.

Special coverage/Sections/Without ads

Lori Montoya, Designer; **Steven R. Nickerson,** Photographer; **Janet Reeves,** Director/Photography; **Randall K. Roberts,** Presentation Director; **Kathy Bogan,** Design Director

El Mundo
Madrid, Spain

Special coverage/Sections/With ads

Carmelo Caderot, Design Director; **Manuel De Miguel,** Art Director & Designer; **Jose Carlos Saez,** Designer

SILVER

The Macon Telegraph
Macon, Ga.

Special coverage, section pages/Inside page or spread

Napo Monasterio, Designer

This is such a simple and elegant solution. Many papers might have thought to use the pencil, but not putting the pencil back together in the end. This series of images tells the story of Americans' lives around March and April — and what the section can help them accomplish.

Ésta es una solución muy sencilla y elegante. Muchos diarios podrían haber optado por usar el lápiz, pero no habrían logrado ensamblarlo completamente al final. Esta serie de imágenes cuenta la historia de vidas norteamericanas cerca de marzo y abril; y lo que esta sección les puede ayudar a lograr.

Savannah Morning News
Savannah, Ga.

Special coverage/Sections/With ads

Stephen Komives, Planning Editor; **Andrea Burg,** News Planner/Designer; **Andrew Ryan,** News Planner/Designer

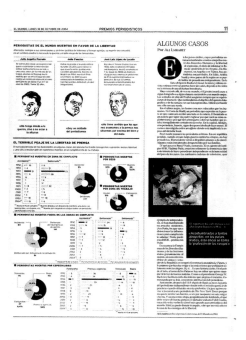

El Mundo
Madrid, Spain

Special coverage/Sections/With ads

Carmelo Caderot, Design Director; **Manuel De Miguel,** Art Director & Designer; **Ulises Culebro,** Illustrator

Sur
Malaga, Spain

Special coverage/Sections/With ads

Alberto Torregrosa, Editorial Design Consultant; **Rafael Ruiz,** Designer; **Baldomero Villanueva,** Section Designer; **Fernando González,** Director/Photography; **Francisco Sánchez Ruano,** Art Director

SILVER

The Boston Globe
Boston, Mass.

Special coverage, section pages/Cover only

Tito Bottitta, Art Director & Designer; **Doreen Vigue,** Editor; **Dan Zedek,** Design Director

If you choose to show details of automobiles, you have many choices. Here, the cropping and color palette blend perfectly, and the type reads as part of the artwork. The elegant refers also complement the page.

Se dispone de muchas alternativas si se elige mostrar detalles de los automóviles. En este caso, el recorte fotográfico y la paleta de color se funden perfectamente, y la tipografía se lee como si fuera parte del arte. Los elegantes llamados también sirven la página.

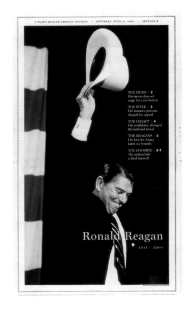

The Plain Dealer
Cleveland, Ohio

Special coverage/ Sections/With ads

David Kordalski, A.M.E./Visuals; **Lisa Griffis,** Designer; **Jeff Greene,** Picture Editor; **Daryl Kannberg,** A.M.E. News

SonntagsZeitung
Zürich, Switzerland

Special coverage/ Sections/With ads

Stefan Semrau, Art Director; **Jürg von Arb,** Designer; **Paolo Friz,** Illustrator

Göteborgs-Posten
Goteborg, Sweden

Special coverage/Sections/With ads

Karin Teghammar Arell, Designer; **Lars Tunbjörk,** Photographer; **Jonny Mattsson,** Photo Editor

Hartford Courant
Hartford, Conn.

Special coverage/Sections/With ads

Tim Reck, Designer; **Suzette Moyer,** Director/Design & Graphics; **Jim Kuykendall,** Graphic Artist; **Alex Nabaum,** Illustrator

The New York Times
New York, N.Y.

Special coverage/Sections/With ads

Wayne Kamidoi, Art Director; **Vincent Laforet,** Photographer; **Fred R. Conrad,** Photographer; **Bob Eckstein,** Illustrator; **Jill Agostino,** Section Editor; **Staff**

San Jose Mercury News
San Jose, Calif.

Special coverage/Sections/Without ads
Staff

The New York Times
New York, N.Y.

Special coverage/Sections/With ads

Lee Yarosh, Art Director; **Wayne Kamidoi**, Art Director; **Bedel Saget**, Graphics Editor; **Joe Ward**, Graphics Editor; **Mika Grondahl**, Graphics Editor; **William McNulty**, Graphics Editor; **Brett Taylor**, Graphics Editor; **Brad Smith**, Graphics Editor; **Jill Agostino**, Section Editor; **Staff**

SILVER

Pittsburgh Post-Gazette
Pittsburgh, Pa.

Special coverage, section pages/Cover only
Daniel Marsula, Artist

The broad-shouldered figure in the illustration and grimy, golden color palette really evoke Pittsburgh. The page has depth through transparency and nuanced typography. It's nostalgic and futuristic at the same time. The line from the tool to the refers is a great touch.

La figura de grandes hombros de la ilustración y la paleta de color lúgubre y dorada realmente evocan la ciudad de Pittsburgh. La página tiene profundidad a través de la transparencia y la sutil tipografía. Es nostálgica y futurística a la vez. La línea de la herramienta a los llamados es un gran toque.

Houston Chronicle
Houston, Texas

Special coverage/Sections/With ads

Dave Wilson, Designer; **Kevin Pender**, Section Editor; **Dan Cunningham**, Assistant Managing Editor/Sports; **Fred M. Faour**, Assistant Sports Editor; **Jay Lee**, Assistant Sports Editor; **Robert Wuensche**, Illustrator

The San Diego Union-Tribune
San Diego, Calif.

Special coverage/Sections/With ads

Greg Manifold, Sports Designer; **Michael Price**, Presentation Editor; **Christina Martinez**, Illustrator; **Doug Williams**, Deputy Sports Editor; **Brian Cragin**, Deputy Graphics Editor

SILVER

The Seattle Times
Seattle, Wash.

Special coverage, section pages/Cover only

Julie Notarianni, Designer/Illustrator

The bull-and-bear imagery has been used over and over again. But this cover, with dusty texture, sophisticated layering, flying numbers and suit-wearing cowboy, is a winner. The implication is that the market is going to be a wild ride, and even if you attempt to control it, it may or may not go your way.

Las imágenes del toro y el oso ha sido usada una y otra vez. Sin embargo, esta tapa, con una textura polvorienta, el uso sofisticado de capas, los números que vuelan por el aire y el vaquero con traje ejecutivo, es todo un ganador. La implicación es de que el mercado accionario va a ser un galope movido, y que incluso si se intenta controlarlo, puede que resulte beneficioso para uno o no.

Chicago Tribune
Chicago, Ill.

Special coverage, section pages/Cover only

Elaine Melko, Art Director; **Stefano Vitale,** Illustrator; **Elaine Matsushita,** Home and Garden Editor

The San Diego Union-Tribune
San Diego, Calif.

Special coverage, section pages/Cover only

Greg Manifold, Sports Designer; **Michael Price,** Presentation Editor

San Francisco Chronicle
San Francisco, Calif.

Special coverage, section pages/Cover only

Dick Krepel, Illustrator; **Matt Petty,** Art Director; **Nanette Bisher,** Creative Director; **Glenn Schwarz,** Sports Editor

El Mundo
Madrid, Spain

Special coverage, section pages/Cover only

Carmelo Caderot, Design Director/Designer; **Manuel De Miguel,** Art Director & Designer; **Chano del Rio,** Designer

SILVER

The Columbus Dispatch
Columbus, Ohio

Special coverage/Sections/With ads

Todd Bayha, Page Designer; **Scott Minister,** Art Director; **Barth Falkenberg,** Photo Director

Each photo takes almost the same amount of space, but one hardly notices. The restraint in design, excellent organization and deft spacing make all images stand out. Also worth recognizing are the items identifying the photographers and explaining their point of view.

Cada foto toma casi el mismo espacio, pero eso apenas se nota. La restricción en el diseño, la excelente organización y el correcto espaciamiento hacen que todas las imágenes se destaquen bien. También vale la pena reconocer los ítemes que identifican a los fotógrafos y que explican sus puntos de vista.

El Mundo

Madrid, Spain

Special coverage, section pages/Cover only

Carmelo Caderot, Design Director/Designer; **Manuel De Miguel,** Art Director & Designer; **Ulises Culebro,** Illustrator

San Francisco Chronicle
San Francisco, Calif.

Special coverage, section pages/Cover only

Mark Ulriksen, Illustrator; **Matt Petty,** Art Director; **Nanette Bisher,** Creative Director; **Glenn Schwarz,** Sports Editor

SILVER

O Globo
Rio de Janeiro, Brazil

Special coverage/Sections/Without ads

Renata Maneschy, Designer; **Custodio Coimbra,** Photographer; **Marizilda Cruppe,** Photographer; **Alvim,** Associate Art Editor/Infographics; **Fernando Alvarus,** Associate Art Editor/Infographics; **Paulo Motta,** Editor; **Jorge Antonio Barros,** Associate Editor; **Liane Conçalves,** Associate Editor

Smart typography and color add to the rawness of the story. It's an approach that could have come off gimmicky, but the designers here overcame this trap with excellent execution. The photography held the dignity of the subjects.

La tipografía y el color inteligente hacen lucir la crudeza del artículo. Es un enfoque que pudo haber resultado artificioso, pero estos diseñadores sortearon esta trampa con una excelente ejecución. La fotografía mantuvo la dignidad de los sujetos.

La Nación
Buenos Aires, Argentina

Special coverage, section pages/Cover only

Silvana Segu, Graphic Designer

El Mundo
Madrid, Spain

Special coverage, section pages/Cover only

Carmelo Caderot, Design Director/Designer; **Manuel De Miguel,** Art Director & Designer; **Jose Carlos Saez,** Designer

El Mundo
Madrid, Spain

Special coverage, section pages/Cover only

Carmelo Caderot, Design Director/Designer; **Manuel De Miguel,** Art Director & Designer; **Jose Carlos Saez,** Designer

SILVER

Fort Worth Star-Telegram
Fort Worth, Texas

Special coverage/Sections/With ads

Celeste Williams, Sports Editor; **Michael Currie,** Assistant Sports Editor; **Ralph Lauer,** Photographer; **Clif Bosler,** Graphic Designer

The level of detail and work that went into this section is exceptional. To explain each sport using small, photograph-based graphics takes time, coordination and people skills. The results stretch the limits of the genre.

El nivel de detalle y trabajo que tomó esta sección es excepcional. Explicar cada deporte usando gráficos pequeños y basados en fotografías toma tiempo, coordinación y habilidades. Los resultados expanden los límites de este género.

Chicago Tribune
Chicago, Ill.

Special coverage, section pages/Cover only

Chris Soprych, Illustrator; **Michael Kellams,** Assistant Sports Editor; **Bill Adee,** Sports Editor

El Mundo
Madrid, Spain

Special coverage, section pages/Cover only

Carmelo Caderot, Design Director/Designer; **Manuel De Miguel,** Art Director & Designer; **Chano del Rio,** Designer

The Dallas Morning News
Dallas, Texas

Special coverage, section pages/Inside page or spread

Sergio Pecanha, Graphic Artist; **Rob Schneider,** Design Editor/Sports

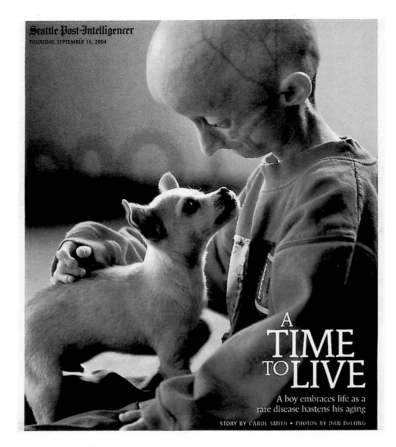

Seattle Post-Intelligencer
THURSDAY, SEPTEMBER 16, 2004

A TIME TO LIVE

A boy embraces life as a
rare disease hastens his aging

STORY BY CAROL SMITH • PHOTOS BY DAN DeLONG

Seattle Post-Intelligencer
Seattle, Wash.

Special coverage/Sections/Without ads

Kurt Schlosser, Designer; **Dan Delong,**
Photographer

'I BETTER EAT IT WHILE I CAN'

Invaders feel right at home in Duluth port

Brown trout, steelhead are
among intentional imports

BARBARIANS AT THE GATE: A LOOK AT THE NEXT ROUND OF POTENTIAL INVADERS

Star Tribune
Minneapolis, Minn.

Reprints

Rhonda Prast,
Assistant Director/
Design/News;
Ray Grumney,
Graphics Director;
Marlin Levison,
Photographer;
Kyndell Harkness,
Photographer;
Mark Boswell,
Artist; **Jane
Friedmann,** Artist;
Vickie Kettlewell,
Photo Editor;
David Shaffer,
Team Leader;
Tom Meersman,
Reporter; **Mi-Ai
Parrish,** A.M.E./
Sunday

CONVENTION 2004

THE *new* BOSTON

PEOPLE • SPORTS • ARCHITECTURE • BRAINS • INNOVATION • YOUTH

A
historic
city
reinvents
itself in
surprising
ways.

**The Boston
Globe**
Boston, Mass.

*Special coverage,
section pages/Cover
only*

Nick King, Editor;
Gregory Klee,
Designer; **Dan
Zedek,** Design
Director

100 años Miranda 1904-2004

Miranda el
periodista

Ideal
Granada, Spain

Special coverage/Sections/Without ads

José Santos, Designer; **Carlos J. Valdemoros,** Designer/Infographics

GRO TESco

KARLA SUCNIT CHÁVEZ

Cariconte

se bajó del bus e inmediatamente
sacó el cigarrillo que llevaba en la
bolsa de la camisa, lo encendió y
aspiró con ansiedad el humo. Era una
desgracia que el bus se tardara más de una hora desde su trabajo hasta su casa, porque la necesidad de nicotina se hacía sentir justo en
medio de sus pulmones. Lo único bueno de ese trayecto de mierda

La Prensa Gráfica
Antiguo Cuscatlán, El Salvador

Special coverage/Sections/Without ads

Gabriela de Vega, Designer; **Mauricio Duarte,** Artist; **Enrique Contreras,** Design Editor; **Héctor Ramírez,** Design
CoEditor; **Florence Natsumy,** Design CoEditor; **Gabriel Trillos,** Newsroom Manager

Sports crazy

The New England Patriots won two of the last three Super Bowls, and the Red Sox last won the World Series in 1918. So who's the reigning king of this sports town? The Red Sox. Go figure. [BY CHARLES P. PIERCE]

The Boston Globe
Boston, Mass.

*Special coverage/
Sections/With ads*

Doug Most, Editor;
Gregory Klee, Designer;
Dan Zedek, Design
Director

The Eagle-Tribune
North Andover,
Mass.

*Special
coverage,
section pages/
Cover only*

Dan Ryan,
Design &
Graphics Editor;
Todd Dybas,
Designer

Star Tribune
Minneapolis, Minn.

*Special coverage,
section pages/Inside
page or spread*

Mark Hvidsten,
Designer; **Jerry
Zgoda,** Writer; **Mark
Wollemann,** Assistant
Sports Editor; **Cory
Powell,** Presentation
Director; **Glen Crevier,**
A.M.E./Sports

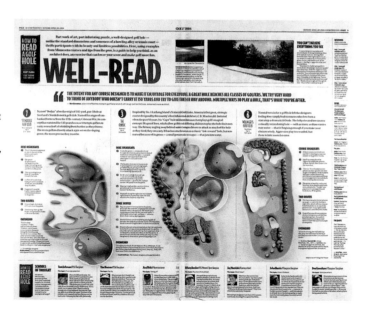

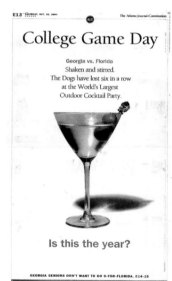

**The Atlanta
Journal &
Constitution**
Atlanta, Ga.

*Special coverage,
section pages/
Cover only*

Vernon Carne,
Artist; **Paul Kasko,**
Assistant Sports
Desk Manager;
Rick Crotts,
Presentation
Editor/News Art
Manager; **Dee Dee
D'Asaro,** Features
Desk/Design
Manager

Récord
México City, México

Special coverage/Single subject

Aarón Zúñiga Castañeda, Section Designer; **Alfredo Kassem,** Photographer; **Alejandro Belman,**
Design Editor/Designer; **José Luis Tapia,** Editor; **Alejo Nájera,** Design Editor; **Alberto Nava,** Art Director;
Alejandro Gómez, Editorial Director; **José Luis Barros,** Graphics Editor

El Diario de Hoy
San Salvador, El Salvador

Special coverage/Single subject

Juan Durán, Art Director & Designer; **Teodoro Lira,** Graphics Editor; **Jorge Castillo,** Infographics Editor;
Lafitte Fernandez, Editor; **Remberto Rodriguez,** Graphics Co-Editor

The Press Democrat
Santa Rosa, Calif.

Special coverage, multiple sections/Without ads

Steve Leone, Designer; **John Burgess,**
Photographer

An 8,400-mile connection

DIFFERENT REALITIES SEPARATE AGILENT WORKERS IN SONOMA COUNTY AND PENANG

OFFSHORING JOBS AND THE NORTH COAST

global shift

FIRST OF FOUR PARTS The reality of a global economy hits home as Agilent moves hundreds of Sonoma County technology jobs to Malaysia

JOBS LEAVE

Story by Erin Allday · Photography by John Burgess

St. Petersburg Times
St. Petersburg, Fla.

Special coverage, section pages/Inside page or spread

Steve Cavendish, Art and Presentation Director; **Don Morris,** Senior Artist

WORST TO FIRST

GAME 7: TAMPA BAY 2, CALGARY 1
JUNE 7, 2004

OFFSHORING JOBS AND THE NORTH COAST

global shift

LAST OF FOUR PARTS Educated workers in India and elsewhere overseas compete for jobs once thought to be deeply rooted in America

THE FUTURE

Story by Erin Allday · Photography by John Burgess

DISRUPTIVE & DARING

the ENDS

the SECONDARY

Seattle Post-Intelligencer
Seattle, Wash.

Special coverage/Sections/With ads

Mark Evans, Designer; **Scott Eklund,** Photographer

THE OSCARS

Really winging it

Los Angeles Times
Los Angeles, Calif.

Special coverage, section pages/Inside page or spread

Joseph Hutchinson,
Deputy M.E.; **Bill Gaspard,**
News Design Director;
Paul Gonzales, Designer;
Calvin Hom, Photo Editor;
Kirk McKoy, Photo Editor;
Cindy Hively, Photo
Editor; **Anacleto Rapping,**
Photographer; **Gary
Friedman,** Photographer;
Kelli Sullivan, Deputy
Design Director; **Michael
Whitley,** Deputy Design
Director

Récord
México City, México

Special coverage, multiple sections/With ads

Ulises Bravo, Photographer; **Alejo Nájera,** Design Editor/Designer;
Alejandro Belman, Design Editor; **Alberto Nava,** Art Director;
Alejandro Gómez, Editorial Director; **José Luis Barros,** Graphics
Editor; **José Luis Tapia,** Editor; **Iván Pirrón,** Section Editor

The Baltimore Sun
Baltimore, Md.

Special coverage, section pages/Cover only

Derrick Barker, Designer

La Presse
Montréal, Quebec, Canada

Special coverage, section pages/Inside page or spread

David Lambert, Designer; **Benoit Giguere,** Art Director;
Sebastien Rodriguez, Journalist; **Agnes Gruda,** A.M.E. News

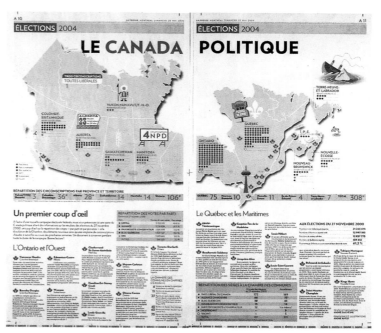

La Presse
Montréal, Quebec, Canada

Special coverage, section pages/Inside page or spread

Andre Rivest, Designer; **Benoit Giguere,** Art Director; **Andre
Duchesne,** Journalist; **Agnes Gruda,** A.M.E. News

Heraldo de Aragón
Zaragoza, Spain

Special coverage/Single subject

Javier Errea, Art Director; **Ana Perez**, Designer; **Kristina Urresti**, Designer; **Asier Barrio**, Designer; **Pilar Ostale**, Designer Manager; **Carmelo Roy**, Designer; **José Miguel Marco**, Photographer; **Oliver Duch**, Photographer

La Nación
Buenos Aires, Argentina

Special coverage, section pages/Cover only

Silvana Segu, Graphic Designer

El Diario de Hoy
San Salvador, El Salvador

Special coverage/Sections/Without ads

Juan Durán, Art Director & Designer; **Teodoro Lira**, Graphics Editor; **Jorge Castillo**, Infographic Editor; **Lafitte Fernandez**, Editor; **Remberto Rodriguez**, Graphics Co-Editor; **Álvaro López**, Photographer

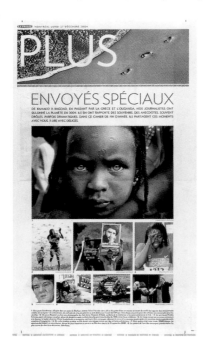

La Presse
Montréal, Quebec, Canada

Special coverage/Sections/Without ads

Helene De Guise, Designer; **Benoit Giguere**, Art Director; **Michele Ouimet**, A.M.E./News

Sunday Herald
Glasgow, Scotland

Special coverage, multiple sections/With ads

Richard Walker, Editor; **Allan Burnett**, Page Editor

PORTFOLIOS

chapter 9

SILVER

Zaman
Istanbul, Turkey

Combination/Individual/175,000 and over

Mustafa Saglam, Designer

These pages are very traditional in their form, but they explode with color, humor and energy. Photos and illustrations are used in innovative ways. Each page is easy to approach and read.

Estas páginas son muy tadicionales en su formato, pero explotan de color, humor y energía. Las fotos y las ilustraciones se usan de forma innovadora. Cada página es fácil de abordar y leer.

El Diario de Hoy
San Salvador, El Salvador

News page designer portfolio/Individual/50,000-174,999

Edgardo Mendoza, Designer

The Boston Globe
Boston, Mass.

News page designer portfolio/Individual/175,000 and over

Vic DeRobertis, Art Director & Designer

The Seattle Times
Seattle, Wash.

News page designer portfolio/Individual/175,000 and over

Paul Morgan, News Designer

The Palm Beach Post
West Palm Beach, Fla.

Sports page designer portfolio/Individual/50,000-174,999

Chris Rukan, Sports Design Director

El Mundo
Madrid, Spain

News page designer portfolio/Individual/175,000 and over

Carmelo Caderot, Design Director

The State
Columbia, S.C.

Sports page designer portfolio/Individual/50,000-174,999

Merry Eccles, Sports Designer

Detroit Free Press
Detroit, Mich.

Sports page designer portfolio/Individual/175,000 and over

Christoph Fuhrmans, Sports Designer

El Mundo
Madrid, Spain

News page designer portfolio/Individual/175,000 and over

Carmelo Caderot, Design Director

SILVER

Dagens Nyheter
Stockholm, Sweden

Illustration/Individual portfolio

Jesper Waldersten, Illustrator

These illustrations take me to another space. The use of color is dark and magical. The range of the artist is fascinating — from fun to whimsical to sensual to macabre to mysterious.

Estas ilustraciones me llevan a otro espacio. El uso del color es oscuro y mágico. El rango de variedad del artista es fascinante; de divertido a misterioso, pasando por mágico, sensual y macabro.

The New York Times
New York, N.Y.

News page designer portfolio/Individual/175,000 and over

Nicholas Blechman, Art Director

The State
Columbia, S.C.

News page designer portfolio/Individual/50,000-174,999

David Montesino, Design Director

San Jose Mercury News
San Jose, Calif.

News page designer portfolio/Individual/175,000 and over

Chuck Burke, Designer

Chicago Sun-Times
Chicago, Ill.

News page designer portfolio/Individual/175,000 and over

Eric White, Design Director

Hartford Courant
Hartford, Conn.

News page designer portfolio/Individual/175,000 and over

Ryan C. Healy, Business Designer

The Oregonian
Portland, Ore.

News page designer portfolio/Individual/175,000 and over

Mark Friesen, Designer

The Boston Globe
Boston, Mass.

News page designer portfolio/Individual/175,000 and over

David Schultz, Assistant Design Director/News

The Laser as Inchworm, Sizing Up Caves and Crevices

Headphones That Make the World Go Away

SILVER

The New York Times
New York, N.Y.

Information graphics/Portfolios/Non-breaking news (individual)/175,000 and over

Frank O'Connell, Graphics Editor

These luscious cutaway renderings are supported by consistently well-layered graphic information that is not too text-heavy. The content is uniformly superb, with expertly written text and excellent headlines. There's not much room to improve on these. The commitment to this beat is a credit to the publication.

Estos seductivos dibujos recortados se sostienen gracias a la bien diseñada información gráfica que no es muy intensiva en texto. El contenido es uniformemente excelente, con textos y titulares expertamente escritos. No hay mucho que mejorar aquí. La dedicación a este tema es un crédito a esta publicación.

International Press
Tokyo, Japan

Sports page designer portfolio/Individual/50,000-174,999

Douglas Okasaki, Graphic Designer

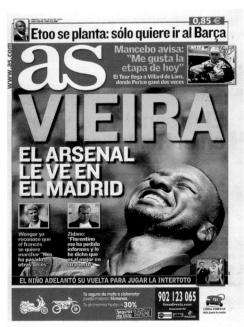

AS
Madrid, Spain

Sports page designer portfolio/Individual/175,000 and over

Julián Perez-Diaz Hernandez, Designer

The New York Times
New York, N.Y.

Sports page designer portfolio/Individual/175,000 and over

Wayne Kamidoi, Art Director

Fort Worth Star-Telegram
Fort Worth, Texas

Sports page designer portfolio/Individual/175,000 and over

Seth Schrock, Design Editor

The Boston Globe
Boston, Mass.

Sports page designer portfolio/Individual/175,000 and over

Grant Staublin, Designer

Diário de Notícias
Lisbon, Portugal

News page designer portfolio/Individual 50,000-174,999

José Maria Ribeirinho, Art Director

The Boston Globe
Boston, Mass.

Sports page designer portfolio/Individual/175,000 and over

Brian Gross, Designer

The Seattle Times
Seattle, Wash.

Sports page designer portfolio/Individual/175,000 and over

Mark McTyre, Desk Editor

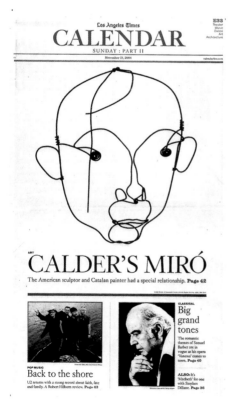

Los Angeles Times
Los Angeles, Calif.

Features page designer portfolio/Individual 175,000 and over

Steven E. Banks, Design Editor

Zaman
Istanbul, Turkey

Sports page designer portfolio/Individual/175,000 and over

Selim Simsroglu, Designer

Toronto Star
Toronto, Ontario, Canada

Features page designer portfolio/Individual/175,000 and over

Spencer Wynn, Designer

The Denver Post
Denver, Colo.

Features page designer portfolio/Individual/175,000 and over

Jeff Neumann, Designer

The Seattle Times
Seattle, Wash.

Features page designer portfolio/Individual/175,000 and over

Boo Davis, Designer/Illustrator

South China Morning Post
Hong Kong, China

Features page designer portfolio/Individual/50,000-174,999

Troy Dunkley, Features Art Director

The Boston Globe
Boston, Mass.

Features page designer portfolio/Individual 175,000 and over

Cindy Daniels, Designer

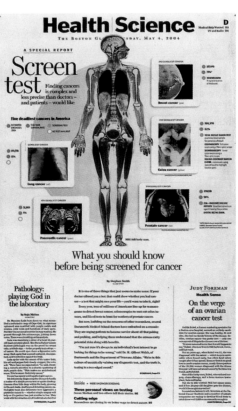

El Mundo Metropoli
Madrid, Spain

Magazine designer portfolio, combination/Individual 175,000 and over

Rodrigo Sanchez, Art Director & Designer

El Pais
Madrid, Spain

Illustration/Individual portfolio

Agustín Sciammarella, Illustrator

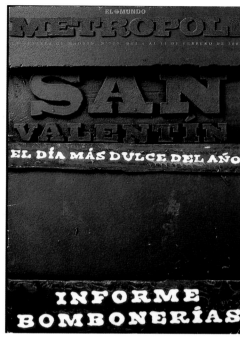

San Francisco Chronicle
San Francisco, Calif.

Features page designer portfolio/Individual 175,000 and over

Elizabeth Burr, Designer

El Mundo
Madrid, Spain

Magazine designer portfolio, combination/Individual 175,000 and over

Carmelo Caderot, Design Director; **Manuel De Miguel,** Art Director & Designer

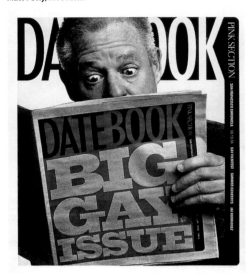

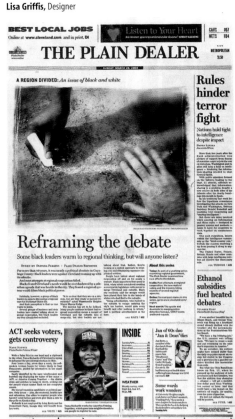

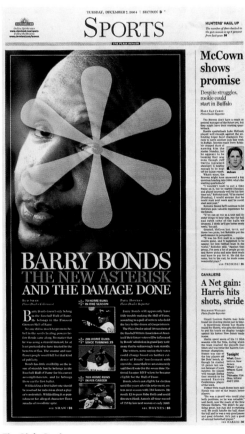

Welt am Sonntag
Berlin, Germany
Combination/Individual/175,000 and over
Jördis Guzmán Bulla, Page Designer

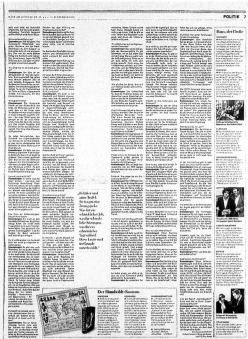

The Buffalo News
Buffalo, N.Y.
Illustration/Individual portfolio
Phillip Burke, Illustrator

International Press
Tokyo, Japan
Combination/Individual/50,000-174,999
Roger Hiyane Yzena, Graphic Designer

Los Angeles Times
Los Angeles, Calif.
Features page designer portfolio/Individual/175,000 and over
Wes Bausmith, Design Editor

Heraldo de Aragón
Zaragoza, Spain
Illustration/Individual portfolio
Luis Grañena, Illustrator

The Seattle Times
Seattle, Wash.
Illustration/Individual portfolio
Boo Davis, Illustrator

The Denver Post
Denver, Colo.
Illustration/Individual portfolio
Jeff Neumann, Illustrator

La Vanguardia
Barcelona, Spain
Illustration/Individual portfolio
Patrick Thomas, Illustrator

La Presse
Montréal, Quebec, Canada
Illustration/Multiple
Bruce Roberts, Illustrator; **Annie Lachapelle,** Art Director; **Celine Tremblan,** Editor-in-Chief; **Lis Keifer,** Writer

Dagens Nyheter
Stockholm, Sweden
Illustration/Individual portfolio
Stina Wirsén, Illustrator

Los Angeles Times
Los Angeles, Calif.

Photography/Portfolio/Individual

Damon Winter, Photographer

Heraldo de Aragón
Zaragoza, Spain

Illustration/Staff or team portfolio

Javier Errea, Art Director; **Ana Perez,** Designer; **Kristin Urresti,** Designer; **Asier Barrio,** Designer; **Pilar Ostale,** Designer Manager; **Carmelo Roy,** Designer

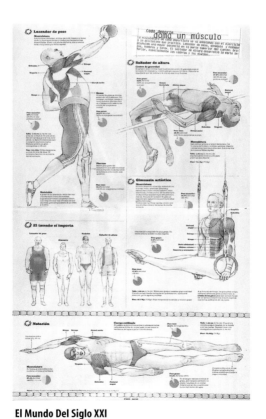

Rocky Mountain News
Denver, Colo.

Information graphics/Portfolios/Non-breaking news (individual)
175,000 and over

Michael Hall, Graphic Artist

Chicago Tribune
Chicago, Ill.

Photography/Portfolio/Individual

Bob Fila, Photographer

El Mundo Del Siglo XXI
Madrid, Spain

Information graphics/Portfolios/Non-breaking news (individual)/
175,000 and over

Emilio Amade, Graphic Artist

San Jose Mercury News
San Jose, Calif.

*Information graphics/Portfolios/Extended coverage/
175,000 and over*

Javier Zarracina, Deputy Graphics Director; **Andrea
Maschietto,** Graphic Artist; **Karl Kahler,** Graphics
Coordinator; **Phil Loubere,** Graphic Artist; **Pai,** Graphics
Director; **Matt Mansfield,** Deputy M.E.; **Kris Viesselman,**
Creative Director

South Florida Sun-Sentinel
Fort Lauderdale, Fla.

Photography/Portfolio/Individual

Mike Stocker, Photographer

The Oregonian
Portland, Ore.

Photography/Portfolio/Staff

Ross William Hamilton,
Photographer;
Rob Finch, Photographer;
Olivia Bucks, Photographer;
Doug Beghtel, Photographer;
Bruce Ely, Photographer;
Patty Reksten, Photo Editor;
Randy Cox, Photo Editor;
Lisa Cowan, Designer

Mount St. Helens

The
beauty
of the
beast

See anyone you know?

The Oregonian
Portland, Ore.

Photography/Portfolio/Individual

Rob Finch, Photographer

The New York Times
New York, N.Y.

Information graphics/Portfolios/Extended coverage/175,000 and over

William McNulty, Graphics Editor; **James Bronzan,** Graphics Editor; **Joe Burgess,** Graphics Editor

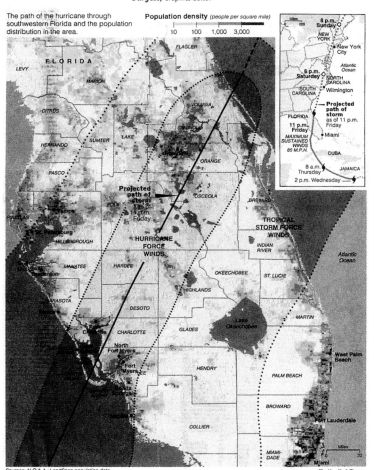

The path of the hurricane through southwestern Florida and the population distribution in the area.

Population density *(people per square mile)*
10   100   1,000   3,000

Projected path of storm as of 11 p.m. Friday

MAXIMUM SUSTAINED WINDS 85 M.P.H.

Projected path of storm 11 p.m. Friday

HURRICANE FORCE WINDS

TROPICAL STORM FORCE WINDS

Sources: N.O.A.A.; LandScan population data

The New York Times

South Florida Sun-Sentinel
Fort Lauderdale, Fla.

Information graphics/Portfolios/Extended coverage/175,000 and over

Belinda Long, Graphics Reporter; **Edward Bremner,** Graphics Reporter; **Cindy Jones-Hulfachor,** Senior Graphics Reporter; **Daniel Niblock,** Senior Graphics Reporter; **Hiram Henriquez,** Senior Graphics Reporter; **Karsten Ivey,** Senior Graphics Reporter; **Len De Groot,** Assistant Graphics Director; **R. Scott Horner,** Assistant Graphics Director; **Don Wittekind,** Graphics Director

Forecasting a storm's path

Meteorologists at the National Hurricane Center study a wide array of data and use experience and intuition to predict a hurricane's future path. Computer-generated weather models and measurements gathered by "Hurricane Hunter" aircraft play a major role. Here's a look at some of the computer-generated tracks the NHC used to create Friday's 11 a.m. forecast for Hurricane Ivan.

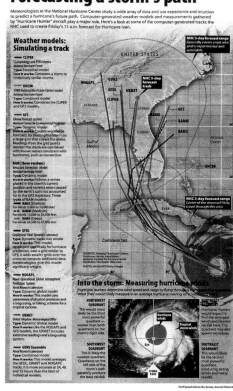

Weather models: Simulating a track

Into the storm: Measuring hurricane winds

Staff graphic/Len de Groot, Daniel Niblock

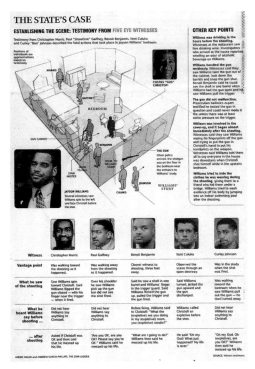

THE STATE'S CASE

ESTABLISHING THE SCENE: TESTIMONY FROM FIVE EYE WITNESSES

OTHER KEY POINTS

	Christopher Morris	Paul Gaffney	Benoit Benjamin	Kent Culuko	Curley Johnson
Witness					
Vantage point					
What he saw of the shooting					
What he heard Williams say before shooting					
... after shooting					

The Star-Ledger
Newark, N.J.

Information graphics/Portfolios/Extended coverage/175,000 and over

Andre Malok, Graphic Artist; **Andrew Garcia Phillips,** Graphics Editor; **George Frederick,** Graphics Editor; **Matthew J. Dowling,** Reporter; **Matthew Reilly,** Reporter; **Mary Yanni,** Reporter

---

CIUDADANOS

El 'Diana Uno' perdió casi todo su combustible durante el naufragio

Los buzos de Salvamento Marítimo confirman que los tanques quedaron «muy afectados» al partirse el carguero

ÍÑAKI CASTRO BILBAO

EL HUNDIMIENTO DEL 'DIANA UNO'

El fuerte viento provocó que el carguero de bandera portuguesa escollara y posteriormente se fuera a pique en el exterior del Puerto de Bilbao

EL ACCIDENTE

EL 'DIANA UNO'

EL RESCATE

EL NAUFRAGIO

EL CORREO
DOMINGO, 8 DE FEBRERO DE 2004

El Correo
Bilbao, Spain

Information graphics/Portfolios/Breaking news (staff)/50,000-174,999

Fernando G. Baptista, Editor; **Gonzalo De Las Heras,** Infographic Artist; **José Miguel Benítez,** Co-Editor; **José Maria Estébanez,** Infographic Artist; **Daniel García,** Freelance Artist; **Leire Fernández,** Infographic Artist; **Sandra Serrano,** Infographic Artist

The New York Times
New York, N.Y.

Information graphics/Portfolios/Breaking news (staff)/175,000 and over

Matthew Ericson, Graphics Editor; **Archie Tse**, Graphics Editor; **Hannah Fairfield**, Graphics Editor; **William McNulty**, Graphics Editor

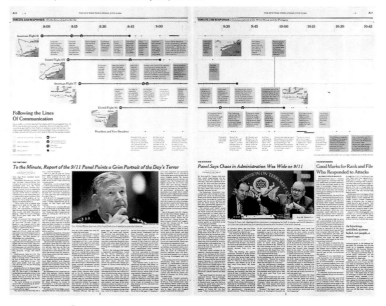

Clarín
Buenos Aires, Argentina

Information graphics/Portfolios/Breaking news (staff)/175,000 and over

Gustavo Lo Valvo, Art Director; **Alejandro Tumas**, Graphic Director; **Pablo Loscri**, Graphics Editor; **Staff Artists**

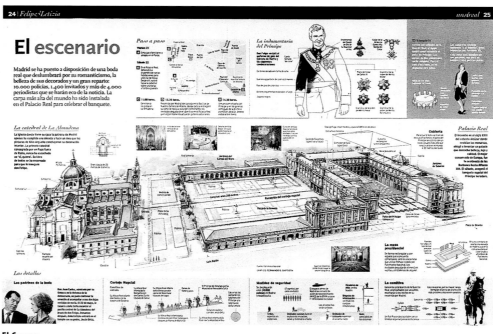

El Correo
Bilbao, Spain

Information graphics/Portfolios/Non-breaking news (individual) 50,000-174,999

Fernando G. Baptista, Editor

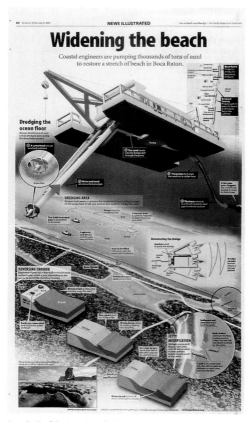

South Florida Sun-Sentinel
Fort Lauderdale, Fla.

Information graphics/Portfolios/Non-breaking news (individual)/ 175,000 and over

Belinda Long, Graphics Reporter

REDESIGNS

Het Parool
Amsterdam, The Netherlands

Redesigns/Overall newspaper

Mario Garcia, Designer; **Erik van Gruijthuijsen,** Editor-in-Chief; **Frits Campagne,** Publisher; **Jan Kny,** Designer; **Henk Koetzier,** Designer; **Frank Hylkema,** Designer; **Hugo Kunz,** Production Editor; **Lucy Prijs,** Design Editor

The publication took the format change as an opportunity to start over completely. The pacing is energetic while maintaining consistency. Welcome surprises come within an established structure. It uses a consistent and pleasing color palette and well-designed labeling from front to back.

El diario aprovechó su cambio de formato para partir completamente desde el comienzo. El ritmo es energético a la vez que mantiene la consistencia. Las bienvenidas sorpresas vienen dentro de una estructura establecida. Usa una paleta consistente y agradable, y un etiquetado bien diseñado desde el comienzo hasta el final.

After

Before

El Diario de Hoy
San Salvador, El Salvador

Redesigns/Overall newspaper

Carlos Perez-Diaz, Innovation Consultant; **Montserrat Ortiz,** Innovation Consultant; **Innovation Staff**

After

Before

After

After

After

Columbia Missourian
Columbia, Mo.

Redesigns/Overall newspaper

Staff

Before

The Buffalo News
Buffalo, N.Y.

Redesigns/Overall newspaper

Margaret Sullivan, Editor; **John Davis,** Design Director;

Before

The Eureka Reporter
Eureka, Calif.

Redesigns/Overall newspaper

Kevin Bell, Graphic Artist; **Alan Jacobson,** Consultant

Before

After

After

After

Before

Before

Before

Anderson Independent Mail
Anderson, S.C.

Redesigns/Overall newspaper

Kristen Powell, Design Consultant; **Leah C. Daniels,** Lifestyle Editor; **Staff**

Zycie Warszawy
Warszawa, Poland

Redesigns/Overall newspaper

Andrzej Zalucki, Editor-in-Chief; **Jacek Utko,** Design Consultant

Eesti Päevaleht
Tallinn, Estonia

Redesigns/Overall newspaper

Priit Hobemagi, Editor-in-Chief; **Merike Pinn,** Design Director; **Cases Associates**

SUNDAY
Star-Telegram
FORT WORTH

Candidates focus on terrorism threat

A CLASSIC FINISH

HOUSTON ★ CHRONICLE

What a blast!

■ **UP 3-2:** Kent homers Astros to brink of World Series

■ **PITCHING:** Backe, Lidge combine for one-hitter

TEXAS REMAP SENT BACK TO LOWER COURT

Seeing is believing in this magic show

Bush, Kerry sharpen attacks on each other

Fending off a flu 'disaster'

A new arm for Asra'a

Fallujah's negotiator obeying insurgents

The Seattle Times
Sunday
Seattle Post-Intelligencer

AUGUST 15, 2004
$1.50

Olerud's 8th-inning hit lifts Yankees over M's

"Our worst fears have come true"

Thousands homeless, 15 dead from Charley

Phelps gets first gold

Real life a tough role for Seattle actors

Talks with rebel cleric collapse; showdown likely

Cowboys vs. Giants · **FAMILY AFFAIR**

Star-Telegram
FORT WORTH

Next round to begin in redistricting fight

Powell sees gains in Iraq

Up, up and away

Bringing the sea to Grapevine isn't easy

Talks skid to a halt at WTO meeting

Houston Chronicle

Religious leaders prepare for *Passion*'s impact

Seeds of discontent

Haiti peace talks shaky

Long, dirty campaign anticipated

Beef bans to have little effect on rodeo

The Seattle Times
Sunday
Seattle Post-Intelligencer

APRIL 25, 2004
$1.50

Dozens die in multiple attacks

Midway into darkness

How two women, one photo stirred national debate

Fort Worth Star-Telegram   Before
Fort Worth, Texas

Redesigns/Overall newspaper

Redesign Team

Houston Chronicle   Before
Houston, Texas

Redesigns/Overall newspaper

Susan Barber, Art Director; **Dan Cunningham,** Project Manager; **Roger Black,** Consultant

---

The Seattle Times   Before
Seattle, Wash.

Redesigns/Overall newspaper

Tracy Porter, Designer; **Jeff Neumann,** Designer; **David Miller,** Design Director; **Susan Jouflas,** Assistant Art Director; **Liz McClure,** Presentation Director; **Celeste Ericsson,** Designer; **Heidi de Laubenfels,** Assistant Managing Editor

After

After

After

The Times of Northwest Indiana Before
Munster, Ind.

Redesigns/Overall newspaper

Matt Erickson, Assistant Sports Editor/Design; **Theresa Badovich,** M.E./
Visuals; **Erica Smith,** News Design Team Leader; **Gladys Rios,** Design
Director; **Karin Lowe,** Features Design Team leader; **Gregg Gearhart,**
Acting Director of Photography; **Bill Thornbro,** Graphics Director; **Design
Staff**

The Denver Post Before
Denver, Colo.

Redesigns/Overall newspaper

J. Damon Cain, M.E./Presentation; **Jeff Neumann,** Lead Designer; **Blair
Hamill,** Graphics Editor; **Jim Carr,** Features Design Editor; **Ingrid Muller,**
Design Director; **Linda Shapley,** Designer; **Leanna Efird,** Designer

The Scotsman Before
Edinburgh, Scotland

Redesigns/Overall newspaper

Palmer Watson, Consultant; **Ross Russell,** Design Editor

After

After

After

Before

Infobae
Buenos Aires, Argentina

Redesigns/Overall newspaper

Carlos Perez-Díaz, Innovation Consultant; **Montserrat Ortiz,**
Innovation Consultant; **Innovation Staff**

O Dia   Before
Rio de Janeiro, Brazil

Redesigns/Section

André Hippertt, Art Director; **Luisa Bousada,** Art Editor; **Carlos
Mancuso,** Designer; **André Gomes,** News Editor; **Claudia Cecilia,** News
Editor; **Alessandro Matheus,** Designer

The Bend Bulletin   Before
Bend, Ore.

Redesigns/Section

Renee Fullerton, Features Designer; **Anders Ramberg,** Presentation
Editor/Design; **Sheila Timony,** Designer; **Denise Costa,** Features Editor

After

After

After

The Eureka Reporter
Eureka, Calif.
Before

Redesigns/Section

Kevin Bell, Graphic Artist; **Alan Jacobson,** Consultant

The Atlanta Journal & Constitution
Atlanta, Ga.
Before

Redesigns/Section

Rick Crotts, Presentation Editor; **Mark Wallgore,** Suburban Editor;
Patty Murphy, Designer; **Todd Duncan,** North Fulton Bureau Chief

El Comercio
Quito, Ecuador
Before

Redesigns/Section

Ponto Moreno, Graphic Director; **Jorge Mantilla,** Graphics Editor;
Guilleermo Corral, Photo Director; **Juan Carlos Morales,** Designer

SECTION D

NFL MONDAY

The Buffalo News

Punt and kickoff runbacks spark victory as Bills take advantage of the windy confines of home

RETURN TICKET

Bills view themselves as a team on the rise

Extra-special teams knocks wind out of Cards

Tonight's game | Week Eight | What's Inside

REPORTAGE   INTERVJU   ESSÄ   BÖCKER   VETENSKAP

SÖNDAG

HBL

En fråga om tro

Allt fler unga i väst konverterar till islam. Det har varit en trend redan en längre tid, men efter attackerna den 11 september 2001 steg antalet. "Föräldraoppror" säger en del, andra säger att det helt enkelt handlar om att muslimerna blivit in synlig del av samhället också här.

After

IMOBILIÁRIO

Espaços & Casas

Expresso

Antiga fábrica transformada em 'lofts'

PARA SOLUÇÕES IMOBILIÁRIAS COMPETITIVAS

SIL   **FALE CONNOSCO**

213 555 555

After

SPORTS

Lowest of the low

Bills keep sinking with home loss to Texans. Page 3

The Buffalo News   Before
Buffalo, N.Y.

Redesigns/Section

Vincent J. Chiaramonte, Designer

SÖNDAG

HUFVUDSTADSBLADET
Andra sektionen
25 januari 2004

Reportage & Analys • Liv & Lust • Hem & Fritid • Resor

Hårfin skillnad

Så skön och så bedräglig. Skiftande i allt från svart och grått till vitt och blått. Blank och glansig eller grov och skrovlig. Is är lite som eld, fascinerande och farlig. Is förtjänar all respekt, säger Patrick Eriksson, iskännare och forskare på isstjänsten vid Havsforskningsinstitutet.

Forskaren som brinner för is

Hufvudstadsbladet HBL   Before
Helsinki, Finland

Redesigns/Section

Marita Granroth, Head of Layout Dept.; **Jesper Vuori,** Layout; **Kristofer Pasanen,** Layout Journalist; **Ally Palmer,** Design Consultant; **Terry Watson,** Design Consultant

---

Expresso
IMOBILIÁRIO

Escritórios

Investimento de 8,5 milhões de euros

MERCADO
Investir na qualidade

Monte Gordo vai ser requalificado

Marinha–Guincho supera a crise

EDIFÍCIO CRISTAL

OFFICE HALL

• 10.989 m² DE ESCRITÓRIOS
• 411 LUGARES DE ESTACIONAMENTO
• EXCELENTE LOCALIZAÇÃO E ACESSOS

ESCRITÓRIOS
ARRENDAMENTO

Expresso   Before
Paco de Arcos, Portugal

Redesigns/Section

Pedro Pimentel, Page Designer

THE BEST OF NEWSPAPER DESIGN 26 | REDESIGNS | **255**

After

After

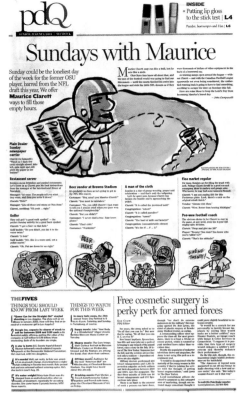

After

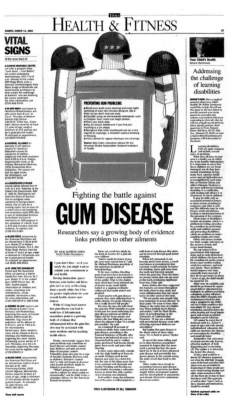

The Times of Northwest Indiana
Munster, Ind.

Redesigns/Section

Matt Erickson, Assistant Sports Editor/Design; **Theresa Badovich,** M.E./ Visuals; **Karin Lowe,** Features Team Leader; **Features Staff**

Before

The Denver Post
Denver, Colo.

Redesigns/Section

Jeff Neumann, Designer; **Ed Smith,** Arts & Entertainment Editor; **Ray Rinaldi,** A.M.E./Features & Arts; **J. Damon Cain,** M.E./Presentation & Design

Before

The Plain Dealer
Cleveland, Ohio

Redesigns/Section

Emmet Smith, Designer; **Staci Andrews,** Designer; **Kim Crow,** Deputy Features Editor; **David Kordalski,** A.M.E./Visuals; **Elizabeth McIntyre,** A.M.E./Features

Before

AT HOME

HOMING IN ON HOLIDAY GIFTS

Photos by MICHAEL McANDREWS

Escapes & Getaways

THE BUFFALO NEWS

Sunday, December 13, 2004

Spared by storms, Cayman Brac is a big draw for ecotourism

Undersea adventures

By GRETCHEN ALLEN
ASSOCIATED PRESS

A diver surfaces with stingrays off of Cayman Brac, Cayman Islands.

An instant landmark is created by $425 million expansion and remodeling

The new MoMA is a visitor's delight

By ROBERT TAYLOR

"Wall Drawing" by Sol LeWitt is reflected in the floor of the newly renovated Museum of Modern Art.

INSIDE: One-Tank Trip: Toronto's artistic triple play / Page 15
Cruising / Page 13 • Travel Planner / Page 14 • Vegas lights up for New Year's Eve / Page 16

WEEKEND 06.11.04

S&P/TSX	DJ Ind	Nasdaq	Dollar	Gold

REPORT ON BUSINESS

CANADA'S NEW STOCK EXCHANGE
WWW.CNQ.CA

IN BREWING

Brewers sweeten faltering deal

Molson, Coors kick in $388-million in special dividend in effort to win shareholder support for merger

Cover Story

The once feisty tabloid is raising its price, but what readers may not know is that ...

SHOCK, HORROR: SUN'S IN TROUBLE

Paper faces tough challenges in a brutal market, RICHARD BLACKWELL reports. B7

Features

IN TAKING STOCK | MATHEW INGRAM

Economic data sunny, but outlook remains cloudy

Dividend-growth stocks offer a lifetime of returns

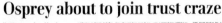

After · After · After

HOME

TODAY'S BACHELOR PAD

By JAMES A. MARKETTI III

Sleek, Modern Style Shows A More Elegant Touch, Replacing Cinder-Block Furnishings, Empty Pizza Boxes Of Yesteryear

BACHELOR CHAD

Solar Homes In The Spotlight

Penny Toys From 1890s Now May Be Worth Thousands Of Dollars

By RALPH and TERRY KOVEL

Antiques Prices

Travel

Inside Section G
Marcia Schnedler / 62
Mini Page / 65
Poetry / 66

HAWAII

Kayaking along the Na Pali coast of Kauai allows a lucky few to enjoy sights others never get to see, including sea caves that are inaccessible when the surf is up.

Exercising smiles

Sea-kayaking off Kauai is a swell way to develop seamanship

By PAUL WEST
L.A. Times-Washington Post

A marathon in paradise

By MICHELLE RUBINO

HONOLULU

Honolulu surf school rolls in fun

Copley News Service

HONOLULU — "The Kyle?!"

REPORT ON BUSINESS

CANADA'S BUSINESS NEWSPAPER • FOUNDED 1862 • GLOBEANDMAIL.COM • SATURDAY, FEBRUARY 11, 2004

Osprey about to join trust craze

Newspaper group formed from former Hollinger papers to go public in weeks

BY DEREK DeCLOET
AND ANDREW WILLIS

Finding the right finishing touches

Attention female shoppers

MARINA STRAUSS

Microsoft rushes to plug Windows leak

Pieces of code prove popular on the Net

Canadian recording industry hopes to inspire fear over file swapping

BY KEVIN MARRON

REPORT ON BUSINESS

WEEKEND

Hartford Courant
Hartford, Conn.

Before

Redesigns/Section

Chris Moore, Designer; **Suzette Moyer,** Director/Design & Graphics;
Thom McGuire, A.M.E. Graphics/Photography

The Buffalo News
Buffalo, N.Y.

Before

Redesigns/Section

Vincent J. Chiaramonte, Designer; **John Davis,** Design Director; **Toni Ruberto,** Travel Editor; **Elizabeth Kahn,** A.M.E./Features

The Globe and Mail
Toronto, Ontario, Canada

Before

Redesigns/Section

David Pratt, Executive Art Director

SECTION F

Arts & Entertainment

THE BUFFALO NEWS   *Sunday, April 18, 2004*

The Albright-Knox makes room for two shows of sculpture — one classic, one contemporary

EXHIBITS TO PONDER

BY RICHARD HUNTINGTON / NEWS CRITIC

There's probably not much going on beyond the furrowed brow of Ron Mueck's "Big Man."

Rodin's famous "The Thinker" contemplates more of life's mysteries.

Dazzling displays — what you need to know

Rodin: A Magnificent Obsession, Sculpture from the Iris and B. Gerald Cantor Foundation

Bodily Space: New Obsessions in Figurative Sculpture

Book marks/ *Today's reviews* | Nonfiction | For Children | Nonfiction | Editor's Choice | Also inside...

The Buffalo News
Buffalo, N.Y.

Redesigns/Section

Vincent J. Chiaramonte, Designer

After

■ BUFFALO ■ NEWS

Arts & Books

THE CITY WITHIN

In only 35 pages, writer Nicholas Howe makes one of the great contributions to the growing 'literature of Buffalo'

Exciting Tick season is a steal for patrons

Big-screen heroics are the summer rage

Before

Sports

U.S. golfers fall further behind
The Americans need an unprecedented comeback to keep the Europeans from winning another Ryder Cup

Sunday
September 13, 2004

TOMORROW: A look at Mariners outfielder Ichiro Suzuki's run at the record for hits in a season.

GameDay SECTION CC

TECH ENDS TCU'S BCS TALK

MOTORSPORTS NASCAR CUTS TO THE CHASE

NBA TRADES CHANGE LOOK OF MAVS

BOXING HOPKINS BEATS DE LA HOYA

NHL LOCKOUT COULD BURY LEAGUE

BASEBALL AMAZING ASTROS CLOSE THE GAP

NFL THE MOST-HATED COACH ANYWHERE

SCORES

INDEX

SCORELINE

HECKLING

FAIR OR FOUL BAWL?

Shouting at opposing players is just part of the game, but when does fun turn into unacceptable abuse?

BY DAVID THOMAS

IN MY OPINION

Big Bill puts us in a fog

Good luck figuring out the Parcells plan

Randy Galloway

Cowboys vs. Browns

IN MY OPINION

Rangers manage to do it right

Jim Reeves

Rangers at Angels

After

Fort Worth Star-Telegram
Fort Worth, Texas

Redesigns/Section

Celeste Williams, Sports Editor;
Michael Currie, Assistant Sports Editor; **Ellen Alfano,** M.E./Sports;
Cody Bailey, Senior Deputy Sports Editor; **Staff**

Sports
WWW.STAR-TELEGRAM.COM

Today

Rangers fall back out of 1st

WHO'S THE GUY?

Quincy says it's him. Vinny says maybe not. And Big Bill's watching.

Frogs aim to climb food chain

It's not improvement without winning more

TOMORROW | Twenty things to watch for in college football's 2004 season ...

Before

Dagens Nyheter
Stockholm, Sweden

Before

Redesigns/Section

Ebba Bonde, Art Director; **Lotta Ek,** Art Director; **Mattias Hermansson,** Editor

After

After

Before

The Times of Northwest Indiana
Munster, Ind.

Redesigns/Page

Matt Erickson, Assistant Sports Editor/Design; **Theresa Badovich,** M.E./Visuals; **Erica Smith,** News Design Team Leader; **Design Staff**

Dagens Nyheter
Stockholm, Sweden

Redesigns/Section

Pompe Hedengren, Art Director

After

Before

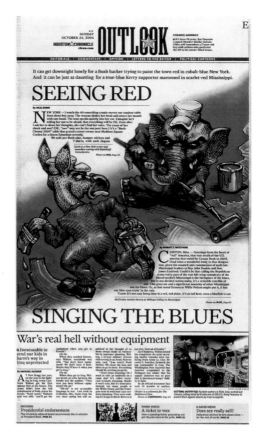

After

After

After

Houston Chronicle
Houston, Texas

Redesigns/Page

Kellye Sanford, Designer/Illustrator

Before

The Virginian-Pilot
Norfolk, Va.

Redesigns/Page

Deborah Withey, Deputy M.E./Presentation; **Ann Marie Griffith,** At Home Editor

Before

Tabasco Hoy
Villahermosa, México

Redesigns/Page

Isaac De Coss, Art Director/Redesigner; **Lizzeth Huerta,** Designer/Photo Artist; **Miguel de la Cruz,** Designer

Before

After

After

After

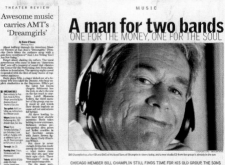

San Jose Mercury News
San Jose, Calif.
Before

Redesigns/Page

Kris Viesselman, Creative Director/Designer; **David Frazier,** Features Design Director; **Matt Mansfield,** Deputy M.E.

The Virginian-Pilot
Norfolk, Va.
Before

Redesigns/Page

Judy Le, Designer; **Deborah Withey,** Deputy M.E./Presentations

Fort Worth Star-Telegram
Fort Worth, Texas
Before

Redesigns/Page

Broc Sears, A.M.E. Graphics/Design; **Sarah Huffstetler,** Executive News Design Director; **Jessica Felkel,** News Designer; **Ryan Peterson,** News Designer; **Meredith Poldrack,** News Designer; **Amanda Reiter,** News Designer; **Spencer Skelley,** News Designer; **News Design Staff**

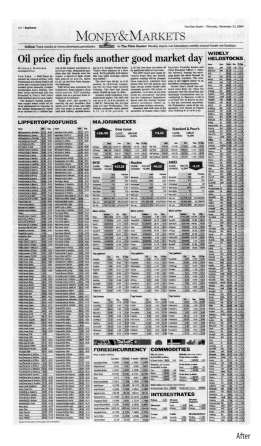

After

After

After

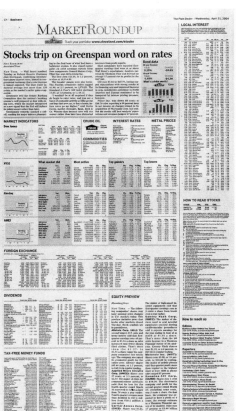

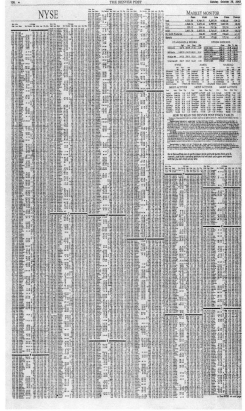

The Plain Dealer
Cleveland, Ohio

Before

Redesigns/Page

David Kordalski, A.M.E./Visuals; **Debbie Van Tassel,** Business Editor;
John Kroll, Deputy Business Editor

The Globe and Mail
Toronto, Ontario, Canada

Before

Redesigns/Page

David Pratt, Executive Art Director; **Michael Bird,** Presentation &
Production Editor; **Randy Volocci,** Assistant Photo Editor

The Denver Post
Denver, Colo.

Before

Redesigns/Page

J. Damon Cain, M.E./Presentation; **Jeff Neumann,** Lead Designer

PEOPLE • PUBLICATIONS

Index

PEOPLE

PEOPLE

Fraser, Matthew, 58-59, 104-105, 108, 113, 135, 146, 159, 180
Fratus, Ken, 54, 96
Frazier, Craig, 80
Frazier, David, 142, 261
Freaner, Ariel, 207
Frederick, George, 102, 107, 195, 245
Freijo, Julia Ma. Crespo, 200
Freye, Anja, 145
Friebe, Richard, 124
Friedman, Gary, 228
Friedmann, Jane, 226
Friesen, Mark, 88, 235
Friis, Jesper, 132
Friz, Paolo, 220
Froelich, Janet, 125-127, 148, 150-152, 154, 156, 159, 161-162, 174, 176-177
Frohman, Susanna, 106
Fuentes, Javier, 206
Fuhrmans, Christoph, 95, 233
Fullerton, Renee, 253
Funch, Fredrik, 126

G

Gallagher, Charles M., 131
Gallardo, Alex, 117
Gallardo, Vicente, 206
Galván, Ernesto, 106
Gámez, José Juan, 149, 205, 213, 214
Gámez, Silvia I., 103
Gannaway, Preston, 164
Garbers, Sandra, 120-121, 134
Garcia, Adrianna, 85, 110
García, Daniel, 245
Garcia, Delgar, 206
Garcia, Leslie, 142, 147, 154, 171-173
Garcia, Mario, 248
García Macías, Mikel, 109, 114
Garcia Phillips, Andrew, 107, 245
García Rivera, Cristina, 78, 213-214
García Rodríguez, Edgar, 132
Garda, Jaun Carlos, 208
Garduño, Karla, 208
Garrido, Guillermo Chávez, 93
Garrote, Aurelio, 109, 114
Garrow, Dan, 185
Gaspard, Bill, 64-65, 67-69, 115, 216, 228
Gauthier, Robert, 64
Gavidia, Raúl, 203-204
Gearhart, Gregg, 252
Gehrz, Jim, 180
Geib, Phil, 182, 187, 189
Gensheimer, Jim, 49, 173
Gentile, Massimo, 107

Giguere, Benoit, 97, 99, 101, 116, 229, 230
Gil Sáenz, Jesús, 155, 157, 160, 184
Gilbert, Susan, 80, 173-174
Gilbertson, Ashley, 39
Gilmore-Barnes, Catherine, 151, 156
Gimenez, Josemar, 84, 89, 93, 113
Giron, Arthur E., 159
Glass, Jon, 191
Glendenning, Jeff, 126, 159, 161, 174
Goertzen, Jeff, 183, 193
Gogick, John, 94
Goldman, Scott, 99
Goldstrom, Robert, 54
Golscher, Fernando, 204
Gomes, André, 253
Gómez, Alejandro, 92-93, 168, 227, 229
Gómez, María Virgen, 200, 207
Gonzales Besada, Agusto, 109
Gonzalez, Andres, 76
González, Antonio, 155, 157, 160
Gonzalez, Carlos Avila, 173
González, Fernando, 109, 111-112, 219
González, Isabel, 75, 183
González, Jesús, 202
Gonzalez, Maria, 125-126, 144-145, 148, 150-152
Gonzáles, Mario, 87
González, Néstor, 206
Gonzales, Paul, 68, 170, 171, 216, 228
González, Xoan, 184
González, Xóchitl, 103
Good, Greg, 115
Gorman, Kate, 182
Gormus, Mark, 165
Gorski, Pete, 78, 199, 204
Gosfield, Josh, 54
Gottschalk, Angela, 97
Gozblau, Alejandro, 209
Gram, Marianne, 141
Grañena, Luis, 241
Granroth, Marita, 255
Graulich, Rich, 77
Gray, Joe, 139-140
Grayson, Mark, 117
Greenberg, Jill, 149
Greene, Jeff, 61, 174, 220
Greener, Stormi, 178
Greenwell, Randy, 80, 173-174
Grewe, Dave, 108, 112
Griffis, Lisa, 61, 86, 220, 240
Griffith, Ann Marie, 260
Grin, Gayle, 58-59, 85, 104-105, 108, 111, 113, 135, 146, 159, 180
Grinbergs, Linda, 79
Griswold, Doug, 51, 130
Grondahl, Mika, 221
Grosner, Patrick, 36
Gross, Brian, 54, 96, 237
Gruda, Agnes, 116, 229

Grumney, Ray, 226
Guadarrama, Arcelia, 201-202, 210
Guerrero, Genoveva, 74
Guerrero, Ignacio, 90-91
Guerrero, Tadeo, 74
Gugliotta, Bill, 61, 174
Guimarães, Jorge, 41, 138
Guise, Helene De, 230
Gurbani, Roger, 154
Gutiérrez, Carlos René, 206-207
Gutierrez, Lisa, 155
Gutiérrez, Luis Enrique, 92
Gutierrez, Mauricio, 136
Guzy, Carol, 173

H

Haag, Jim, 117
Habib, Dan, 164
Haddix, Carol, 72, 139-140
Haffey, Sean M., 53
Hagel, Keith, 78, 199
Hager, Gretchen, 117
Hagin, Anita Sue, 90
Hagman, Alan, 69, 114
Hairston, Kim, 163
Hall, Michael, 243
Hamada, Kyoko, 173
Hamann, Amanda, 141
Hamill, Blair, 252
Hamilton, Ross William, 244
Hancock, John, 181
Hansen, John, 167-168
Hansen, Søren, 132
Harkness, Kyndell, 226
Harmel, Greg, 87, 108, 112
Harris, Doug, 98
Harris, Nancy, 127, 152, 161, 177
Hastings, Sid, 116
Hawkins, Steven, 68
Hayner, Don, 115
Headcase Design, 146
Healy, Ryan C., 100, 102, 235
Heath-Rawlings, Jordan, 91
Hedengren, Pompe, 259
Heisler, Stephanie, 87, 181
Heisler, Todd, 163, 168, 179
Hennessy, Kathleen, 80, 125-126, 173-174
Hennrikus, Kathleen, 185
Henriquez, Hiram, 245
Heras, Gonzalo De Las, 245
Herman, Mike, 57
Hermansson, Mattias, 259
Hernández, Ricardo, 200
Hervás, Antonio Martín, 149
Heumann, Thomas, 124, 142, 144, 146
Hewitt, Roy, 95, 118
Hickman, Roadell, 164
Higgins, Damon, 77, 91
Hildebrandt, Edel, 141

Hill, Angela, 110
Hindenach, Jeff, 50, 89
Hine, Chappell, 49
Hippertt, André, 110, 253
Hively, Cindy, 68, 170-171, 216, 228
Hively, Ken, 140
Hjerpe, Mikael, 122
Ho, Huei-tse, 208
Ho, Rick Ngoc, 137
Hobemagi, Priit, 250
Hoffmeyer, Dean, 165
Höglund, Anne-Marie, 217
Hogue, Michael, 118
Holden, Alfred, 100
Holland, Brad, 156
Holley, Jason, 159
Holmelid, Oddmund, 82, 109
Holt, Jerry, 79
Holzer, Jurek, 131
Hom, Calvin, 68-69, 114, 116, 160, 171, 228
Horn, Anja, 124, 142
Horn, Dave, 76
Horner, Jeff, 182
Horner, R. Scott, 188, 245
Hossain, Farhana, 189
Hovasse, Alain-Pierre, 116
Hovden, Anne, 82, 109
Howell, Joe, 168
Howitt, Keith, 120
Hsiu, Polo Fu Ta, 112
Hsu, June, 208
Hu, Ev, 91
Huand, Lena Huang Yi, 112
Hubbard, Tim, 68
Huerta, Lizzeth, 212, 260
Huff, Bruce, 53, 113
Huffstetler, Sarah, 182, 261
Huffy, Sean M., 113
Hughes, Brian, 57
Humphrey, Eustacio, 174
Hundley, Sam, 188
Hurtado, Juan Luis, 202
Huschka, Robert, 86, 181
Hutchinson, Joseph, 64-65, 67-69, 106, 114, 122, 128, 134, 139-142, 155-156, 191, 216, 228
Huwiler, Edith, 143
Hvidsten, Mark, 227
Hylkema, Frank, 248

I

Igartua, Pacho, 109, 114
Ilic, Mirkoj, 156
Ilsøe, Christian, 133
Imes, Jennifer, 187
Ingram, Bill, 182
Innovation, 248, 253
Ischay, Lynn, 145
Ittner-McManus, Renee, 179
Ivey, Karsten, 245

PEOPLE

PEOPLE

Spengler, Margaret, 133
Spirito, Louis, 189
Spratt, Gerry, 202
Standish, Tim, 186
Stanfield, Chris, 116
Starrett, Sabrina J., 85
Staublin, Grant, 54, 90, 96, 98, 237
Stein Burbach, Ellen, 174
Stein, Jason, 80
Steketee, Sid, 132
Stensrud, Whitney, 115
Stephens, Brendan, 146, 148, 157-158, 171
Stephens, Chris, 61
Stermer, Dugalo, 154
Stevens, Heidi, 72, 123, 136-137
Stewart, Todd, 161
Stocker, Mike, 76, 117, 244
Stollorz, Volker, 124
Stoneman, Sher, 167
Straker, Matthew, 52
Strazzante, Scott, 72
Strean, Linda, 202
Strickland, Dee Dee, 190
Strotheide, Guido, 211
Stroud, Steve, 69
Stubbs, Barbara, 133
Stuenkel, Nancy, 115
Sudnik, Janet, 208
Sugano, Dai, 177
Suhay, Robert, 117, 216
Suils, Mercedes, 205
Sullivan, Joe, 96
Sullivan, John, 129-130
Sullivan, Kelli, 68, 128, 134, 141-142, 155-156, 228
Sullivan, Margaret, 249
Sureck, Shana, 181
Swaroop, Shraddha, 103
Swenson, Daniel, 85, 110
Swift, Elvis, 72
Swinden, Keith, 72
Syrek, David, 149, 157

T

Tajes, Luís, 89, 93
Tapia, José Luis, 92, 227, 229
Taylor, Brett, 221
Taylor, Elizabeth, 149, 157
Taylor, Jeff, 70
Teghammar Arell, Karin, 122, 220
Tejada, Victor Manuel, 200, 207
Telfer, Jerry, 125-126
Terán, Pedro, 168
Thiede, Ed, 110
Thole, Tippi, 133-134
Thomas, Patrick, 242
Thornbro, Bill, 252
Thorp, Gene, 192
Thurston, Scott, 96
Tideman, Pontus, 100

Tiffet, Christian, 201, 205
Timmons III, Lonnie, 61-62
Timmons, Sue, 68
Timony, Sheila, 253
Toledano, Phillip, 150
Tonia Cowan, 57
Torregrosa, Alberto, 109, 111-112, 114, 219
Torres, Hugo, 131, 140, 196
Tortosa, Manuel Romero, 78, 213-214
Tovar, Miguel Angel, 202
Tozer, Tom, 190, 192
Tremblan, Celine, 242
Trevan, Dan, 163
Trevino, Jessica, 174
Treviño, Martha, 132
Trillos, Gabriel, 226
Tsai, Pricilla, 165
Tse, Archie, 73, 246
Tuma, Rick, 129
Tumas, Alejandro, 184, 246
Tunbjörk, Lars, 220
Turbett, Peggy, 145
Turhan, Osman, 127, 145, 154
Turner, Lane, 98

U

Uecker, Tom, 134
Ulriksen, Mark, 54, 223
Unruh, Jack, 134
Uribarri Paguillo, David, 78, 213
Urresti, Kristina, 86, 104, 109, 127, 230
Utko, Jacek, 78, 200, 205, 250

V

Vadillo, Miguel, 194
Valdemoros, Carlos J., 226
Valencia, René, 201
Valentin, Angel, 115
Valenzuela, Milagros, 135
Valiño, Álvaro, 160, 184
Valles, John T., 71
van Gruijthuijsen, Erik, 248
Van Hemmen, Pim, 79
Van Lamsweerde, Inez, 162
Van Tassel, Debbie, 262
Vander Brug, Brian, 167
Vargas, Luis Alberto, 165
Varney, Dennis, 86
Vaughan, Victor, 87
Vázquez, Carlos, 184
Vega, Francisco, 84
Vega, Gustavo, 201-202, 210
Velasco, P., 112

Velázquez, Patricia Maciel, 201
Velez, Chris, 118
Vene, Elisabeth, 100
Ventura, Marco, 154
Verde, Amaya, 205
Vergara, Camilo Jose, 91
Viana, Gonçalvo, 209
Viesselman, Kris, 50-51, 124, 139, 143, 244, 261
Vignoles, Mary, 76, 85, 115, 117
Vigue, Doreen, 217, 220
Villalta, Cristian, 70, 118, 203
Villanueva, Baldomero, 111-112, 219
Vitale, Stefano, 222
Volk, Bryan, 93
Volocci, Randy, 262
von Arb, Jürg, 220
von Rauchhaupt, Ulf, 142
Voros, Robert D., 191
Vuori, Jesper, 255

W

Wa, Ben Wong Kam, 112
Wai, Danny Wong Shu, 115
Waldersten, Jesper, 122, 234
Walgren, Judy, 163, 169
Walker, Chris, 72
Walker, Richard, 230
Wallen, Paul, 78, 199, 203-204, 210
Wallgore, Mark, 254
Walsh Infanzon, Anastasia, 76, 162
Walter, Ralph, 45, 115, 143
Wang, Chin, 56, 147
Wang, Lorraine, 114
Ward, Joe, 221
Ward, Sam, 155
Wasserman, Jeff, 104-105, 108, 111
Watson, Palmer, 252
Watson, Terry, 255
Webbeking, Anne, 85
Weil, Bernard, 91
Weinberger, Peter, 165
Weiss, Diane, 86, 95, 167, 181
Welin, Cissi, 137, 147
Wells, Hal, 68, 128, 167
Wendt, Kevin, 49-51, 89, 94, 103, 106, 130
Wernhamn, Gunilla, 122, 138, 143, 151
Wheatley, Tim, 99
White, Carolyn, 166
White, Eric, 115, 235
Whitley, Michael, 64-65, 67, 69, 93, 106, 114-115, 117, 228
Whitty, Michael, 120
Wilhelm, George, 117
Wilkins, Chris, 70, 118, 181
Wilkins, Sarah, 155
Williams, Celeste, 113, 225, 258
Williams, Charean, 99

Williams, Doug, 53, 113, 221
Willms, Russ, 56
Wilmsen, Steve, 90
Wilner, Paul, 132
Wilson, Dave, 53, 113, 221
Wilson, DeWayne, 89
Wilson, Wade, 74, 104-105, 116, 193
Winsa, Patty, 57
Winter, Damon, 115, 160, 170-171, 242-243
Winters, Dan, 177
Wirsén, Stina, 242
Wishna, Robyn, 130
Withey, Deborah, 117, 188, 191, 216, 260-261
Wittekind, Don, 188, 245
Woike, John, 96
Wollemann, Mark, 227
Woodside, David, 126
Workman, Michael, 96, 130
Wright, Mandi, 167
Wuensche, Robert, 221
Wynn, Spencer, 57, 127, 129, 238

Y

Yan, Kelly, 91
Yanni, Mary, 245
Yarosh, Lee, 83, 221
Yazici, Fevzi, 127, 145, 154
Yeh, Thomas, 138
Yemich, Sharon, 174
Yoder, Chad, 199
Young, Lloyd, 165
Yourish, Karen, 189
Yung, Daniel Wong Chi, 115
Yzena, Roger Hiyane, 241

Z

Zalucki, Andrzej, 250
Zambrano, Jaun Carlos, 109
Zarracina, Javier, 51, 139, 143, 186, 188, 244
Zazueta, Alfredo, 207
Zedek, Dan, 54-56, 88, 90, 96, 98, 99, 101, 122, 128-131, 146-148, 155, 157-158, 171, 217, 220, 226-227
Zeff, Joe, 92, 118
Zelz, Eric L., 190
Zgoda, Jerry, 227
Zisk, Molly, 196
Zoll, Adam, 182
Zúñiga Castañeda, Aarón, 92-93, 227
Zúñiga, Diego, 109, 114

PUBLICATIONS